"This is a wonderful book. It takes us backstage with a keen insight on the writing, directing, and casting of one of the best television shows, ever. I didn't want it to end, any more than I wanted *The Mary Tyler Moore Show* to end."

—Carol Burnett, author of *Carrie and Me*

"I tried to skim this book, but failed miserably, finding I couldn't put it down. In case you're wondering how we got from *I Love Lucy* to *Girls*, the answer is: "*The Mary Tyler Moore Show*, stupid!" Jennifer Keishin Armstrong's deft weave of social history and sharp entertainment reporting explains how this revolutionary show made the world safe for Lena Dunham."

—Peter Biskind, author of *Easy Riders, Raging Bulls*

"*Mary and Lou and Rhoda and Ted* hurt my face. Jennifer Keishin Armstrong brought back memories and laughs from one of the best eras in television. She made me stay up all night and by the morning my face hurt from smiling. I forgive her because I enjoyed the book so much."

—Gail Parent, author of *Sheila Levine Is Dead and Living in New York*

"Pop-culture gold: a can't-put-it-down history of *The Mary Tyler Moore Show* and the misfit genius women (and men) who made it. *Mary and Lou and Rhoda and Ted* is essential reading if you love *The Mary Tyler Moore Show*, or TV comedy wizards, or things that are awesome."

—Gavin Edwards, author of *'Scuse Me While I Kiss This Guy*

"Armstrong's history of '*Mary Tyler Moore*' is warm and funny and rife with juicy details . . . a group portrait of the talented, ambitious young women who maneuvered, wangled, and pleaded their way into writing for the show. It is about secretaries who transformed themselves into writers, and helped to transform Mary Richards into the closest 1970s television came to a feminist icon."

—*Boston Globe*

"A rich chronicle of women making history."

—TheAtlantic.com

"A delightfully thorough history of the show, evoking in detail the making of a piece of pop-culture history and . . . the story of the women in the writers' room."

—*New York Daily News*

"A superb, highly entertaining history of one of television's most beloved sitcoms. . . . A terrific pop-culture history—well-written, lovingly researched, and chock full of great stories from the *Mary Tyler Moore Show* set."

—Shelf Awareness for Readers

"Compelling and highly readable, this book is as informative as it is charming. . . . As enjoyable as reruns of the classic show."

—*Bust*

"Armstrong takes us back to a golden age of comedy."

—*Washington Post*

"For those who truly appreciate great timing (think of Lou Grant announcing he's not as hungry as he thought he was after taking half of Mary's dinner party veal Prince Orloff), the must-read of the summer is *Mary and Lou and Rhoda and Ted.*"

—*Detroit Free Press*

"Delicious. . . . For any fan of the show or TV history in general, this book is pure pleasure."

—*Kirkus Reviews* (starred review)

"Fast-paced and charming. . . . Armstrong's absorbing cultural history offers the first in-depth look at a series that changed television."

—*Publishers Weekly*

"Poor dead Chuckles the Clown might be squirting seltzer water down the angels' robes, but as long as intelligent comedy has a role in our lives, the chuckles and change that *The Mary Tyler Moore Show* wrought will never die. And Armstrong, in this smart and charming history, shows us why."

—*Richmond Times-Dispatch*

"A perfect microhistory of television and feminism and writing and money and pressure and the joy of creativity and those capri pants she wore."

—*The Hairpin*

MARY AND LOU

MARY AND LOU

MARY AND LOU

MARY AND LOU

MARY AND LOU

MARY AND LOU

MARY AND LOU

MARY AND LOU

MARY AND LOU

and all the brilliant minds who

MARY AND LOU

MARY AND LOU

MARY AND LOU

MARY AND LOU

MARY AND LOU

simon & schuster paperbacks

NEW YORK   LONDON   TORONTO   SYDNEY   NEW DELHI

MARY AND LOU

and rhoda and ted

MADE *THE MARY TYLER MOORE SHOW* A CLASSIC

Jennifer Keishin Armstrong

Simon & Schuster Paperbacks
1230 Avenue of the Americas
New York, NY 10020

First Simon & Schuster paperback edition October 2013

SIMON & SCHUSTER PAPERBACKS and colophon are registered trademarks of
Simon & Schuster, Inc.

For information about special discounts for bulk purchases, please contact
Simon & Schuster Special Sales at 1-866-506-1949 or business@simonandschuster.com.

The Simon & Schuster Speakers Bureau can bring authors to your live event. For more
information or to book an event contact the Simon & Schuster Speakers Bureau at
1-866-248-3049 or visit our website at www.simonspeakers.com.

Designed by Ruth Lee-Mui

Manufactured in the United States of America

10 9 8 7 6 5 4 3 2 1

Library of Congress Cataloging-in-Publication Data

Armstrong, Jennifer Keishin.
   Mary and Lou and Rhoda and Ted : and all the brilliant minds who made The Mary
Tyler Moore show a classic / Jennifer Keishin Armstrong. — First Simon & Schuster
hardcover edition.
      pages cm
   Includes bibliographical references and index.
   1. Mary Tyler Moore show (Television program) I. Title.
   PN1992.77.M285A76 2013b
   791.45′72--dc23
                                                                            2013009294

ISBN 978-1-4516-5920-7
ISBN 978-1-4516-5922-1 (pbk)
ISBN 978-1-4516-5923-8 (ebook)

To A. Jesse Jiryu Davis. Obviously.

CONTENTS

CONTENTS
CONTENTS
CONTENTS
CONTENTS
CONTENTS
CONTENTS

PART THREE

PART FOUR

PART FIVE

iNTROduCTiON
iNTROduCTiON
iNTROduCTiON
iNTROduCTiON
iNTROduCTiON
iNTROduCTiON
iNTROduCTiON

COMEdy ANd THE SiNqlE qiRl

Treva Silverman had always wanted to be the beautiful, funny, smart heroine of a 1930s screwball comedy. In that world, the woman bantered with the man; the woman was independent, sexy, desirable, witty. Idiosyncratic actresses like Jean Arthur, Carole Lombard, Rosalind Russell, Claudette Colbert, and Margaret Sullavan were the leading ladies there. Unfortunately, in the 1950s, when Treva was a twelve-year-old in Cedarhurst, Long Island—the time when this desire took hold of her—the movie world had moved on from fast-talking comediennes to man-pleasing models of femininity like Doris Day, who seemed to have endless hang-ups about being good and pure, and Marilyn Monroe, who was the quintessential dumb blonde. The idea of an equal partnership between equally bright men and women trading quips had all but disappeared from films. And TV was even worse: *Father Knows Best* and *The Donna Reed Show* featured "dialogue" in which the woman's only role was to say, "Yes, dear." The most popular

TV comedy heroine was Lucy, who wanted to be in show business but had to hide it from Ricky, who didn't approve. The central joke of the show hinged on the fact that male approval ruled.

Magazines bombarded Treva with advice to young women—*talk about his interests, don't be competitive, learn how to make his favorite meals.* To get the guy, she learned, she had to be all about him. At her grammar school, PS #3, her girlfriends chastised her for winning a spelling bee over Jerry Yaeger, the very boy she had a crush on. She'd never have a chance with him now, they lamented.

So Treva would settle for sitting next to her older sister, Corinne, in the moth-eaten seats of her neighborhood's only revival movie house, watching and listening to her idols, Jean Arthur and Carole Lombard. Jean Arthur, in her day, made a name for herself as a funny leading lady in the Frank Capra films *Mr. Deeds Goes to Town, Mr. Smith Goes to Washington,* and *You Can't Take It with You.* Lombard was once described by Graham Greene as "platinum blonde, with a heart-shaped face, delicate, impish features, and a figure made to be swathed in silver lamé, [who] wriggled expressively through such classics of hysteria as *Twentieth Century* and *My Man Godfrey.*" When Treva watched Jean Arthur and Carole Lombard, she wanted to soak up every last bit of them, the way her movie-house popcorn soaked up melted butter.

Treva had one other escape route from suburban ennui: Every week, she took the train from her family's home in Cedarhurst for more than an hour to get to New York City. It was where she belonged, she was sure. For now, though, she'd settle for going there weekly for her piano lessons at Columbia University. Two officials at the Juilliard School had declared her a "genius" at age five. She had perfect pitch and could play almost any piece by ear after hearing it once; she could transpose into any key. A unique talent, to be sure. But besides her music, something else was becoming a passion.

After her piano lesson every week, she'd race down to the New York Public Library in midtown Manhattan to read her way through the vast stacks of the humor section, in alphabetical order: Robert

Benchley, Dorothy Parker, S. J. Perelman, James Thurber. There, at the Forty-second Street library, she had found her people: the humor writers for the *New Yorker*. Along with some journalists, critics, and actors, they had met daily throughout the '20s for lunches at the Algonquin Hotel, forming a loose camaraderie called the Algonquin Round Table. They were known for their sharp witticisms and one-liners, which were quoted all over the newspaper columns. More importantly, the Algonquin Round Table consisted of men and—yes!—women. Not only Dorothy Parker, one of the wittiest of them all, but also Edna Ferber, Tallulah Bankhead, and Beatrice Kaufman.

Treva read on and on, as afternoon turned into dusk, the shadows cast by the library's stone lions growing longer until they dissolved. She wished she could travel back to the days of the Algonquin Round Table, overhearing them from a neighboring table, or, even better, somehow getting a seat at that table.

When Silverman graduated from Bennington College nearly a decade later, even though the joke of the day was to try to graduate with an "M.R.S. degree," she had nestled nicely into a Manhattan creative life on her own. She had broken into comedy writing and rejoiced when, one by one, a sketch or song of hers was accepted for an off-Broadway show or for Upstairs at the Downstairs, a topical revue nightclub that featured future stars like Lily Tomlin and Madeline Kahn. The rest of her evenings were spent using her musical talent: She played and sang show tunes—Rodgers and Hart, Cole Porter, Gershwin—anywhere around town that had a piano and offered the chance to make a few bucks.

She played at bars, bowling alleys, Japanese restaurants. She got to meet people she never would have met otherwise, who lived the kinds of lives she'd only read about. There was the guy who pulled up his jacket sleeve to reveal five men's watches and whispered to her, "You got a boyfriend who needs a Patek-Philippe timepiece?" There was the guy in the strip joint who wore a black eye patch—he had lost his left eye in a knife fight—who asked her, "Are you a sport, or are you a good girl?" She had only a hazy idea of what a sport was, but she knew she didn't want to be one, and replied that she was a good girl. He gave her a twenty anyway. This piano-playing stint wasn't exactly the way to find a husband, but at least it left her days free to write her songs and sketches, and she was making enough money to survive.

Her colorful life was radically out of step with those of her girl-friends from high school and college. Not only did they have respect-able jobs in publishing and in advertising where nobody asked them to buy stolen watches, but most of them were gradually being whisked away to the magical never-never land called married life. You had to get there by age twenty-five or else—*or else* . . . well, nobody knew ex-actly what the *else* was, but it wasn't anything a good girl wanted. Treva did want a long-term relationship, but in the meantime she wanted everyone who asked her why she wasn't married to shut up.

Her parents believed in her talent but were nervous for her. They saw her life as all promise and hope, with no guarantee of a stable future. "Treva," her mother suggested one day, "why don't you take a shorthand course? Just as a fallback, honey."

Treva rolled her eyes. "Mom, I don't want to learn shorthand so that I can take down some man's ideas. I want someone taking down *my* ideas."

Once she was playing at a restaurant on Fifth Avenue, a place high-priced and elegant enough that, finally, she could invite her par-ents to see her perform. Seated at a flower-laden table listening to her play and sing, her parents watched while a man came up to the piano, spoke a few words to her, and put a ten-dollar bill in her glass piggy bank. Her father rushed to his daughter. "What did that man want?" he demanded.

" 'My Funny Valentine,' Dad," she sighed.

The good news was that the women's lib movement was starting to percolate. The Pill had been introduced in 1960, freeing women from pregnancy fears. And Helen Gurley Brown's 1962 bestseller, *Sex and the Single Girl,* had recently scandalized the nation, making women like Silverman feel *a little* less alone in their singlehood while emboldening them to wear shorter skirts and sleep with any man they pleased. Not every woman had to be Jackie Kennedy, for Chrissake. Brown rallied the single-girl troops to pursue their sexual desires, even giving them advice on the art of pleasuring men. "Theoretically a 'nice' single woman has no sex life," she wrote. "What nonsense!"

Brown saw the single woman as a "glamour girl," contrary to many other contemporary writers, who seemed to pity and fear any unmarried women who displayed both sex drive and career drive. Unmarried women were characterized as spinsters, unmarried men characterized as bachelors-around-town. Brown would soon revamp the magazine *Cosmopolitan* as a haven for sexually liberated women. Her proposal for the makeover said that her *Cosmopolitan* would tell an aspiring actress "not to stay back home in Lima, Ohio, like most articles on the subject do, [but would offer] practical advice. Where to live. How much money to save up first." Treva was beyond the *Cosmo* girl already—she had loads of practical advice she could give such a creature—but it was comforting to know there were girls who dreamed of the exact kind of life she already had.

One night in 1964, Silverman was playing at a piano bar in Manhattan's theater district—it was another one of those dark, smoky places, but this one had a well-tuned baby grand. She took her requisite set break, listening to the glasses clink and the patrons murmur in the absence of her playing. Still energized from her performance, she struck up a conversation with an intense, bearded, hippie-ish guy and his girlfriend sitting near her at the bar. Soon they were chatting about their mutual love of F. Scott Fitzgerald and J. D. Salinger. Beards were only just on the brink of acceptable mainstream grooming at the time, a signal of a certain kind of rebelliousness that endeared this guy to Silverman. Guys with beards tended to smoke weed, be creative, listen to cool music. They were Silverman's people. Even more so when they could talk Fitzgerald and Salinger. It figured that he was there with a woman, though. Those guys were always taken.

The guy, Jim Brooks, worked at CBS as an assistant in the newsroom. Treva and Jim talked about their mutual ambition to write for television. Brooks was intrigued with the sketch comedy work she was doing; his admiration for her was instant. He knew Upstairs at the Downstairs and its reputation for sharp, topical work. She was attracted to the way his mind worked, his quick, easy, funny conversation, his split-second responses. Something clicked between them: that feeling that says, *We're going to matter in each other's lives.*

She stayed in touch with Jim as she got more and more of her comedy sketches and songs performed in New York cabarets. Then came the day she received word that not one, not two, but five sketches of hers were going to be featured at Upstairs at the Downstairs. Five! She had been elevated to being the only sketch writer in the show. She was glowing with success when she ran into the mother of her best friend from high school. What luck, Treva thought—someone with whom to share her excitement. "Mrs. Bernstein, I just found out!" she said. "I have five sketches in the new Upstairs at the Downstairs!"

Treva waited for that spark of respect to alight in the older woman's eyes. Instead, she got: "How nice that you're keeping busy. . . . Are you seeing anyone?" Treva wondered if she would ever go a day again without hearing that question, dripping with passive-aggressive judgment.

But comedian Carol Burnett walked into Upstairs at the Downstairs a few months later with a different attitude toward talented, funny women like herself. Not long after Treva had talked to Jim about wanting to break into TV, Burnett came down to Midtown from her Upper East Side apartment to check out new talent at the revue; it was similar to the one in which Burnett had gotten her own start, the Blue Angel, nearly a decade earlier. Burnett liked Silverman's sketches so much that she invited her to write for a variety show she was about to star in, CBS's *The Entertainers,* along with Bob Newhart and Dom DeLuise. Writing comedy on a network TV show! Treva had arrived.

Silverman's work there led to a job in Hollywood writing for the television show *The Monkees*. She moved west in 1966 to craft scripts for the made-for-TV band that was aiming to replace the Beatles in teen girls' hearts, even as posters for the edgier Who and the Kinks, David Bowie and Jefferson Airplane, vied for the poster space on those same teenagers' walls. When Silverman got to her new gig, she found she was once again, as she had been on *The Entertainers*, the only woman writer on staff. The only other women she encountered were secretaries who typed up what the funny guys wrote and mimeographed copies for the producers and cast.

At that point, Treva was one of only two or three women writers in TV comedy who worked without a male partner; she was such an anomaly that *Mademoiselle* magazine did an article on her. She was part of a sociological phenomenon, a generation of new feminists being profiled in newsmagazines, who prioritized their careers over marriage and were often the only women wherever they went, their miniskirts, high boots, and tent dresses distinguishing them from the cinch-waisted, full-skirted secretaries who came before them. Later, interviewers would always ask Silverman, "How did you survive in such an atmosphere? How did you make it in a profession that had only been men?" The truth, however, was that she just *did* because she *had* to if she did the job she wanted. If the cherubic, soft-spoken Treva Silverman had to sit in rooms full of bearded men to be a comedy writer, then that was what she would do.

Then the original bearded guy in Silverman's life, Jim Brooks, reappeared in the summer of 1969. Treva had written for several sitcoms during the two years since *The Monkees* went off the air, including a few episodes of Brooks's groundbreaking high school history class comedy, *Room 222*. They'd stayed in touch since meeting in New York, and he had even introduced her to his fellow producer on *Room 222*, the short-haired, clean-cut Allan Burns. Now Brooks was calling her with a rather existential question: "What are you doing right now?"

"Washing my hair."

"No," he said, "I mean *with your life*. Our pilot is going to se-ries—the one I'm doing with Allan Burns—and we want you to come on board. It's with Mary Tyler Moore." With the woman from *The Dick Van Dyke Show*, the one who was pretty *and* funny? Like Jean Arthur and Carole Lombard? There was nothing Silverman wanted more. That was quite a relief to Brooks and Burns, who needed writers who could understand their kind of show. They could also use some estrogen-fueled help with their female lead character. No one knew whether the show would last beyond CBS's initial thirteen-episode commitment to it, but Brooks offered her all he could: "We want you to write for this series," he told her, "and we want you to write as many episodes as you want."

As Brooks, Burns, and Silverman carefully wrote and rewrote the early scripts for *The Mary Tyler Moore Show* in 1970, they didn't dream their show would have any long-lasting effect on the world. They just sat at their typewriters and pounded away, trying to write the best they could and hoping the show didn't get canceled. At times the series *would* veer awfully close to ending prematurely. But instead, the writers' and producers' ideas and actions—some smart, some not—piled on top of each other, mixed together, and made history. They pulled star Mary Tyler Moore out of a perilous career slump. They weathered attacks from network executives who said the program was too different to succeed, or just plain rotten. They survived cast members' insecurities and jealousies, divorces and diets, and scream-ing matches between producers and directors. Along the way, they made several unlikely stars, changed the fates of a dozen female TV writers who spun their everyday lives into comedy gold, helped usher in a more woman-friendly era in the television industry, elevated the sitcom to an art form, and killed a clown.

This book tells their story: how they made a classic, and how it changed their lives, and the lives of those watching, forever.

PART ONE
PART ONE
PART ONE
PART ONE
PART ONE
PART ONE
PART ONE

"I'm an experienced woman. I've been around . . .
Well, all right, I might not have been around,
but I've been . . . nearby."
—Mary Richards

ONE
ONE
ONE
ONE
ONE
ONE
ONE

THE COMEBACK

(1961–70)

There is a certain trajectory your life takes when you create a classic book or movie, song or television show. It's a path followed by all those who accomplish this rare feat, and yet they never know they're on it at the time. And thus they never know if the vision they're fighting for is valid, much less great. They don't know of the accolades, or the difficulties, that are to come. They don't know how hard it will be to move on from such a rarefied experience, nor how hard it will be to duplicate it, but they will try, because, let's face it, they won't have much choice. Most of them will find out that comebacks are hard to come by. Then they will, if they are lucky, come to accept that even one classic in one's life is quite enough, and they will sit back and enjoy all the glory that gives them before their time is through.

It is not, all in all, a bad life. But it's not as easy as it looks, either.

Jim Brooks was on his way to such a fate, though he never would have guessed it, when he was spending his days writing copy for CBS

News in New York—reports on the Bay of Pigs, Andy Warhol, Beatle-mania, anything and everything that came through on the clanging wire service machines.

It was 1961, and some form of network news had been a standard part of American life for nearly forty years, since the days of radio. Now television had taken over the country, but it was only just hitting its stride. News was at the forefront of every development in television: The first national live television broadcast in the United States was President Harry Truman's 1951 speech in San Francisco at the confer-ence for the Treaty of Peace with Japan. A then–cutting-edge micro-wave relay system allowed viewers in local markets across the country to hear the president's words at the same time, united, as a nation. Two months later, commercial television had its first live national broadcast with CBS's *See It Now,* a newsmagazine series that opened with a split screen of the Brooklyn Bridge and the Golden Gate Bridge—look! Both coasts! See it now! As the 1960s began and Brooks got hired at CBS, more developments in technology allowed the news to be almost up-to-the-minute when it aired. He had timed his stumble into the business well.

The job required a lot from a guy without a news background, without even a college diploma—Brooks had dropped out of New York University. Now twenty-one, he had lucked into the gig with help from a friend of his sister. The job was exhausting, but he found refuge in watching television when he got home. Not the news—no more news, please—but comedy, *The Dick Van Dyke Show* in particular. While *I Love Lucy* had perfected the sitcom, *Dick Van Dyke* made it more realistic, wringing its comedy not from far-fetched shenanigans but from everyday situations. Brooks liked that *Dick Van Dyke* was about a TV writer, Rob Petrie; even though Rob wrote for a variety show, Brooks could relate at least a little.

More importantly, this show had more believable characters than the sitcoms that came before it, even if they were funnier than ordinary people. When Rob's wife, Laura, ruined a sexy weekend getaway by getting her toe stuck in a bathtub faucet, the incident made audiences laugh, but it also made (some) sense—more sense than Lucille Ball stomping grapes or working at a chocolate factory, in any case.

Female viewers could imagine being Laura, because the woman playing her, Mary Tyler Moore, was vulnerable and goofy along with being pretty; male viewers wanted to be Rob for the same reasons. Laura was never more adorable than when she called out, from behind a closed door, to explain her stuck toe: "I was playing with a drip."

Moore could make a toe stuck in a faucet sexy *and* funny. She was a twenty-five-year-old actress with a brunette flip that women across the country were asking their hairstylists to re-create, a huge smile, gorgeous legs, and impeccable comic timing. The former dancer had grown up in Brooklyn Heights watching Milton Berle on television in the early '50s and aspiring to perform like Mr. Television himself. Her grandfather, watching her prance around the house one afternoon in her youth, had cracked, "This child will either end up onstage or in jail." She'd known even before then—from the age of about three, when she discovered her love of showing off—that it would be the former. By about the age of nine, just after World War II ended, she had moved with her family to Los Angeles at the urging of an uncle who was doing well there working as a music agent. Little Mary welcomed the move, figuring that it would bring her closer to being discovered by Hollywood.

She was, as it turned out, right. She'd gotten her first breaks on such television dramas as *77 Sunset Strip* and briefly as Sam, the sultry secretary on *Richard Diamond* who was known to audiences only by her voice, lips, and legs. Moore was originally uncredited in the role but soon demanded a place in the credits and a raise when the character became a sensation. The producers turned her down, so she quit, then revealed her identity to the world in a small publicity coup. Soon after, she'd been chosen to play Laura Petrie as a "straight woman" to Van Dyke's goofy charmer in his sitcom.

Nonetheless, *Dick Van Dyke*'s creator, Carl Reiner, had seen some inkling of humor in the actress and first tested it out in an early episode called "My Blonde-Haired Brunette," in which Laura bleaches her hair to ridiculous effect in an effort to spice up their marriage. When she's forced to explain the debacle to her husband, she tells him in a masterful monologue-cum-crying-jag about what she's done. In that moment, Moore felt the first thrill of making the audience laugh instead of simply setting up Van Dyke's lines. The cry would become her trademark comedy move, reminiscent of Ball, and the incident proved to Reiner that Moore was a real comedian. The producer began gearing episodes more toward the couple at home than he had originally planned when conceiving the show, and eventually even gave her a catchphrase: "Oh, Rob!"

Everyone who watched fell in love with her, including Brooks. He fantasized about being a TV writer who worked with such people—comic geniuses and pretty brunettes alike—but for the moment he'd have to settle for writing about the news of the day.

On the opposite coast, a comedy writer named Allan Burns had similar thoughts as he watched *The Dick Van Dyke Show*. Burns worked on cartoons like *Rocky and Bullwinkle* and had helped create the sitcom *The Munsters,* but he saw himself as a better writer than any of his projects showed so far. He wanted to understand how *The Dick Van Dyke Show* elevated itself above other comedies of its time, so he watched it closely. He wanted to be Carl Reiner.

The melding of Rob's work and home life, Burns thought, added a new dimension to the traditional home-based sitcom, as did Reiner's clever writing and Van Dyke's exceptional comedic skill. But Moore definitely stood out as special.

As stay-at-home mom Laura, Moore became a hit by forging a "very egalitarian and very sexual" relationship with on-screen husband Rob, as Moore explained it in interviews. The two clearly loved each other and didn't get their comedy from fighting the way Lucy and Desi or *The Honeymooners* did. Laura's formfitting Capri pants—which set off a nationwide trend with their daring show of calf—boosted the show's sex appeal even more. So did the genuine romantic tension between the two stars, who clearly had a crush on each other no matter that both were married off-screen. The network and its sponsors still went to extremes to scrub the show of sexual implications: Rob and Laura had to sleep in separate beds, the word *pregnant* was not allowed (the censors preferred the more decorous "with child" or "expecting," lest one link the lady's condition with sex), and even getting Laura into pants was a hard-fought battle. But the show broke boundaries by subtle implication. Burns admired that.

He wasn't alone in his admiration. In fact, Moore got an unforgettable vote of confidence from none other than Lucille Ball. The cast knew that occasionally, the sitcom queen—whose company, Desilu, owned the lot where the show shot—would lurk about. One day, Moore ran into her role model as Ball descended from a perch on the catwalk above where the *Dick Van Dyke* cast had just been rehearsing. Ball walked by Moore, then backtracked a few seconds later, looked her in the eye, and said, "You're very good," before she left. Moore would think of that whenever she felt unsure of herself.

Burns would have been shocked to learn Moore ever doubted her talent. He couldn't believe, quite frankly, that a woman that good-looking could be that funny. Surely she had a stellar career ahead of her.

Five years later, that career didn't look so good anymore, even when it was dressed in Audrey Hepburn finery. Broadway producer David Merrick's public statement said it all: He had shut down production of his new play, a musical version of *Breakfast at Tiffany's* starring Mary Tyler Moore, "rather than subject the drama critics and the public to an excruciatingly boring evening."

Things had clearly not gone as planned for the much-anticipated 1966 musical, nor for Moore's post–*Dick Van Dyke* career. Earlier that year, *The Dick Van Dyke Show* had ended its five-year run when Reiner and Van Dyke started craving more variety in their work. They felt the show starting to get repetitive, and furthermore, wanted both Van

Dyke and Moore to have a chance at bigger (that is, movie) stardom. Moore felt insecure about leaving her cozy nook at *Dick Van Dyke,* where her costars, the writers, and the crew all cared about her.

But life was pushing her in a clear new direction: Her husband, TV executive Grant Tinker, got a new job with NBC's programming department that forced him and Moore to move to New York City. Tinker hated being back east, but Moore looked forward to testing out her new stardom, even though she still thought of herself, she said, as "a nervous chorus girl from Studio City, California."

Moore planned to take advantage of their new home by giving the Broadway stage a try. She had originally studied ballet, and her first professional showbiz job had been, just a few months out of high school, as the dancing elf "Happy Hotpoint" in stove commercials featured during *The Adventures of Ozzie and Harriet.* Now that she'd moved to New York, she wanted to return to dancing and her dream of starring in a musical, seeing her name on a Broadway marquee. When she got an offer to play Holly Golightly in the stage adaptation of *Breakfast at Tiffany's,* it seemed like her chance to pursue her musical dreams.

It could have been the perfect vehicle for a svelte brunette who could sing and dance and had an Audrey Hepburn–like combination of sweetness and sex appeal. *Newsweek* at the time described Moore, in a '60s version of a compliment, as "the fantasy girl of the American dream . . . bright but not aggressive, wholesome but not puritanical, funny but not slapstick." In *Breakfast at Tiffany's,* she could put those qualities to use and be part of a team that seemed like it couldn't miss. The handsome Richard Chamberlain, known as TV's Dr. Kildare, was cast opposite Moore on the stage. David Merrick, a mustachioed maverick producer, had a flair for dramatic publicity as well as onstage artistry. In 1961, he'd won a special Tony Award just for his exemplary production record.

But Merrick's career had taken a dip the last year or so. The entertainment world was changing, and, like many of his contemporaries in the business, he hadn't figured out how to catch up. Graphic violence and existential ennui were raking it in at the box office with *Bonnie and Clyde* and *The Graduate*. The Beatles had gone from teen-pop idols who took *The Ed Sullivan Show* by storm to music revolutionaries with the release of their innovative *Revolver* and *Sgt. Pepper's Lonely Hearts Club Band*. In the theater world, *Cabaret*—the tawdry story of a lady lounge performer of ill repute in Nazi Germany—was all the rage. Merrick tried to stay with the times, but found that depressing drama didn't always translate into admirable edginess: The same year he planned to launch *Breakfast at Tiffany's*, his production of *The Loves of Cass McGuire*, Brian Friel's play about an Irishwoman who becomes an alcoholic in America, closed in sixteen days. *We Have Always Lived in the Castle*, about a teenager who kills her parents, lasted only a week.

The problems on *Breakfast at Tiffany's* proved far worse, far higher-profile, and they started almost as soon as rehearsals began at the Mark Hellinger Theatre, on Fifty-first Street. The idea for the production had its inauspicious beginning in an airplane-ride argument between Merrick and songwriter Bob Merrill, known for his work on *Funny Girl*, about whether it was a good idea to do a musical version of *Casablanca*. Merrick said yes, Merrill said no. To punctuate his point, Merrill gestured to a guy across the aisle reading Truman Capote's novella *Breakfast at Tiffany's* and said even that would make a better musical than *Casablanca*. Next thing Merrill knew, Merrick was convincing him to write songs about Holly Golightly.

Screenwriter Nunnally Johnson and director Joshua Logan soon joined the team. But they quickly began to argue over how to approach the difficult material. It was a sign of things to come: The crux of *Breakfast at Tiffany's* was its tug-of-war between dark and light, and that had played out to brilliant effect in the 1961 movie version. Audrey Hepburn had solidified her star status by bringing a sweetness and vulnerability to a character who's a kept woman at best, a high-class hooker at worst. Johnson and Logan soon quit the project. To take over the writing and directing duties, Merrick brought in Abe Burrows, who'd written and directed *Cactus Flower*, a farce that was still playing on Broadway after opening two years earlier, and who'd won Tonys for writing and directing the 1962 production *How to Succeed in Business Without Really Trying*. Burrows had become so well-known for his script-doctoring skill that "Get me Abe Burrows!" was a standard cry among bereft producers. Burrows, upon taking the *Breakfast at Tiffany's* job, decided to favor the novella's darker tones rather than the movie version's sparkle.

After harsh reviews in Boston and harsher reviews in Philadelphia for the show's on-the-road previews, Moore grew terrified to return to New York, dreading the looks of pity she'd get at theater district hangout Sardi's. She felt desperate to clear her name. She took on the look of someone who was about to jump out of a skyscraper window at every rehearsal and performance. The lack of TV's retakes, camera work, or directors and writers she knew and trusted made things even worse. The men in charge of the production—Merrill and Merrick— admired her intense work ethic, but they weren't Carl Reiner and John Rich from *Dick Van Dyke*. She missed being surrounded by people who knew how to guide her to her best work.

Merrick trashed the original script by Burrows. He needed a script doctor for the celebrated script doctor, and he was looking for Moore's old boss, Reiner. But Reiner was vacationing in Europe with his wife after five years of round-the-clock sitcom work, so there was nothing Merrick or Moore could do to lure him back to the States to fix *Breakfast at Tiffany's*. Instead, Merrick brought in the renowned—and quite serious—Edward Albee to take on the ill-fated rewrite. "Why drown in two feet of water?" Merrick said, explaining his choice of the *Who's Afraid of Virginia Woolf?* playwright. "We might as well swim out and take our chances."

But Albee began disparaging the current script in public: "All those awful jokes will be thrown out," he told the *Boston Globe*, "and I hope to substitute some genuine wit." An angry Burrows left as the production's director, replaced by *110 in the Shade* director Joseph Anthony.

Actors often received new script pages mere hours before curtain time during the preview shows, which caused major problems even though much of the material, Moore thought, was "masterful," ahead of its time. Still, it was excessive. Sometimes the show ran four hours.

Moore, despite her best efforts, was at least part of the problem. In Boston, she had "a vocal range of about six notes," as she later recalled, and a temperature of 103 as she battled the flu. Audiences in Philadelphia booed her, shocking the cast and crew. Who on earth boos the sweetest sitcom wife on television? Answer: people who want to see the darling star they fell in love with playing someone darling, not playing this dark lady of the night. If Moore had been given the role Audrey Hepburn had playing Holly Golightly, she may have been able to nail it. But she'd been given the part of a complicated, opportunistic hooker with more emphasis on how she made her living (collecting "fifty dollars for the powder room" from her dates)—and sometimes broke out into song. And other times swore. It was a dramatic challenge for which Moore was not prepared. Cast members started calling the show *Who's Afraid of Holly Golightly?*

The implied answer was Mary Tyler Moore. "She was a dream to work with, inexhaustible," Merrill said. "She was a good egg, but you always had a sense you knew you weren't getting all out of her." Every time Moore left the stage, she felt so terrible that she'd throw her arms around the stage manager, Burrows's son Jim, for comfort. Once, she collapsed to the floor, sobbing, "What have I done wrong?" She thought she was always about to be fired from the project. Merrick showed no ill will toward the actress, however. Despite rumors that Tammy Grimes or Diahann Carroll might take her place, Merrick never recast the role.

Instead, Merrick put Moore and the rest of the cast out of their misery. On December 15, 1966, he canceled the show before it officially opened in New York, despite having to refund $1 million in advance ticket sales. He referred to the incident in the press as "my Bay of Pigs." Moore later admitted to *Time* magazine, "I told everybody that doing *Breakfast at Tiffany's* had strengthened and enriched me and that I had developed valuable scar tissue to make me tougher. Except that none of that was true."

Holly Golightly, the character who had redefined single womanhood in America and made an icon of Audrey Hepburn, would not be doing the same for Mary Tyler Moore. Since *The Dick Van Dyke Show,* Moore had acted only in a handful of disposable movies for Universal that she'd been contractually obliged to make. The least offensive of the roles was as the naïve Dorothy, a supporting character in the film version of *Thoroughly Modern Millie,* starring Julie Andrews as the aggressive flapper. The most infamous was as a nun in *Change of Habit,* in which Moore, as Sister Michelle, falls in love with a doctor played by Elvis Presley.

Moore knew how far she'd fallen when she attended a movie premiere and was shoved out of the way by a pack of photographers. "Step aside, lady," one of them said to her, "here comes Marlo Thomas." Thomas was becoming a trendsetter as the star of a new sitcom, *That Girl,* about a single girl trying to make it in the big city. Moore was becoming a no-name, a has-been.

Soon after that, Moore suffered a miscarriage. She had a ten-year-old son from her first marriage, Richie, who shuttled between living with her and with his father, Dick Meeker, whom Moore had married straight out of high school. She had continued smoking and drinking after she found out she was pregnant with her and Tinker's first child—still a common practice at the time—and later wondered if her bad habits contributed to her miscarriage. At the hospital after losing the fetus, her body dealt her another blow: Her doctors discovered she was diabetic. Frustrated, she "caved in to an assault of self-pity," as she would later call it, after her diagnosis: She bought a dozen doughnuts, then drove around Beverly Hills eating all of them.

When the *Van Dyke* producers contacted Moore soon after that, with the offer to reunite her with her former TV husband in a variety special called *Dick Van Dyke and the Other Woman,* she grabbed the chance. At best, it would help fans—and, perhaps more importantly, show business—to forget about the *Breakfast at Tiffany's* debacle. At worst, it would end up a night of fun with old friends.

It got Moore far more than fun, though. The special didn't just feature Moore, it presented her as at least an equal to Van Dyke. In fact, it often played like a celebration of her, a reminder through song, dance, and comedy of all the assets that had been buried under the rubble of the last few years of her career. The opening number, "On the Other Hand," had Van Dyke singing about Moore's wonderfulness while dancing with dozens of different cardboard cutouts of her looking sexy in a bikini, seductive in a glittery gown, cute in a summer frock. Their first performance together, "Life Is Like a Sitcom," poked a bit of good-natured fun at their previous life as a TV couple. It was a special that challenged every TV reviewer *not* to use the word *charming*. Moore looked fresh, funny, talented, and totally in her element.

As soon as CBS executives saw the ratings for *Dick Van Dyke and the Other Woman,* and heard fans' enthusiastic response to seeing Moore on television again, they offered her the exact chance at career redemption she needed. How would she like to have her own sitcom, to be the headliner instead of the "other woman"?

Moore saw her way out of the career slump and personal disappointment she'd been stuck in for the last few years; she didn't hesitate to sign the deal. She'd missed TV comedy since leaving *Dick Van Dyke.* But she also knew she needed this new sitcom of hers to be special.

Under the circumstances, with her career comeback so fresh and still delicate, CBS likely assumed she'd hire Carl Reiner to make her another show in which she played an adorable housewife. That way, everyone—the network and viewers—would get what they expected. If there was a lesson to be learned from the *Breakfast at Tiffany's* debacle, it was that audiences did not enjoy the element of surprise when it came to Mary Tyler Moore.

But that was not what Moore would do. Instead, she allowed Tinker, with his eye for both the business and content of television, to take care of the details. Her strategy was to surround herself with talented people she trusted and let them do their thing—exactly what she'd wished she could have done on *Breakfast at Tiffany's*. She chose well: Her husband was not only running a major television studio at the time, but he was the kind of guy so perfect you wanted to hate him, except that you couldn't because he was so darn nice. He was known for hitting the home run at company softball games, for winning every tennis match, and for charming his associates with generosity, kindness, and class. He was good at everything he tried. If anyone had a chance at knocking her new sitcom out of the park, it was Tinker.

The couple had just returned to the welcoming warmth of Los Angeles to escape from the tribulations of the previous few years and for Tinker to start a new job as the head of Twentieth Century Fox Television. It was the perfect time for both Moore and Tinker to start life anew. What better way than working on her comeback project together?

Jim Brooks was hanging out at a laid-back New Year's Eve party in Los Angeles given by a guy named Bud Wiser—yes, the man, a fellow documentary writer, shared his name with a brand of beer. A Clark Kent type in a tuxedo showed up among the jeans-and-T-shirt crowd as champagne-popping time drew near. Allan Burns had arrived at the party with his wife, Joan, armed with a joke about their stuffy wardrobe, and the stuffier party he'd attended beforehand. "Now can I start having fun?" Burns said, chafing in his tux jacket. He and Joan had been at her friends' formal shindig ahead of this one. Brooks couldn't get over someone walking into that Bud Wiser party in black-tie gear.

Brooks and Burns, who'd known of each other through mutual friends, soon started chatting, and Brooks admitted to Burns that he didn't much like the documentary work he had been doing since moving to Los Angeles. What he wanted to do was comedy, great comedy. Brooks had quit his job in New York as a copywriter in the CBS newsroom a few months earlier, thinking he'd find a larger sense of purpose writing documentaries in Los Angeles for producer David Wolper. Brooks surprised himself by making the move; he hadn't thought of himself as someone with enough ambition to do such a thing.

His instinct to move toward the source of media power was a good one. The television business was truly taking over the country now. In the depths of North Dakota, three steel beams connected by a metal grid and painted in alternating red and white bands stretched above the surrounding farmland for 2,063 feet in what was now the tallest man-made structure in the world, the KTHI-TV mast, built for one reason: to broadcast network programming to the widest possible swath of households. To be in on the business that provided that programming, these days, one had to be in Los Angeles.

But since coming to Hollywood, Brooks, a quietly funny guy who enjoyed the work of comedians Mike Nichols and Elaine May, found himself more and more interested in the world of television comedy, rather than documentary. He didn't dare think he could get a job writing that sort of thing, but it intrigued him. "I want to get into TV," Brooks told Burns. "Sitcoms."

Burns's tux looked to Brooks like a sign of his success in the television business. He knew Burns's résumé, which spanned the impressive breadth from cartoon *George of the Jungle* to sophisticated sitcom *He & She*, which focused, *Dick Van Dyke*–like, on a cartoonist and his wife (played by real-life couple Richard Benjamin and Paula Prentiss). The show had gone off the air after just one season but had gotten loads of industry attention and won Burns an Emmy. By Brooks's count, Burns had about a million shows on the air at the time. Brooks wanted to be the next Carl Reiner, and this guy was in the right line of work to get him there.

Burns didn't impress himself quite so much. Though he worked steadily, the work didn't make him very proud. He was known for, among other things, co-creating the sitcom *My Mother the Car*, which was as ridiculous as its title: It starred Dick Van Dyke's brother, Jerry, as a guy whose deceased mother speaks to him through the radio of his antique car. At the same time that hippies were taking LSD and advocating for socialism and protesting war and making free love and *wondering what it all meant,* network television was trying to sell America a show about a guy whose car radio talks to him. The series became an instant, and lasting, punch line about everything dumb and crass and uncool and out-of-touch about TV. In any case, Burns's television work wasn't his focus. He was working on a screenplay on the side. He *really* wanted to be a respected film writer. Five years of television had worn him out, and it was time to follow his dream.

That night, as Brooks and Burns rang in 1966, Burns agreed to help secure his new friend a gig writing for *My Mother the Car.* It would be a good and obviously low-pressure place for him to start. The job marked Brooks's first break into Hollywood writing, and he was grateful for the opportunity, even if *My Mother the Car* was no *Dick Van Dyke.* "Pillar of the Community," Brooks told him. "That's my new nickname for you."

Thanks to the break Burns gave him, Brooks went on to write episodes of *That Girl, The Andy Griffith Show,* and *My Three Sons* before he was hired as a staffer on the short-lived comedy *My Friend Tony.* Jim Brooks was finally on his way to the career he wanted. Or at least he hoped so.

Three summers later, Jim Brooks—now officially James L. Brooks, television writer—called Allan Burns, eager to impress his old pal. He'd just helped develop a pilot—a test episode, which determines whether the network will buy the show and air it—for a new series called *Room 222.* The groundbreaking program would follow an African-American high school teacher played by the suave Lloyd Haynes, among the few black lead characters in TV history. ABC, the show's network, was in third place of three networks, and its programming department was run by the audacious Barry Diller, so it was scrappier than its competition and willing to take chances. The show had gotten picked up and was going into production. "I want you to come see it," Brooks told Burns. "I'm really proud of it."

"You want me to write for it, don't you?" Burns said, already worried he'd get sucked in. "And I'm not going to because I want to devote time to writing screenplays."

"No, no, no!" Brooks protested. "Not at all. I just want you to see it—I'm screening it for a bunch of people. Would you come over and look at it?"

Burns agreed to go to the Fox screening room, to show his support for Brooks's enthusiasm. He watched the show—an hour-long drama that focused on an American history class at the fictional Walt Whitman High School in Los Angeles—with Brooks and executive producer Gene Reynolds, along with four other producers and writers. *This is about the best thing I've ever seen,* Burns thought as he watched. It addressed the race issues at its core, but subtly. The cast, from Haynes to Michael Constantine, who played the principal, to Karen Valentine, who played a teacher, to the kids in the class, was impeccable. Burns could tell Brooks had done his homework before writing the script. Brooks had spent time at Los Angeles High School, and had gotten this portrait of a modern school just right. ABC had wanted to put a laugh track behind the show, but Brooks and Reynolds had refused; Burns thought that was admirable. He couldn't wait to tell his friend how terrific he thought the show was. When it ended, he didn't hesitate. "Okay, Jim, where do I sign up?" he said. "Because I'm not going to get the chance to write on anything anywhere near this good for a while."

Burns became one of the show's first freelance writers, still keeping his options open to write screenplays. The series gave him an office, even though he insisted he wasn't technically on staff. He wrote half a dozen scripts.

Then, when Reynolds left *Room 222* to work on some other pilots, Burns gave in and became a producer, always happy to help out. He and Brooks now produced and wrote, side by side, for the first time.

They grew closer; they liked each other and everyone they now worked with, a great feeling. All of the writers and producers partied with each other. They had their dream jobs. Everything seemed to be working according to plan.

Brooks, however, couldn't quite settle for just a dream job. Looking to expand on his newfound success, he worked on some other pilot projects. Burns stepped up to run *Room 222* full-time while Brooks pursued those other ideas. By fall of 1969, Burns was once again saddled with a television show he hadn't meant to run. He'd been trying to avoid exactly this—a committed, full-time involvement that took him away from his movie writing projects—but it was worth it to work on a great show and help his buddy Jim Brooks achieve the visions of TV greatness that had once seemed so far out of his reach.

The two made an unlikely pair. Brooks, a thirty-year-old hippie artsy type, had a beard and beads that belied his past life in a New York newsroom. Burns, a clean-cut thirty-five-year-old, sported side-parted hair and Buddy Holly glasses. But they had the kind of working chemistry that won Emmys and soon attracted the attention of Grant Tinker, now the vice president of Twentieth Century Fox Television, the studio that produced *Room 222* for ABC. He was also the husband of Mary Tyler Moore, that comedic vision both Brooks and Burns had admired from afar a decade earlier.

That fall, Burns found himself sitting across a restaurant table from Grant Tinker, a quietly handsome man who looked exactly like you imagine a great TV executive would look—graying hair, a few perfectly placed wrinkles, dimples, aquiline nose. The lunch, per Tinker, was to be a secret. Burns wasn't sure why, but he went along with it, since Tinker was something like his boss's boss's boss.

Tinker asked Burns whether he'd ever thought about doing another sitcom. Burns responded by complaining about the tough six-day-a-week, sixteen-hour-a-day schedule. "Grant, I've done it," he told the executive, thinking of his wife and young children. "It's hard work. I don't want to do another one."

"Well, think about it," Tinker said. "If you're running it, you can dictate your own schedule." Burns foolishly bought that argument and went back to his own office, near his home in Brentwood, agreeing to give it some thought.

Then he got a phone call from Brooks. "Have you been talking to Grant at all?" he remembers Brooks asking. "About doing another pilot?" The secret lunches had made Burns nervous. And now he was worried his buddy had gotten wind that he was engaged in discussions about another job behind his back.

Burns took his chances that the curious tone in Brooks's voice meant this was no accusation of treason. "As a matter of fact, I have," Burns replied, still playing it cool.

"Well, me, too. He's been talking to both of us. What do you think he's getting at?" Brooks asked, then answered his own question: "I think Mary's going to do a TV series and he's feeling us out. He loves us. He loves *Room 222*. That would be his style."

"You're right," Burns said, relieved they were on the same side. "Let's call him."

Brooks put Burns on hold while he patched Tinker in for a three-way conference call. Then they confronted the executive: "Mary's doing another show, right?"

Tinker confessed: He'd tried to handle the proceedings in what he called a "dark of night kind of way. I shouldn't even be talking to you about this on my Twentieth Century Fox phone." But he'd have to tell his prospective writer-producers eventually, so it might as well be sooner than later. "We've made a deal. But not at Fox. Let's get together and talk about it."

As it turned out, Moore had signed on for thirteen episodes with CBS; the network had jumped at the chance to work with her, without even the faintest hint of a premise. Tinker wanted creative minds with a fresh vision of what Moore could do, and he hoped Brooks and Burns would team up for the job. He wanted the kind of writers he could trust while he got out of the way. If one terrific writer was a good thing, he thought, two would make things even better.

Tinker, whom Brooks describes as a "heroic figure" for using his business acumen for artistic good, had made one crucial decision when his wife had signed with CBS: Moore and Tinker would form their own production company, called MTM Enterprises, to maintain some control of the show to which she'd hitch her fortunes. Of course, this meant funding their own production, making the series an awfully large gamble for its star. Her money, her reputation, and her future now depended on its success. Failing to make good would provide one more dramatic wallop to the star's fragile state. But succeeding would make Moore not only a star, but a pioneer. At the time, female producers were rare. Putting Moore's name on the new venture could still go either way—yes, she had some star power, but many men in the business still resisted the idea of women with real, executive power.

Moore had given Tinker a few stipulations about what she wanted in her new show, Tinker now told his producers. She wanted to play someone close to herself, because she didn't trust her acting skills to go much further. For the same reason, she also wanted to make it an ensemble show; even if it was named for her, as was typical for sitcoms of the time, she wanted to surround herself with great supporting actors. Allowing focus to routinely pull back from its marquee star would become the show's first major innovation, and its hallmark.

Brooks and Burns agreed to the job. Burns would have to postpone his movie-writing dreams yet again. He hoped this show was worth giving that up—and that it lived up to the faith Tinker had placed in them.

This kind of project could catapult Brooks's and Burns's careers to the next level of greatness, even the *Dick Van Dyke* level of Emmy-winning prestige, or it could flop quite prominently. But the pressure didn't end there. As they brainstormed ideas, they also found themselves heading a production company, since Tinker didn't want his name on it until the show was ready to go and he could leave his job at Fox.

Tinker secured offices for Brooks and Burns, then turned them loose to do the rest of the work. They put in long hours, getting to their new office in the early morning Southern California sun and heading home well after dark. They hired the new production company's accountant, as well as other employees. Most writers, even executive producers, did not take on this level of responsibility at a production company. But Brooks and Burns hardly knew any better. The arrangement, luckily, worked well, with Burns's experience and pragmatism balancing Brooks's visions of greatness.

Among their first hires was their secretary, Pat Nardo, who'd recently relocated from New York. Back east, the twenty-nine-year-old had been working for Talent Associates, a production company known for its work on Broadway as well as its gritty TV drama, *East Side/West Side,* starring George C. Scott. When Nardo left high school ten years earlier, she'd been the only girl in her class who wasn't engaged. Her friends had been in awe of her: "I don't have your courage," they said. "I want to know what I'm doing every Saturday night for the rest of my life." When she started working at Talent Associates, she considered it the most exciting place to work in the world. There she got to be far more than a secretary, and she learned what went into high-quality producing. The company hired a fair number of women (which is to say, more than one), though Nardo suspected that was because women made less money and seemed less threatening to David Susskind, the prolific producer and talk show host who ran the place.

In any case, the job allowed her a surprising amount of responsibility and adventure. Susskind would send her on last-minute trips with F. Lee Bailey—a lawyer famous at the time for defending Dr. Sam Sheppard, who was convicted, then later acquitted in a retrial, of killing his pregnant wife (and whose story became the basis for *The Fugitive*). Bailey was now hosting a talk show, *Good Company,* meant to emulate Edward R. Murrow's successful '50s interview show, *Person to Person*. Nardo got her first passport as a one-day rush job so she could jet to London for shoots with J. Paul Getty and Sean Connery. On another trip, she flew, with a scotch-sipping Bailey at the controls, in a private plane to Chicago for a tour of the Playboy Mansion.

But recently she'd met someone. Chuck Barris ran ABC's daytime programming department, creating hot new game shows such as *The Newlywed Game* for the network, and she'd fallen for him. He asked her to move out to Los Angeles to be closer to him, and she found a job on a film that was about to start shooting. When that fell through, one of Barris's colleagues suggested she interview with these two comedy writers he knew who were developing a show. He'd heard they needed a secretary.

At first, she wasn't impressed with the idea of working for Brooks and Burns. Before working for Susskind, she'd been secretary to the charismatic producer Bob Rafelson, who created *The Monkees* TV show in 1966. Nardo hadn't watched *The Dick Van Dyke Show*, so she had only the vaguest idea of who this Mary Tyler Moore was, and she had no idea who Brooks and Burns were.

When she met with them, she couldn't even believe these two guys could work together—they were the definition of "odd couple." Brooks's desk was a mess of papers and stray pieces of clothing; Burns's was impeccable. Brooks slumped over and spaced out during the interview; Burns directed the questioning. When Burns asked what brought her to California, she didn't want to say she'd come for a man, so she ranted in her Bronx accent about how sick of New York she'd gotten. Brooks, finally roused, looked right at her and said, "She's Rhoda."

She had no idea what he meant—that she was the embodiment of the outspoken, Jewish girl from New York they'd been envisioning as the character of Mary's best friend. But her Rhoda-ness sold Brooks on Nardo. Burns, on the other hand, liked her Gucci shoes. She got the job, whether she wanted it or not. She didn't—she was sure she would be miserable at it. She was above this. But she took it to make money and stay close to Barris.

It helped, however, when Brooks and Burns offered to get the *New York Times* delivered to the office every day for her. She'd read the paper every day of her life since her teenage years, but she couldn't afford it now. She'd considered it her college. If Pat Nardo was going to be a secretary, she needed at least a little bit of intellectual stimulation. The *New York Times* was a good start. She had no idea at the time that she'd be among the show's several influential women behind-the-scenes— and one of its many secretaries-turned-TV-writers who would help make Mary Richards into a feminist icon.

Just when Nardo was starting to warm to her new job, she managed to offend her new bosses. Brooks and Burns were going to a meeting across town, and they felt bad that their secretary would be alone in the office all day, so they invited her to join them. She climbed into the backseat. As they drove, they were discussing how awful most of television was. "Talk about a bad show," Nardo cracked, "how about that *My Mother the Car*?" Brooks and Burns froze, suddenly silent. She knew what she'd done just by the way they acted. "And you wrote it," she concluded.

In case there had been any lingering doubt, this served as a reminder to Brooks and Burns: If their secretary didn't know who they were, if her only knowledge of their body of work was their laughable mother-as-motor-vehicle scripts, they still had a long way to go to conquer Hollywood.

TWO
TWO
TWO
TWO
TWO
TWO
TWO
TWO

tHE pRODUCERS

(1969–70)

The character who could change all of their fates, Mary Richards—who could give Treva Silverman something to write about, could make Jim Brooks and Allan Burns the innovative producers they wanted to be, could give Mary Tyler Moore the comeback she needed—began her fictional life in a room full of men. And that life began with one dreaded word: *divorce*.

Brooks and Burns sat in a conference room at CBS's New York headquarters, known as Black Rock. The network had just built the structure—the only skyscraper ever designed by Finnish architect Eero Saarinen, famous for his stark aesthetic. The black granite building at Fifty-second Street and Sixth Avenue rose thirty-eight stories from midtown Manhattan's Television Row, where CBS, ABC, and NBC all plotted their gambits to dominate the country's 83 million TV sets. The building seemed fittingly ominous for this nightmare of a business meeting. A fall chill settled over the shedding trees in nearby Central Park.

The producers were now trapped in one of the upper floors, surrounded by black-paneled walls and network executives, as the lights in the ceiling burned into the tops of their heads. CBS was the Establishment, where executives wore pin-striped suits and had gray hair. Both Brooks and Burns had been to other pitch meetings before in their careers, but this felt different, more menacing. As Burns later remembered, "It was like something straight out of Kafka."

Brooks and Burns had flown across the country from Los Angeles with Arthur Price, Moore's business manager and now the de facto vice president of her production company, to share their vision for the new series with programming executive Mike Dann and his colleagues. The destiny of the show rested with Brooks and Burns, in this room, as the faces of MTM Entertainment. They wished Tinker, with his magical way of smoothing over any business interaction, were there with them. But Tinker remained in Los Angeles, staying in the background for now.

"You want to *divorce* Mary?" Michael Dann asked, incredulous.

Dann was known for his obsession with ratings numbers, and particularly his competition with NBC's vice president for audience measurement, Paul Klein. As technology made the numbers increasingly parsable, network executives had begun to worship the god known as Nielsen, the company that tracked viewership numbers for the networks. Ratings were born in the days of radio, back in 1930, when a group of advertisers met with an opinion researcher to form the Cooperative Analysis of Broadcasting. The group decided to use telephone polling to determine which shows were most popular; researchers would call a sampling of potential viewers and ask what they'd listened to the day before. Nielsen began offering ratings services in 1942, replacing phone polling with a device that was installed in selected homes to photograph and time-stamp which channel the device was tuned to at a given time. The national numbers were extrapolated from the sampling of about 1,200 homes. Eventually, Nielsen moved into the burgeoning world of television.

Now, in the late '60s, Nielsen raked in an estimated $10 million a year from the networks, local affiliates, and advertising agencies. And for good reason: The numbers were growing ever more sophisticated, allowing networks to determine their audiences' location (goal: big cities), age (goal: younger than forty-nine), income (goal: higher than the $8,389 annual average), and level of education (goal: college or better). This information was gold to advertisers hoping to target their messages. And it led networks to promote themselves with laughably specific boasts: NBC's 1970 "Product Usage Highlights" packet, for example, proudly announced, "Audiences of 12 returning NBC shows reveal high usage of dry dog food."

Dann and NBC's Klein, as the two most ratings-obsessed men in a ratings-obsessed business, had become infamous in their enmity. The two often traded barbs in the industry press, as well as via personal correspondence. They'd never met in person, but regularly exchanged notes bearing messages such as, "You are scum!" The battle had heated up in the last two seasons of television: After thirteen straight years of CBS dominance, NBC started winning in the demographic most important to advertisers—young, wealthy, educated consumers. To pull off a last-minute victory for the 1968–69 season, Dann threw out his network's weakest regular shows and subbed in specials: a documentary about Eskimos, another about a veterans' hospital; a broadcast of British drama *Born Free* and its sequel, *The Lions Are Free*.

Things got so desperate that the entire season's success ended up riding on a CBS *Cinderella* special. Dann wired CBS's two hundred affiliates: "My [contract] option is coming due shortly. . . . And how you promote *Cinderella* will tell me something about your personal feelings toward me." CBS came out ahead of NBC, 20.3 percent to 20 percent.

Now, however, as calendars flipped to the last page of 1969, Dann's position at CBS was far from solid. The ratings wars had continued the previous fall, with NBC doing so well that it called a press conference where it handed out bright yellow buttons that said HAPPINESS IS BEING NO. 1. "I've never known what it is to lose," Dann kept muttering to colleagues, flabbergasted. "I've never lost a season."

Dann wasn't taking any chances with his programming, and he and the New York suits hadn't laughed at a thing Brooks and Burns had said in their comedy pitch so far. The word *divorce* hung in the air. The network executives saw nothing funny about divorce. The divorce rate in the country was skyrocketing. It was a serious problem, not a sitcom premise. They would sooner fill the time period allotted for this show with that American-flag footage that signaled the network had signed off for the night than they would sanction a comedy about a divorced woman played by Mary Tyler Moore. "Yes," the producers said. "We want to divorce Mary."

A silence.

Then, the onslaught of objections. "The audience will think she divorced Dick Van Dyke!" one executive said.

The producers ran through their prepared response: They would show her husband. He would be nothing like Dick Van Dyke. They promised. The script would make it clear that Mary was not at fault, that she was so likable even her ex's parents couldn't stay away from her after the divorce.

"Why not make her more like Doris Day or Lucille Ball?" another executive asked.

Doris Day, they explained, was somehow playing an ingénue even though she was forty-eight. That might have flown once, in the '60s, but it was hardly the way to make a statement at the beginning of a new decade. Movements for women's independence, free love—these weren't even *new* anymore, and yet TV was still trying to sell shows about happy couples and "innocent" grown women and life down home on the farm. And Lucy, a national treasure, could do what she pleased and still draw an audience. Brooks and Burns wanted reality with this show. Funny reality, but reality. And a lot of viewers would likely relate to a thirty-year-old divorced woman, the producers argued.

"Why *do* you have to say her age?" another executive wondered. "You don't have to *say* it. Lucy never says her age."

But, the producers replied, they wanted to say Mary's age. If she was thirty, and single, and divorced, wouldn't she be inherently more interesting than the ageless wives who had populated television since its inception?

"We have a man here from our research department," Dann said, "and I'd like him to say a few things."

Research Department Man chimed in. "Our research says American audiences won't tolerate divorce in a lead of a series any more than they will tolerate Jews, people with mustaches, and people who live in New York."

Brooks and Burns could form no logical response to this, except, perhaps, to note that Mary would be none of the other three. The writers refused to back down. The executives implied that if they went ahead with their current plans, the show wouldn't last past its thirteen-episode commitment. This, and Brooks and Burns hadn't even gotten past the "divorce" part of their pitch to discuss Mary's proposed job as a gossip columnist's assistant. The matter of her career and the rest of her life would have to wait until her complicated marital status was settled.

Dann, meanwhile, rolled his eyes at another pair of creative types gone haywire in a pitch meeting: This was a pretty typical day at the office for him, especially when dealing with the unique breed of individuals known as comedy writers. He imagined them all immediately heading to their analysts' offices between meetings to deal with their intense *feelings*. He always felt like they were about to strangle him with their enthusiasm for their own ideas. "If you guys are determined to go with this," he told the producers, "it's Grant's call."

As Brooks, Burns, and Price turned to leave, Dann asked Price to stay behind. "Arthur," he said, "there are a few business things I'd like to discuss if the guys want to wait outside for you." Once the door closed, he had one item of business: These guys, whoever they were, could very well end up killing Moore's show, he warned.

Price told him he'd discuss the matter with Tinker, but he didn't think a change of producers was likely. He didn't, however, sugarcoat things when he met Brooks and Burns at the elevator. "Guys," he said, "that did not go well."

A few weeks before the New York meeting with the network, newly minted producers James L. Brooks and Allan Burns had arrived at Mary Tyler Moore and Grant Tinker's home in the tony Hollywood Hills—a neighborhood full of winding roads and panoramic views made famous by resident George Harrison's song "Blue Jay Way." The producers came armed with a bold idea, and some trepidation. They knew how important this show was to Moore, and thus to Tinker. And they knew their idea wasn't quite what most people expected from Moore's return to television. But they also thought it was a terrific idea, the next step beyond *The Dick Van Dyke Show*.

When Moore appeared atop the grand staircase to make her movie-star entrance, the producers had to choke down their nerves. When she got to the bottom of the stairs, however, she wobbled a little, pretending she was drunk, drugged, or otherwise unstable, here in the middle of the day. Then she laughed.

Burns and Brooks laughed in response, more at ease. She was genuinely funny.

They didn't know if she would find their proposal for her show quite so amusing. Writers renowned for their Emmy wins, critical lauds, and realistic approach to issues on *Room 222*, Jim Brooks and Allan Burns did not court the masses with middlebrow humor. They tackled modern problems. Brooks's old boss on *Room 222*, Gene Reynolds, had instilled in him the value of research—lots and lots of research. Brooks would tell him, having visited a school for a day, "I'm done." Reynolds would say, "Go back." At first, Brooks grew annoyed, but once he learned to stop resisting the extra work, he started to enjoy it. He'd since adopted that approach to all of his work.

Critics seemed to like that approach, though *Room 222* was hardly a smash hit with viewers. The duo knew Tinker liked them, but they had no idea yet what to expect of their star. They also weren't sure how much she wanted to risk on her comeback show. For their part, however, they wanted this series to be a step forward from *Room 222*, to be even better and bolder than their first risky enterprise together was. They could only hope Moore and Tinker gave them that chance.

Moore's character, they now told their new bosses, should be divorced and starting a new life. Her name would be Mary Richards, a smart, nice girl from Roseburg, Minnesota—and she would be unapologetic about her age, about being single, and about her independence. Popular culture was changing: Woodstock had rocked the music world earlier that year. The Beatles had given their last concert together. Brooks and Burns wanted to make a show that could finally pull television into modern times, they explained to the couple.

The idea went over better than they dared hope.

Moore herself had gotten divorced, eight years earlier, from the man she'd married straight out of high school, Richard Meeker. She could relate to the character they were now proposing, a woman who had chosen the wrong man when she was too young to know better and was now starting over. Their idea also seemed like a fresh concept for television, she told them, with lots of story possibilities. That the character was a single woman, and thirty, felt new for the lead of a sitcom.

Brooks and Burns's pitch also called for Moore's character to be an assistant to a prickly gossip columnist modeled after the *Los Angeles Times'* Joyce Haber. Moore and Tinker went for the whole thing. "I hired you because you did stuff that seemed to be in the real world," Tinker told the producers. "And that's what I want this to be."

What Grant Tinker wanted and what CBS executives wanted, however, was not necessarily the same.

Next Brooks and Burns had to present their Moore-approved premise to CBS's Los Angeles–based vice president, Perry Lafferty. If he liked it, they'd head to New York for what would be that ultimately disastrous final approval meeting. Over a tense lunch at the network's Television City headquarters, Lafferty was already anticipating the cold reception their idea would receive at CBS's East Coast headquarters. This was, after all, the network of *I Love Lucy*. "Divorced?" he asked. His boyish face went slack and pale with disbelief as commissary knives and forks clanged against commissary plates. "No, you can't do this. You cannot have Mary Tyler Moore divorced. People hate divorce and there's no way that anybody is going to accept her that way."

Lafferty was known for being slick and modern himself—his meticulously side-parted hair, dark-framed glasses, and tailored suits made him look like a handsome, serious version of a *Get Smart* agent. But he'd risen through the ranks at CBS on a straightforward philosophy: Series concepts should be as simple as a paper clip, "a bit of wire adroitly twisted into useful form," but capable of infinite variations, like a great piece of classical music. More practically speaking, scrapped series pilots cost the network up to $750,000 each year. Lafferty didn't like missteps.

On the other hand, critics were grumbling about CBS's successful, but wildly out-of-touch, lineup of silly, backwoods-set shows: *Green Acres, The Beverly Hillbillies, Petticoat Junction*. "A stirring up of the schedule, particularly with some contemporary material among all that rural corn pone, would be good for television," *Los Angeles Times* columnist Cecil Smith had written of the network's current offerings. Lafferty wanted to take a few creative chances with some new shows—but big gambles were better off made in summer programming, not in series featuring major stars, with major commitments, and major fall launches. He was currently considering seventeen possible new shows for the fall, but he had only four open spots on his schedule. One of those *had* to go to Moore, so Lafferty preferred her series concept be ironclad.

But it was hard to tell anymore what was ironclad in the TV business. The medium had tentatively pushed boundaries in the past year, though not in a very artful way. The sketch comedy series *Turn-On* turned into a notorious flop, airing just once in February 1969 on ABC with gratuitous bits that expected audiences to guffaw over uses of the word *titular* and a pregnant woman singing "I Got Rhythm" as a reference to (lack of) birth control. NBC's . . . *Then Came Bronson* tried to be *Easy Rider* for TV but came off as a toothless wannabe starring one of many Steve McQueen lookalikes who populated the airwaves that season.

Overall, though, networks continued to offer either the same old predictable standards or fluff for prime-time, scripted programming in 1969: *The Brady Bunch,* that happy, blended television family resplendent in trivial problems and loads of double-knit polyester, premiered; *My Three Sons* and *Bewitched* remained staples. The formula for success espoused by former CBS president Jim Aubrey—"broads, bosoms, and fun," a nonstop beach party—had yet to leave the airwaves completely even though times had changed since the early '60s, when he'd given the green light to *Hillbillies, Gilligan's Island,* and the like. Aubrey had great success with that programming throughout the decade, even though he had great contempt for his audience: "The American public," he once said, "is something I fly over."

Television's untapped power grew more evident through its role in real events: The moon landing was viewed by 720 million people around the world; Senator Edward Kennedy addressed the fatal car crash on Chappaquiddick before a national audience; film director Roman Polanski discussed the brutal murder of his pregnant wife, Sharon Tate, by followers of Charles Manson. All these real events kept viewers riveted, and had them talking for days about what they'd seen on television.

It seemed like TV had the power to effect genuine change, to push culture forward instead of holding it back. Producers like Brooks and Burns were trying to move the medium in that direction—the trick was to do so without scaring network executives and alienating advertisers. Joining them in their crusade was film director Norman Lear, who wrote and produced the Dick Van Dyke movies *Divorce American Style* and *Cold Turkey.* He had been struggling to get his progressive sitcom about a blue-collar family with political differences onto the air. Based on the British series *'Till Death Do Us Part,* which featured a working-class Tory battling with his socialist son-in-law, the U.S. version had gone through two failed pilot episodes at ABC, but Lear, who felt that no one was depicting American life candidly on television, was determined to make it work. Comedy writer Garry Marshall had a pet project, too: bringing a TV version of Neil Simon's acclaimed Broadway play and film *The Odd Couple* to life. They all hinted at TV's potential to turn toward the smarter.

Now, however, Brooks and Burns tried to reason with Lafferty on a more basic level. They just wanted him to consider the divorce idea for the moment; changing television history could come later. "Look, everybody, including all the executives at CBS, has been divorced," they told him. "It's not this terrible stigma. It's not like divorced people are lepers. Why are you so afraid of it?"

Lafferty started to warm to the idea, even though it still made him nervous. "Listen," he said, "what you're saying makes sense. But we have to go and pitch it to Mike Dann in New York."

That, of course, didn't turn out so well.

After the New York meeting, Arthur Price called Grant Tinker to tell him what the CBS executives had said about Brooks and Burns. Tinker wasn't interested. Firing Brooks and Burns was out of the question as far as he was concerned. He knew he still had leverage—he had Moore, with whom the network wanted to be in business. Moore and Tinker were willing to reconsider the divorce angle if their producers were, but the producers themselves would stay.

Dann just wanted to protect Moore's persona. He'd done battle for years with Reiner over *The Dick Van Dyke Show* upholding Standards & Practices edicts: Yes, the Petries would need to sleep in separate beds, with nightstands between them. If Lucy and Desi had to do it, so did Rob and Laura. Dann's standards hadn't changed much since then. He worried that Moore's loyal fans would react badly to her being a divorcée, a status he thought implied a woman of lesser morals.

"I think you could classify me as a prude at that point," he explains. "I was worried about keeping a perfect image of her." He wanted to maintain leverage for the network as well: "You're negotiating with [producers] for a major commitment of a couple million dollars," Dann says. "You never are *too* enthusiastic [about their show] when you're dealing with them. As a consequence, the creative people think they know everything, but they don't. While my career depends upon them, at the time they make the deal, they're the opposition."

And in this case, the opposition—Moore and Tinker—wouldn't back down. "They knew exactly what they wanted to do and they were going to do it," says Fred Silverman (no relation to Treva), who at the time worked under Dann as the network's vice president of development. "After that the network threw its hands up." The couple proved a formidable team, Dann recalls: "Grant played a strong role in getting Mary what she wanted. Mary was lady-like and could cook dinner for you, but she was firm about protecting her career."

Jim Brooks and Allan Burns got on a plane back to Los Angeles together after their New York meeting, exhausted and dejected. The five-hour flight felt twice as long, Burns recalls, as they relived the horrible feeling of a room full of network executives who seemed to hate them. Soaring over the patchwork quilt of midwestern states, they discussed quitting the Moore project, knowing they could always go running back to *Room 222*. That show was struggling in the ratings, but it was still getting solid critical notice and had a shot at some Emmy nominations. "And I've got my movie career," Burns reasoned, trying to see the bright side. Why not make everyone's lives easier, they thought, and back out now? They figured that if they did stick around, Dann would just make their lives miserable.

But after they got home, they reconvened in their shared temporary office at CBS Studio Center and thought better of their decision. The news of their quitting would come out in *Variety*, they figured, and it would seem like they didn't get along with Moore and Tinker. It would look bad for everyone involved. So they decided that since they still had Moore's and Tinker's backing, they would brainstorm a new concept for the show to address some of the network's concerns while still making a series that felt contemporary for 1970 *and* worthy of Moore's big comeback.

They thought about Moore's strongest qualities, about what she was best at. There was no reason she had to be in a typical domestic sitcom as a wife to use the traits that made Laura Petrie a sensation—just the right balance of sexy and innocent, sweet and tough, independent and vulnerable. After a week, they came up with a compromise of sorts: Mary would still be single. And, yes, still thirty. But she wouldn't be going through a divorce; she would simply be recovering from a big breakup.

They also took the opportunity to rethink the idea of putting her at the mercy of a bitchy boss in a Los Angeles newspaper office. They had never loved that concept to begin with, so they felt lucky to replace it. Now Mary would live in the city—Minneapolis, they decided, to get away from overplayed Los Angeles and New York. Minneapolis's bad weather could provide plot points and visual interest. Mainly, snow. And lots of coats. It would also allow for a bit of character illumination. What seemed like a big city to Mary would be a small town to her New York transplant best friend, Rhoda.

Mary would work in a local TV newsroom based on Brooks's experiences at CBS News in New York. A newsroom would lend a sense of everyday reality to the series, as well as provide conflict—it would be a loser station constantly struggling with ratings. For research, Brooks and Burns spent time at the local Los Angeles news affiliate, KNXT, where CBS president Robert D. Wood had once worked, and where Moore's aunt, Alberta Hackett, also used to work. The station's anchor, Jerry Dunphy, known for his authoritative voice, became the model for the vacuous character of Ted Baxter. Brooks and Burns saw producers with bottles of liquor in their desks and thought, *Our producer character must do that.*

To make sure Moore was surrounded by a strong ensemble cast, they created two separate worlds for Mary, her workplace and her home life—a similar model to *The Dick Van Dyke Show,* but this time, with a single woman at its center. To populate these worlds, the writers dreamed up the kind of strong characters they were known for: an overbearing, semi-alcoholic newsroom boss; a kindly newswriter; that Dunphy-like newscaster; a perfectionist neighbor; and that tough best friend.

The friend was to be a particularly important part of the cast. Brooks and Burns based Rhoda Morgenstern on a friend of Brooks's sister named Rose Goldman. Rhoda got her last name from the title character of the Herman Wouk novel and subsequent film *Marjorie Morningstar,* about a Jewish girl who changes her name to become an artist. But Goldman provided Rhoda's generous heart and soul. Brooks had met Goldman when he was newly married and looking for an affordable apartment in New York. Goldman did the impossible by finding him one. Her secret: bribing the doormen of a rent-controlled apartment with the promise of brides. *That* was Rhoda.

Mary would need help from a friend like that. She'd be starting over after a major breakup with a longtime boyfriend who refused to propose, even after she'd supported him through medical school. The script would imply that she had possibly lived with him, though it would never make it clear. Given that she was thirty and had been "supporting" him, audiences could surmise the obvious. CBS, in turning down divorce, had settled for living in sin.

Brooks liked the idea of a character who was "an independent single woman, who had spent her life wanting to be a dependent married woman up until that point." That premise struck him as rife with fresh comedic possibilities and dramatic conflicts alike. Brooks and Burns's original twenty-one-page proposal for the show summed up her character: "Mary is open and nice. That's why she's in trouble. It's also why she's still single. If she had been less open she could've maneuvered that doctor into marrying her. In the world of the seventies, openness is for national parks; niceness is for Betty White, who can turn a buck with it; and trust is something the President asks for and doesn't get. Lest you be left with the picture of Mary with warm apple pies cooling on her windowsill, singing duets with her pet squirrel, that's not our girl. It's just that she seems especially wholesome when contrasted with those around her. (We'll let you in on a secret that's for our eyes only. Mary is not a virgin. This becomes a very wholesome quality when you realize that Rhoda is not a virgin many times over.) . . .

"This series will, as we hope you have noted, be comedically populated. But it is clearly about one person living in and coping with the world of the 1970s . . . tough enough in itself . . . even tougher when you're 30, single, and female . . . when, despite the fact that you're the antithesis of the career woman, you find yourself the only female in an all-male newsroom."

This described the fate of more than a few real women at the time, but it was a scenario that had never been depicted on television. When Moore read it, she told the producers she loved it enough to take the risks involved. "This is what I wanted to do," they recall her saying. "I would have loved to have been divorced. But this is great."

THREE
THREE
THREE
THREE
THREE
THREE

THREE

NOT QUITE MAKING IT YET

(1970)

James L. Brooks and Allan Burns were still toiling over their pilot script for *The Mary Tyler Moore Show* during the spring before the series was to air. On another day of not quite finishing, they got a call at their office. It was Moore's manager, Arthur Price. He asked, not just out of curiosity, "Do you have any ideas on the theme?" Since Brooks and Burns were still recovering from their battle with the network and coming up with their living-in-sin compromise, they'd had time to write only a brief outline of the show's pilot. They were still concentrating on Mary's words—and the occasional foosball game—not her song.

But Price was always looking for opportunities for his music business clients. It just so happened that he'd passed the series outline on to one of them, a singer-songwriter named Sonny Curtis. The thirty-three-year-old southern "shitkicker kind of a guy," as Burns describes him, had been born in a dugout—a hole in the ground with a roof over it, his family's makeshift house—in Meadow, Texas. He had played with Buddy Holly back home, where the only way boys like them could get themselves out of their fleck of a town was to play some good country-and-western on the guitar. Curtis had found his way to fame when he met Holly in the '50s at a local radio station's "Sunday Party" open mic in Lubbock, Texas. Curtis, a good-looking bluegrass singer with a smooth voice, had driven thirty miles to pick for whoever would listen. He could also fiddle a hoedown like nobody's business. Buddy took notice, and soon the two were swapping R&B records, drinking beer, chasing girls, and occasionally playing actual music together.

Because of this close friendship, Curtis later went on to play in Holly's band, the Crickets, when the band members continued on after Holly's death in 1959. Curtis also became a successful songwriter, whose hits included the much-covered rock anthem "I Fought the Law." Now he lived in Los Angeles, and he was looking for work.

Curtis, who'd been spending most of his time writing jingles, had gotten a call from his agent that day, at around eleven in the morning, telling him about the new sitcom in the works for Mary Tyler Moore. Someone from the agency dropped off a four-page outline for the show at his house, which proved to be just enough detail. He didn't want too much information to "muddy the waters," as he says, of his creativity. First he thought of the gentle cascading notes of the guitar lick that would become the opening of the song. Then he contemplated what he knew about the show: It was to follow a young woman from the Midwest moving to the big city—which, to her, was Minneapolis—and renting an apartment almost beyond her means. The first lyrics began to flow: "How will you make it on your own? This world is awfully big, and girl, this time you're all alone."

By 2 p.m., he called his agent and said, "Who do I sing this to?"

Then Price called Burns, who remembers him saying, "There's this guy who used to be with Buddy Holly. He's a songwriter and he plays guitar. He's written something I think is pretty good."

"That's kind of putting the cart before the horse, but okay," Burns said.

At 4 p.m., Curtis sat in an iron chair in the middle of Brooks and Burns's temporary office at CBS's Studio Center, cradling his guitar, ready to make a buck or two on his new song. He laid a sheet of paper on top of his guitar case and sang the freshly written lyrics. Brooks and Burns looked at each other with mutual disbelief: Could it be this easy? How did a Texas farm boy understand their show about a modern midwestern woman so well when they still couldn't seem to complete their script? This song would speak directly to the young women starting to enter the workforce in larger numbers.

Brooks got on the phone. The room filled with MTM staffers. He asked someone to bring him a cassette recorder; once it appeared, Curtis sang the song again.

Next Curtis found himself at Price's office meeting with lawyers and the producers. They told him they wanted the song but would hire someone else to sing it. "You can't have it then," Curtis said. "If you're gonna get someone that's not-known to sing it, that not-known person has to be me." They revealed that they were considering crooner Andy Williams for the job, who was, as Curtis says, "hotter than soap at the time," and one of Price's clients. Curtis's only capitulation: "If you can get him," he said, "you can have it. But otherwise it has to be me."

Andy Williams declined the gig, so the songwriter got to sing his song, turning his gritty twang into a creamy city-boy baritone. Now Brooks and Burns had to write a character who lived up to every word of Curtis's hopeful and hopelessly catchy tune, "Love Is All Around."

Burns passed the song along to his friend, composer Patrick Williams (no relation to singer Andy)—who'd done music for several TV shows, including *Columbo*—and asked if he could work out some orchestrations to score the show. Curtis went to Williams's house and played the song yet again on Williams's tape recorder, then left. Williams began arranging how it would sound in the opening title sequence and for the end credits. Of course, he had no idea how important the song, or the show, would be at the time. It felt like just another job to him. In fact, he wasn't hearing good buzz around town about the project. As he says, "It wasn't like cymbals crashed and you heard a wild C-major chord from an orchestra when the *Mary Tyler Moore Show* pilot was made."

Still, it needed cue music for however long it stayed on the air, and Williams was happy to do the job. *Mary Tyler Moore,* as Williams saw it, sounded like strings, flutes, clarinets, and flugelhorns, which he considered "a feminine kind of sound. I thought there was a certain vulnerability to the feeling of the show, and that's what I tried to put into the music."

At the time, he and most television composers wrote their scores by hand, and for each individual episode. For *The Mary Tyler Moore Show,* Williams used a twenty-five-piece orchestra, doing about three episodes in a three-hour recording session. He scored every cue as he watched a rough cut of a filmed show, treating it like a mini-movie and working *with* the natural audience laughter. (No laugh tracks allowed.) A fellow composer friend would later call Williams "the undisputed king of the three-second cue."

Next, the producers recruited thirty-nine-year-old, Iranian-born director Reza Badiyi, who'd done some work on *He & She,* to shoot the opening for *The Mary Tyler Moore Show.* He was himself an unusual Hollywood story: He'd moved from Iran to the United States in 1955 after directing documentaries in his native country, and graduated from Syracuse University with a film degree. He eventually befriended director Robert Altman, who hired him as his assistant on his low-budget 1957 debut, *The Delinquents.* Badiyi soon after secured work in the television industry, directing episodes of *Mission: Impossible* and *Mannix*—hardly a natural progression toward *The Mary Tyler Moore Show,* but he'd made a name for himself assembling the distinctive credits for the sensations *Hawaii Five-O* and *Get Smart.*

For *The Mary Tyler Moore Show,* Badiyi conceived a simple-but-sweet opening sequence, featuring Mary driving her 1969 Mustang from her hometown in the Minnesota suburbs down Route 100 toward Minneapolis, intercut with scenes of her leaving her friends behind to start a new life and frolicking about various parts of town looking glamorously independent. In one cut she wore a fox fur–trimmed jacket (which would disappear from the sequence by the second season, when Moore became an animal rights activist). In another she wore an enviable shearling and suede coat lent by Brooks and Burns's new secretary, New York transplant Pat Nardo.

Now Badiyi, the producers, and Moore faced their first major decisions on the look of Mary Richards. Their main concern was distinguishing her from Laura Petrie. Moore wanted very much to prove that she could be more than Laura, since her previous efforts to do so in movies and on the stage had fallen flat. She thought long and hard about her former character's distinctive look, and her own tastes. But in the end, she could think of only one major way to emphasize the new Mary: She would wear a wig to make sure her hair looked nothing like Laura's signature bobbed flip. She hoped Brooks and Burns's script would do the rest of the work to impress her new image upon viewers.

Moore and the crew experienced Minneapolis at its most brutally cold on the February day when they shot the credits. Luckily Moore didn't have to speak for the footage, as most of the time her lips couldn't move enough to form coherent words. But Badiyi had a vision, and most of it involved outdoor shooting. He hoped the final scene of the sequence would become the pièce de résistance: Mary would stop in the middle of an intersection, Nicollet Mall and Seventh Street, and toss the hat she had with her (a knitted black and turquoise beret Moore's aunt had given her) in the air. The beret would serve as the perfect headwear for this, given its associations with rebels (see: beatniks, Black Panthers) as well as girlish dreams of European sophistication. The act, Badiyi reasoned, would symbolize Mary's graduation into her new, single, adult life in the city.

As they wrapped up filming on Nicollet Mall, Badiyi told the shivering star, "Run out into the middle of that intersection and throw your hat up in the air as if this is the happiest moment of your life." As always, Moore did as she was told, even though she wasn't sure what Badiyi was envisioning. The hat flew up in the air, and then plopped down onto the pavement. That was the shot. They wrapped.

Once they returned to Los Angeles and Badiyi showed Brooks and Burns the raw footage on the editing machine, the producers were puzzled. But they had other worries, so they had to trust Badiyi to do something worthwhile. If they hadn't been desperately trying to write a good script, they may have meddled more.

They were happy they didn't. They couldn't believe just how good it looked once it was edited together, freeze-framed at the end with the hat in the air and a scowling older woman who happened to be walking by disapproving of Mary's independence for eternity. "You son of a bitch," Burns said to Badiyi. "You made this work."

But Brooks and Burns, along with their growing crew, still had far more work to do before they had a ready-to-shoot show.

After the scouting trip to Minneapolis, the producers knew what Mary's home would look like: a three-story Queen Anne Victorian house, with the exterior of the real home at 2104 Kenwood Parkway, divided up into apartments. Mary would have the $130 a month studio unit with the grand Palladian windows that the script outline called for: "A room. Actually, an entire apartment, a single large room. There are some—mostly of the working-girl variety—who would consider this a 'great find': 10-foot ceilings, pegged wood floors, a wood-burning fireplace, and, most important, a fantastic ceiling-height corner window. Right now the room is totally empty, but it won't be for long. It will be the main setting for THE MARY TYLER MOORE SHOW. So God Bless It."

Set designer Lewis Hurst and set decorator Raymond Boltz went to work putting this description together with some Mary-appropriate décor. Their crews began constructing sets on the stage at General

Service Studios, where the first season of *The Mary Tyler Moore Show* would go into production. She'd have a hideaway bed, not having much of a choice in such a small apartment. A French armoire would show off her impeccable taste. A wooden *M* on her wall would signify that the place was hers, and only hers. She'd have a kitchenette with a stained-glass window that opened and closed to show or hide it, a walk-through closet that led to the unseen bathroom, and she would, in fact, get her wood-burning Franklin stove in the corner and her vaulted ceilings with beams. Thrift-store finds like her oak dining set and upholstered chairs would nod to her budgetary limits. The pumpkin-shaped cookie jar in her kitchen could hold real cookies for between-scenes snacking.

She would go to work in a building that, in real life, was the twenty-story Midwest Federal Savings and Loan high-rise in down-town Minneapolis. The set designers would create a typical newsroom for WJM-TV: plain, industrial, drab décor with utilitarian desks. Mary's desk would always display her neatly arranged office supplies, as well as a vase that contained a single fresh flower.

At the end of each show, a title card would mark it as the work of MTM Enterprises. The production company's trademark seal would emerge as a hastily conceived parody of the MGM lion, with a fluffy orange cat (named Mimsie, procured from a shelter for the occasion) meowing instead of MGM's definitive roar—ironic, in a sense, given that the once-mighty MGM itself was now gasping for breath as its musical heyday came to an end. Burns had come up with the idea to play off the similarity between the names.

It took Brooks and Burns's team a whole day to get usable footage of the cat—six reels of film in all. In frustration, producer Dave Davis put some milk on the cat's paw so she would lick it. He took that piece of the tape and ran it backward through the Moviola, to look like she was looking up and then meowing. They got the actual "meow" from a sound library and dubbed it in. After at least six hours' more work than they'd planned for the task, the MTM logo came to life.

✦ ✦ ✦

Brooks and Burns, meanwhile, continued to toil away at the actual script. They couldn't force the words until they were willing to come, they reasoned, even if dozens of people were scouting locations, building sets, editing ending titles, and filming a cat in anticipation of those words.

At last, however, it happened. Sometime between foosball matches, words tumbled onto the page, and they . . . weren't bad. In fact, when Brooks and Burns finished the pilot script and passed it around to Mary and Grant, friends, network executives, potential crewmembers, and potential actors, one reaction came back over and over: It was unlike anything anyone in the television industry had ever read in 1970. It was hardly Beckett, yet it broke with traditional television comedy form just enough to surprise audiences, but not enough to scare them. That was where its power lay, as far as its writers and producers were concerned. Not only did it divide Mary's time equally between home and work—an innovation for a female character—but it also combined sophisticated humor with genuine pathos. It didn't just emulate *The Dick Van Dyke Show;* it went beyond it.

To most of the network executives, this was not good news—the humor was too sophisticated to jump off the page at them, and the pathos seemed maudlin. To the rest of the script's earliest readers, this could change everything. But it would require the right cast to do it justice, and enough network support, against all odds, to survive past CBS's original thirteen-episode commitment. In fact, tucked into newspapers' pages alongside news of the Vietnam War's Cambodian campaign and the Kent State shootings were TV business articles in which insiders were already predicting the show's demise. Herb Jacobs, an industry consultant who was becoming known for his preseason predictions of ratings success and failure, pronounced *Mary Tyler Moore*'s fate to the National Association of Broadcasters convention in the spring of 1970: It was likely to be canceled as soon as it could be.

Brooks and Burns took the slight personally, and fired back in a letter to the *Los Angeles Times*' TV critic, Cecil Smith: "We are distressed at the reports of Herb Jacobs's predictions, . . . particularly in light of the fact that we have made no pilot he could have seen nor could he have access to our scripts. This business being as nervous and as timid as it is, we feel that statements like Jacobs's can be harmful. As people trying to do a good television show, we're disappointed to find there are those who smugly wish us failure without any knowledge of what we're doing."

That C-major chord of victory was still a long way off.

four
four
four
four
four
four
four

casting call

(1970)

CBS casting executive Ethel Winant peered through her oversize black-framed glasses at the actor before her, who was pleading for his life. They were always pleading for their lives, or at least for their livelihoods, when they appeared in her office at CBS Studio Center. There, piles of scripts were strewn over every surface, watched over by the framed photos of Peter Lorre, Vincent Price, Jack Palance, Zsa Zsa Gabor, and all the other huge names Winant discovered when she worked on one of TV's earliest drama series, *Playhouse 90*. The struggling actors who came into her office and stood in front of the tiny woman in her Day-Glo, drapey dresses and chunky plastic jewelry wanted to be her next discoveries. They hoped to someday be worthy of framed, autographed photos themselves.

Winant's intuitive kick, the one she got when she saw the right actor standing there, could take them to that next level. She'd developed this sense in the decades since she'd graduated from the University of California, Berkeley, as she'd worked her way through a string of backstage positions at the Pasadena Playhouse. She had to delay her theater dreams when she worked as a riveter during World War II at Lockheed, but even then, she'd started a theater club that produced plays for Los Angeles venues in the afternoon.

After the war, instead of heading to housewifery like many women of the time, she'd moved to New York to work for theatrical agents and for playwright Tennessee Williams. When she visited the set of the television show *Studio One,* she got hooked on the new medium, where she'd eventually make a name for herself casting *Playhouse 90.* She had since risen through the ranks at CBS at a time when most women were lucky to be secretaries and assistants. Other women in the business looked to her as an example—if she could do it, maybe they could, too. Only one other woman at CBS was close: Anne Nelson, the director of business affairs.

Now the handsome fellow before her, the one with silvery hair, ice-blue eyes, newscaster cheekbones, and booming baritone, needed to flip the right switch in her so he could lift himself out of the one-line-part purgatory he had inhabited for his entire acting career. At forty-six, Ted Knight was getting anxious about making this Hollywood thing stick. He'd dropped out of high school once upon a time to fight in World War II and had studied acting when he returned. But he'd spent the early years of his career mastering puppetry and ventriloquism as the host of a kids' show in Providence, Rhode Island, in the 1950s.

Eventually, he moved west to seek his fortune in Hollywood, hoping to finally make a name as a legitimate actor. But since arriving more than a decade before his audition with Winant, his résumé had become an endless list of appearances on the likes of *Bonanza, Combat!, McHale's Navy,* and *Get Smart.* Knight's best-known moment on-screen had come when he played the cop guarding Norman Bates (silently) at the end of Alfred Hitchcock's 1960 classic *Psycho.* Since then, the nation had gone to war in Vietnam, the Beatles had evolved from teenyboppers to musical revolutionaries, and the world had mourned John F. Kennedy and Martin Luther King Jr. Ted Knight, however, had gotten almost nowhere. Now, in the spring of 1970, he was ready for his big break.

He did, in fact, make an impression on Winant, who had one of the sharpest minds, and the best instincts, in the business: It was his cheekbones and his voice. They didn't work for the role he was officially there for (which no one would even remember later); but they were perfect for the role he was now telling her he *really* wanted.

What he really wanted, he said, was to play the hunky lunk of an anchorman in that Mary Tyler Moore series Winant was also in the process of casting. She couldn't blame Knight for hoping for a shot at Moore's show. Mary was a dream, for one thing, just an adorable girl. Winant could tell Moore was willing to work hard to make this a great show. Winant knew showbiz enough to know when someone *wanted* it; this girl did.

Winant would stay up late into the night going over scripts in her bedroom, her stack of player directories at her side, her TV always on, her eyes always scanning for a new discovery, and she'd become obsessed with *The Mary Tyler Moore Show*. She always made herself available, until the latest hours, sitting next to her dedicated business phone line at her home, to argue the show's case. Her young children, lying awake well past bedtime, could overhear her saying, "If you don't do this, I'll put my job and reputation on the line." She believed in *The Mary Tyler Moore Show*, and she was going to do her best to defend it from meddling fellow executives.

The script had impressed her the minute she began reading it. Winant could not resist the idea of this wonderful actress as such a strong, independent, single lead character. The sitcom *That Girl*, which premiered in 1966, had attempted the same territory, but Marlo Thomas's character had remained ditzy and dependent on her boyfriend and father, even if she was technically single. Winant could already envision how terrific this new Mary Tyler Moore show would be, if everything went well, with a thirty-something female character navigating her life and her career on her own terms. But Winant's love for the script went beyond the main character's independence. Some magic was brewing among the supporting characters, each of whom felt like a fully realized person who could be the center of his or her own show.

It baffled Winant, to some extent, that her fellow executives—the male suits who surrounded her—weren't so excited about this series. They didn't hate it, at least not as much as they acted like they did while they negotiated with the producers, but they didn't have the confidence in it that Winant had.

Brooks and Burns appreciated her support—hers was the only positive voice they were hearing from the network at the moment. Once, during a heated discussion with an executive, during which said executive implied that no one at CBS cared for the program, Burns blurted out, "There's one person who likes us. Ethel Winant."

Next thing Winant knew, her secretary was searching the halls for her—Winant was elsewhere in the building at the moment—and, when the secretary found her, she said, "They've been buzzing for you on the executive intercom for the last twenty minutes. You better get up there."

When Winant arrived in her bosses' office, she later recalled, they asked her, "Did you tell Jim Brooks and Allan Burns that you liked their script? Why would you do that?"

"One, because I like the script," she answered. "And two, because I'm casting their show." She had volunteered to handpick the actors for the show, even though her executive position at the network no longer included such direct involvement in shows. She had read five or six of Brooks and Burns's scripts by that time, and loved them all, but dreaded her colleagues' reaction to them. She knew they wouldn't like the character-driven humor. Most of them, she said, didn't even bother to read the scripts—they took the rumors of imminent disaster at face value. "They just accepted that they had this great star at a disastrous production group," she later remembered. "So they didn't pay too much attention to me because they were convinced that nothing I did was going to matter."

She had gotten used to being on her own. As the first female television network executive ever, Winant harbored a particular interest in making this show a success, and she wasn't blind to why she might take the show personally. Winant was married and a mother of three, but, boy, was she happy to see a character to whom she could relate after all this time. Despite Winant's own successes, women were still treated as a second class in Hollywood. CBS had yet to provide a separate ladies' room, or even a simple restroom lock, in the executive dining room. Winant had to place her high-heeled shoes outside the door of the restroom to let the others—all men—know she was inside.

A show like Mary's, however, made all of Winant's sacrifice—of time with her young sons and her actor husband, H. M. Wynant (he'd changed his name from Haim Winant)—worth it. Her husband supported her career drive—he even benefited from her position of power on more than one occasion—but things were often tense at home, and she knew she wasn't the best mother. Family had not turned out to be her strong suit, but she knew good television. And though Winant, as the executive in charge of talent at the network, didn't often cast individual shows at this point, she agreed to take on Moore's sitcom.

When it came to the role Knight wanted, the role of news anchor Ted Baxter, *The Mary Tyler Moore Show*'s producers had thought more along the lines of Lyle Waggoner, the beefcake from *The Carol Burnett Show*. Jack Cassidy, who'd played a similarly buffoonish part on Allan Burns's show *He & She,* was also in contention for the role—it was written with him in mind—but he turned it down. The producers had even considered casting the stately, thirty-six-year-old John Aniston, imagining the character might evolve into a love interest for the leading lady. But after three callbacks, Brooks and Burns still weren't convinced Aniston was their man.

They hadn't been thinking of a silver-haired gentleman, but Winant believed Knight, at forty-six, might lend a whole different dimension to the bumbling newsman. And he sure seemed to want it, at least as far as she could tell. She called Brooks and gushed, "You *have* to see this." He agreed, eager to see anyone who might be the right person to make his show something special. She hoped she was right—she might look a little crazy if his audition for the producers went disastrously.

As it turned out, *Mary Tyler Moore Show* producer Dave Davis had just seen Knight in a local production of the Broadway comedy *You Know I Can't Hear You When the Water's Running*. "This guy is hysterical," he told Brooks and Burns of Knight. "I think you ought to see him." A guy this funny had no business lingering on the sidelines of Hollywood any longer. In fact, anyone who had seen his work would have wondered what was taking his career so long.

Ethel Winant convened with James L. Brooks and Allan Burns, along with director Jay Sandrich, Mary Tyler Moore, and Grant Tinker, to see actors for auditions at the production office's new home, the old-Hollywood holdover General Service Studios. George Burns and Gracie Allen had filmed there. *The Beverly Hillbillies* shot there now.

To sort through potential cast members, the *Mary Tyler Moore* team would meet in a building on the dusty old Desilu lot at General Service, where *I Love Lucy* had been filmed. Desi Arnaz and Lucille Ball's production company had changed television, comedy, and CBS with the couple's classic sitcom. They had virtually invented the modern TV comedy. Arnaz and Ball had since divorced, and Ball sold the company to Gulf + Western, a deal that led to the creation of Paramount Television. She now ran her own Lucille Ball Productions and starred in CBS's *Here's Lucy*.

But the couple's old studio home remained. The building where the *Mary Tyler Moore Show* auditions were being held had once been used as an office by Arnaz. It had been maintained over the years in a house-like building complete with a yard-like plot of grass in front of it. Secretary Pat Nardo, used to cramped New York City, gushed over it, begging Brooks and Burns to get a puppy. It was now Brooks and Burns's working space, with their desks at opposite ends of the room, facing the sofa in the middle. Nardo sat just outside. The producers' cavernous shared office provided the perfect place to pick through their options for the cast.

Knight appeared in front of them as Baxter—no doubt about it— and not just because he shared a first name with the character. He wore a bright blue blazer from a thrift store, looking every bit the local TV news anchor from a low-budget station. Winant, a woman susceptible to vintage and handmade costume jewelry, appreciated the unique effort, as did the producers. This guy wanted the role enough to furnish his own wardrobe. They were touched. They knew that as a struggling actor, he didn't have much money to spend on extras. Knight's performance took the character deeper than they'd envisioned: Ted Knight's Ted Baxter would be arrogant, sure, but anyone who bothered to look closely enough could see through the arrogance to the fragile person inside. In fact, Ted Knight's insecurity pulsed through his performances like an exposed nerve; if he thought he was covering it up, he was wrong. And in this case, that worked in his favor. It would have broken Burns's heart to reject this guy.

Because the *Mary Tyler Moore* producers had originally imagined the part going to someone younger, they asked Knight back three times for additional readings before they gave in. But in the end, he was the one.

Gavin MacLeod showed up in Brooks and Burns's office ready to read for the part of hard-boiled newsroom boss Lou Grant, but he didn't want it.

Though he wasn't a household name, MacLeod had played a long string of thugs in prominent TV guest spots and small-but-memorable movie roles since he came to Los Angeles from New York in 1957. He'd grown up in Pleasantville, New York, home of *Reader's Digest,* for which his mother worked before he was born. He got an acting scholarship to Ithaca College, where he earned a bachelor's degree in drama. He moved to New York City soon afterward and married a Rockette, Joan Rootvik, with whom he lived in a small apartment at Ninth Avenue and Fifty-fifth Street, across from a bus depot. When he'd first graduated from college, he had a simple career goal: to appear in one Broadway play and one movie, then retreat to teaching drama for the rest of his life. But his dreams had since grown, pushing him to move to Los Angeles at the age of twenty-seven, a decade before he appeared in front of Brooks, Burns, and Winant.

His first time in his new Los Angeles agent's office, he met a fellow actor who was also new in town, named Tadeus Wladyslaw Konopka. This guy was also just starting out in Hollywood, but he was seven years older than MacLeod. When they met in 1957, he gave some advice to MacLeod: He himself was getting a business manager, and MacLeod should, too. MacLeod remembers protesting: "I don't have any money!" But they both hired the same man anyway to manage their meager funds, and they remained friends after that, providing mutual respect and support for each other's work. Soon Tadeus Wladyslaw Konopka would start using the same name for his acting career that he'd used on the air as a children's show host in Providence, Rhode Island: Ted Knight.

The move to Los Angeles pushed MacLeod far beyond his inauspicious Broadway debut in a Shelley Winters play (his one line: "Back up, Johnny, back up like a mule"). He'd since become the go-to guy for thug parts thanks to his premature baldness and 260-pound weight at the time. When a critic described one of MacLeod's characters as "something that crawled out from under a wet rock," he summed up MacLeod's entire movie and TV career prior to 1970. MacLeod continued that tradition in prominent TV guest spots, like the part of drug dealer Big Chicken on *Hawaii Five-O*. He had built his résumé on advice he once got from actress Jessica Tandy: "Take what you think is your liability and make it your asset as an actor." MacLeod's baldness plus his girth equaled tough-guy roles that he figured he'd be stuck with for the rest of his career. But his warm smile and kind blue eyes suggested an untapped side to the actor.

Even as MacLeod was auditioning for the part of Lou Grant, growling a convincing, "You've got spunk," his mind was on a different role: Murray Slaughter, Mary's disgruntled coworker—based, though MacLeod didn't know it at the time, on a gay colleague of Brooks at CBS News, who kept a pair of ice skates in his desk drawer to hit Rockefeller Center on his lunch breaks. All MacLeod knew then was that the character was intended to grow into Mary's workplace nemesis. (He would soon be established as straight and happily married.) MacLeod didn't believe himself as Moore's boss. He felt he should be her peer. Even though Murray was a supporting part, MacLeod's offscreen nature lent him a certain kinship with the snarky—but, MacLeod was sure, nice-underneath-it-all—newswriter. In short, he liked Murray. He thought the character had potential.

After getting laughs from the producers and casting director as Lou, MacLeod turned to leave. He had his hand on the doorknob, then reversed course. He took his chances and asked to read for Murray; the producers obliged. MacLeod delighted in what he saw as the poetry of Murray. He loved one of Murray's few lines in the pilot script: "Ah, the Mastroianni of Minneapolis!" he says in a taunting singsong when he sees Ted.

After reading as Murray, MacLeod left, satisfied that he'd at least tried for what he wanted. Burns, in particular, reacted so warmly that MacLeod was sure he'd get at least one of the parts; he just hoped it was the right one. As he headed out the door to his rehearsal for a staging of *Carousel,* he saw actor Ed Asner—a familiar face, as the two often found themselves vying for the same parts—pacing in the waiting room.

A few hours later MacLeod's agent showed up at his rehearsal and beckoned him offstage. "They want you to do the pilot," MacLeod remembers him saying, though the agent was confused: "Is there a guy called Murray in that?"

"Yes," MacLeod said. "There is."

Winant and the producers had been trying to cast the part of Lou Grant for three months. Brooks and Burns had wanted to hire Shelley Berman, a comedic actor who'd made several guest appearances across television. He'd started in Chicago's Compass Players, later to become Second City, along with Mike Nichols and Elaine May, and eventually recorded several hit comedy records. Price, however, begged them to reconsider, noting the actor's reputation for being difficult. Not wanting to take their chances with their precious production, they instead pursued Jack Klugman, who was known for his roles in dramatic films such as *12 Angry Men* and *Goodbye, Columbus*. But he had already committed to a Garry Marshall series, the TV adaptation of *The Odd Couple*. (Berman later played a divorced dentist obsessed to hilarious effect with Mary's impressive teeth in one of *Mary Tyler Moore*'s early episodes.)

In any case, Winant wanted someone else as Lou Grant: Edward Asner, a balding, bushy-eyebrowed, paunchy slab of masculinity. The fifty-year-old midwesterner, known for roles on *The Outlaws, Mission: Impossible,* and *The Invaders,* would contrast nicely with Mary's willowy femininity. Winant's fellow CBS executives expressed skepticism, saying, "Ed Asner's a good actor, but he can't do comedy."

They had good reason to doubt Asner's comedic abilities, or at least no evidence to believe in them. For the past decade, Asner, the fifth and youngest child of a Kansas City junk dealer, had been appearing in television movies and in supporting roles as warrant officers, district attorneys, sheriffs, and sergeants. He'd grown up striving to "sing the loudest and act the loudest," he says. A high school football player, he didn't take to the stage until he was at the University of Chicago, where he fell in love with acting by participating in a school radio program. But, he says, "I was too bourgeois to think people made a living as radio actors, so I studied political science."

Acting sucked him in further when his roommates, who were both, as Asner says, "more cosmopolitan" than he was, bought him a Valenti Angelo–illustrated version of *The Song of Songs Which Is Solomon's,* a gold-edged edition of the famously romantic Old Testament book. They gave it to him for his birthday, he says, "as a counterthrust to my jockiness."

Asner was considering trying out for a radio production of Shakespeare's *King Richard II,* and he practiced reading a passage from *Solomon* for his roommate. "Where did you learn to read like that?" his shocked friend asked. Asner played the Duke of York in the production and got hooked on acting for life.

For a few years, he lived on odd jobs: selling shoes, selling ads. He got occasional stage roles in Chicago. He lived in a one-room apartment that looked out on an airshaft. He took a job driving a cab but found he didn't make much money because he spent all of his time parked and reading scripts. Finally, the army drafted him, and he served in the Signal Corps in postwar France. "The best thing I did for my country was organize the basketball team that played the French and won a lot of French hearts," he says.

When he returned to the States, he spent a few years in New York doing theater before moving to Hollywood in 1961 to seek acting work. He planned to stay for just a week to scout out the options, but at the end of the week he called his wife back east and told her he wanted to stay for another week. "Oh, shit," she said. That week, he got an agent and called his wife again to say he wanted to move to Los Angeles. "Oh, shit," she said again. But they did.

Winant was sure that Asner, as Lou Grant, could keep the *Mary Tyler Moore* cast of characters in line. Tinker backed her up, and urged Brooks and Burns to see Asner's performance as a newspaperman on the political drama *Slattery's People,* which had run on CBS four years earlier. "I think he'd be wonderful," Tinker told the producers. He sent over a few screeners of the show for them to watch, and they agreed that Asner was terrific.

All of the forces had aligned to guide Asner into the part, and Asner wanted it. The *Mary Tyler Moore Show* pilot was the best script he'd read since he moved to Los Angeles. He longed for the challenge of comedy, which made him nervous. He liked to tell a story he heard about English actor Edmund Gwenn, best known for his Oscar-winning role as Kris Kringle in *Miracle on 34th Street*. Director George Marshall, one version of the oft-told Hollywood tale goes, came to visit Gwenn on his deathbed. Gwenn said, "Dying's hard, but comedy's harder." (The same line was also attributed to Peter O'Toole and Edmund Kean over the years. In any case, it seemed to resonate with a number of actors.)

When Asner came in for a reading, he charmed Moore, Brooks, and Burns as soon as he entered the room and made some small talk, so they all figured he'd be just as breezy in the audition. He and Moore read their scene together from the pilot episode: Lou interviews Mary, badgering her about her religion and marital status, and then, when she protests, delivers what would become perhaps the series's most famous line: "You've got spunk . . . I hate spunk."

But Asner roared the line so loudly at the star, gave it so much of his dramatic conviction, that he scared everyone in the room.

Asner knew his performance was off. He could tell he'd blown his audition from the barely concealed scowls and winces on the faces of Moore, the producers, and Winant. "That was a very *intelligent* reading," he remembers one of the producers saying to him. He knew what that meant—it wasn't funny.

Brooks and Burns struggled to cover their horrified reactions with more small talk. However, as Asner walked out to his car, he realized they were just too nice to indicate how rotten he'd been.

Then he had a thought: If he already knew where he'd gone wrong, why couldn't he make it right? Especially since those producers seemed so nice. Asner marched back in and asked Nardo if he could see Brooks and Burns again. When she buzzed the producers and announced that Ed Asner was back, Burns thought, *Awww, shit.* Was this guy going to force them to reject him to his face? But they agreed to see him anyway.

Asner burst back into the office and said, "You just sat there on your asses and let me bomb like that? I was terrible. And you know it was terrible and you were too polite to tell me. Don't be so fucking polite. Tell me what you want in this character." Winant welcomed him, eager to prove her faith in him correct. And the guys, once again too nice to say no, talked him through the character for a half hour. "We want you to read it like a crazy meshugana," they told him. Now they were speaking this Jewish boy's language.

He and Moore did their second take, with Asner dialing the volume—and the palpable *hatred* of spunk—down several notches. The whole room laughed this time, though Moore still didn't see it. "Well, I guess we keep looking, huh?" the producers remember her saying when Asner left the room again.

"Mary, I've got to tell you," Winant said, "the hairs went up on the back of my neck when you were reading together. It was so great."

"Oh, really?" Moore said.

Winant's instincts remained unchallenged once again, and this time, the producers' pathological niceness had saved the day. If Jim Brooks and Allan Burns didn't have such good manners, they never would have seen Ed Asner's second try. And they never would have offered the part to him.

Winant knew whom she wanted for the role of Mary's fluttery, perfectionist neighbor, Marna Lindstrom. She wanted Cloris Leachman, who'd appeared in guest roles on shows such as *The Andy Griffith Show* and was a longtime personal friend of Winant. When Winant told Leachman about *The Mary Tyler Moore Show,* it piqued the actress's interest, even though she encountered plenty of naysayers as she spoke to colleagues about it: "Oh, who wants to watch a show about a single woman?" she remembers someone saying to her. But she forged ahead, hoping to prove that sentiment wrong. More importantly to her, she was hoping to prove she could do comedy.

Although she'd acted for years, she'd always had a hard time convincing casting directors that she could be funny. A casting report from back in her teen years read: "Intelligent reading, good expression, but can only play straight." She'd performed in the musical/comedy review at Northwestern University, *The Waa-Muu Show,* during her time there, but she dropped out of college, put off by all the term papers involved, and became the 1946 Miss Chicago instead. This also did little to add to the perception that she had comedy talent, nor did her time studying at the legendary Actors Studio, run by Elia Kazan. Her stint there did, however, inspire one of her go-to jokes when she was courted by a classmate but declined his advances. "Brando just wasn't my type," she delighted in saying many times afterward.

Instead she'd married movie producer George Englund in 1953, giving up her career for seventeen years of housewifery. She had been taught that *ambition* was a dirty word for a woman. But she loved and missed acting. And now, as the '70s approached, it was occurring to her that ambition was the way to get the work she wanted. But it wouldn't be easy: At forty-three, Leachman had five children, ages three to sixteen. Not only that, but her résumé from the last decade didn't exactly entice sitcom producers. Brooks, Burns, and Sandrich all had the same reaction to Winant's suggestion that they cast Leachman: "Are you kidding? This is a woman who's been on *Lassie* for the last several years."

Winant, however, did not worry. "Trust me on this," they recall her telling them.

Leachman's audition didn't get off to a great start. She arrived a half hour late—the kids were always making trouble when she wanted to leave the house. But when she showed up, she showed the *Mary Tyler Moore Show* producers how funny she could be—and gave them a glimpse of what working with her would be like—before she'd uttered a word of the script. When she entered the room where Moore, Tinker, and the producers waited for her, she asked, "Who makes the decisions here?" Everyone pointed to Brooks and Burns, so she went and sat in Brooks's lap, then flitted, "like a wood nymph," as Moore later said, to Burns's lap. She even twirled Tinker's hair, and this was a man whose meticulously parted hair did not invite twirling, and thus was not often twirled. Moore thought, *How am I ever going to hold my own in a scene with her?*

Once the producers and Tinker assured Moore that she could, in fact, share the screen with Leachman, she saw the potential. The lady from *Lassie* won the role. Leachman, however, refused to sign a long-term contract, agreeing only to an episode-by-episode deal. She'd just shot a movie with director Peter Bogdanovich called *The Last Picture Show,* and she wanted the freedom to do more films. Soon the producers would change her character's name from Marna to the more assonant Phyllis Lindstrom. She was getting funnier already.

Ethel Winant and the *Mary Tyler Moore* boys were still having trouble finding the right actress to play Mary Richards's sidekick, the sarcastic, 150-pound schlub named Rhoda Morgenstern—the kind of big-city girl who wouldn't be ashamed to be on the birth control pill but also wanted to find a husband, and would have to still be likable while doing all of that. It was starting to feel like an impossible task. They thought they'd considered every thirty-something actress in Hollywood, but none was quite right. Then Winant, on one of her standard theater runs—she'd often see up to two plays per night on Los Angeles's "off Melrose" circuit, scouring the casts for talent—spotted a thirtyish woman with brown hair, perfect bone structure, green eyes, a quick wit, and an intriguing combination of warmth and edge. As soon as Winant saw Valerie Harper, she thought, *Wow, this is her. That's our Rhoda.*

It made sense that Harper had the air of Rhoda, an insecure New Yorker. Her family had moved constantly throughout her childhood, with her dad's industrial lighting company always transferring him. But they finally settled in Jersey City, where she spent her teen years, just over the Hudson River from Manhattan. The final move changed Harper's life—after studying ballet since she was nine, she was dancing at Radio City Music Hall by the time she was fifteen, for seventy dollars a week, doing four shows a day, "forming shapes of presidents' heads or twirling umbrellas," she says.

The experience inspired her to move into the city as soon as she graduated, to pursue dancing and show business. At seventeen she landed a part in the chorus of the musical *Li'l Abner,* which played in Las Vegas and then was shot as a movie in Los Angeles in 1959. She didn't get any other jobs while she was in Hollywood at that time—all she got was hepatitis, a condition for which her doctor prescribed eating bread and sugar to keep her strength up. Her weight ballooned from 130 to 150, putting her well beyond ballerina weight and giving her a lifelong image of herself as fat.

Things weren't all bad for Harper, though. When she moved back to New York, her roommate introduced her to actor Dick Schaal. The two got married in 1964, just as she also joined Schaal's touring company, an offshoot of the legendary Second City comedy troupe called Story Theater, in what she calls the role of "the girl." The troupe always had one token woman—Elaine May, Melinda Dillon, Mina Kolb. In this group, it was Harper.

Her parents, in the meantime, divorced. Her father remarried to an Italian woman named Angela from 116th Street in the Bronx, the street known for its connection to the Genovese crime family. The character of Rhoda was Jewish, but she was also from the Bronx, and Harper's stepmother provided the perfect model for her accent and mannerisms. Some of her lines—most notably, "Who do you think you are?"—came out far more Italian than Jewish. So to get the Jewish part down, Harper would add a bit of her dancer friend from New York, Penny Ann Green, a Brooklynite who'd changed her name from Joanna Greenberg.

Somehow, there at the Fountain Theatre in Los Angeles in 1969, as Winant watched Harper perform, the casting director felt all of this potential in the young actress. Winant called her in for an audition the next day, though Harper didn't harbor much hope for winning the role. "Because of my name," she says. "That is, I didn't have one." She also figured she looked too similar to the leading lady—both were brunettes, both had small noses. Basically, she shared Rhoda's lack of self-confidence.

Harper had only minor experience in television—she and Schaal had settled down in Los Angeles just two years earlier. The two had cowritten one episode of the romantic anthology series *Love, American Style,* but aside from that she'd had only bit parts in the TV industry. The couple were renting a small house in West Hollywood and helping each other get their West Coast careers off the ground. So far Schaal had gotten luckier than Harper, snagging speaking roles on *I Dream of Jeannie* and *That Girl.* Harper had even met Mary Tyler Moore in passing once when Schaal did a brief guest spot on *The Dick Van Dyke Show,* though that was before they'd moved to Los Angeles.

Harper was thrilled for the chance to audition for *Mary Tyler Moore,* if only to read for the part opposite Moore, one of her role models. So she prepared as best she could, running her audition lines with Schaal over and over at home and bringing her own prop cloth with which to wash the imaginary window in Mary's apartment in her opening scene.

When Harper read the scene for the producers, complete with prop cloth, Brooks didn't feel it; he loved Harper but didn't think she was Rhoda, and he wanted the absolutely perfect actress for this special role. "She was something we never expected the part to be," Burns says, "which was someone as attractive as she was. But you've got to go with the talent."

And the actress's natural knack for nailing dialects, including the Bronx Jewish intonation she wasn't sure she could master, intrigued the producers and Sandrich enough that they brought Moore in to read with her despite Brooks's misgivings. Sandrich argued in favor of Harper from the beginning, and even called Winant to offer a tip to pass on to the actress for her next reading: "Tell Valerie to dress down and not wear any makeup," he said. She had the necessary body type: chunky by Hollywood standards, at a time when Goldie Hawn and Mary Tyler Moore were the ideal. She just needed to look a little more unkempt, something that might take some effort for such a beautiful woman.

Moore came to Harper's reading straight from ballet class, her hair still damp and in a bun, wearing a pink dance shirt and white trousers. The two women sat and read the scene together, and after more than fifty actresses had sat before Moore reading those same lines with her, she knew what Winant had known: *That's Rhoda.*

By the time Harper had driven the ten minutes from the studio to her house on Westmount Drive, her husband greeted her on the front lawn to tell her she'd gotten the part. The inexperienced actress would make a mere seven hundred dollars a week, but that was fine with her. Winant had finally cast the last major part in the *Mary Tyler Moore Show* pilot.

Throughout these auditions, Moore was going over the script and pondering her own character, eager to nail her first starring role on television. To flesh out Mary Richards, she channeled her own aunt, a successful executive at the Los Angeles news station she'd helped the producers to research for their script. Her name was Alberta "Bertie" Hackett, but she was known as Bertie *Hatchet.* Of course, not too much *hatchet* spirit came through in Mary Richards, but her aunt's liberated attitude did. When Moore was failing in school, her aunt would assure her, "You're going to be a dancer, or you're going to be an actress. Whatever it is, you're going to be very good at it."

Now Moore was hoping to prove her aunt right with the role of her life.

five
five
five
five
five
five
five

TECHNICAL DIFFICULTIES

(1970)

It wasn't until Jim Brooks and Allan Burns had hunky actor Angus Duncan pinned against a wall that they knew for sure their new sitcom was veering off the tracks.

As rehearsals had gotten under way on the set earlier that week, things seemed to be going okay, if not great. The initial read-throughs—the first step in the rehearsal process, where the actors sit at a table reading their parts aloud—went only barely well enough. The producers knew, as they said, that they had "a little bit of work to do." And Moore was struggling with a still-new diabetes diagnosis: She had decided to keep the fact of her disease from everyone but her closest friends and family, always sneaking off to inject herself with insulin, an act that nauseated her every time, careful not to leave stray syringes in a wastebasket where someone else might find them.

But then, the tension erupted. Duncan, the Ken-doll–handsome, clean-cut actor the producers had cast in the guest role of Bill, Mary's noncommittal med student ex, made a dramatic show of expressing his displeasure with the pilot script's rewrites, throwing the pages on the floor when he saw them. Duncan—best known for replacing Robert Redford in the '60s Broadway production of *Barefoot in the Park*, and thus, in a way, one step away from the dreamiest man in the country—had crossed a line. He hit the laid-back producers in the one place it counted: their writing. Burns felt defensive of his own fledgling career, contained, as he saw it, in those precious pages. Brooks was already developing a lifelong, unfailing policy: Always respect the script. No one knew what Duncan was thinking. Perhaps he was showing off for the more famous actors surrounding him on the set. Perhaps he genuinely disliked the new pages.

Either way, in his gesture of disrespect, Brooks and Burns's hopes of greatness seemed to dwindle before them. Suddenly the pair of writer-producers had the tall, chiseled actor cornered against a wall. The uncharacteristic "out-of-body" experience, as Brooks would remember it, forced them to become "atypically he-men." They could see the fear in the actor's blue eyes, and the admiration from the rest of the cast. Brooks told Duncan, "You respect the script. We can replace you."

They'd succeeded in flaunting their masculinity to their new cast, but the chances of Brooks and Burns redeeming their reputations with this show at CBS were diminishing. They'd lost veteran director John Rich, who'd handled most episodes of *The Dick Van Dyke Show*, to CBS's in-the-works comedy *All in the Family*. Rich met with Brooks and Burns to deliver his regrets. "Having worked with Mary on *Dick Van Dyke*, I thought this would be a very good show," he said. "But it has some overtones of reminiscence. It just feels okay, like another comedy that might be good, but this other thing, *All in the Family*, is outrageous." Lear's incendiary dialogue had blown him away, to the point where he'd said to Lear, "You aren't going to make this, are you?" When Lear said yes, Rich asked, "Is anybody going to put it on?" Rich told Moore that he was sorry, but he had to be a part of Lear's show, "even if it's just an exercise."

Brooks and Burns settled instead for the upstart Jay Sandrich, who'd directed a few episodes of *He & She*. Sandrich had no contacts in the industry beyond Burns's acclaimed, ratings-deprived program, so he had a hard time finding work after the show folded. He'd later call the *Mary Tyler Moore* job "the luckiest thing of my career." He adds, "They took a big shot asking me if I was interested in doing the show. I hadn't done anything as a director that had been in that class." As a result, Sandrich felt insecure, but he was determined to hide it.

He developed his own methods to prove to the producers that they hadn't made a mistake by hiring him: The show would employ the "multiple-camera" technique used by most sitcoms that were filmed before a live audience, capturing different angles at the same time to be edited together later. But it wouldn't be filmed like a stage production, as many other sitcoms were, with the actors playing to the audience. It would more closely resemble a short movie, shot on film instead of videotape. Sandrich studied other shows on the air at the time and thought, *Why are they yelling at each other? They're sitting next to each other.* So as he took over directing the *Mary Tyler Moore* cast, he instructed the actors to speak in natural tones and interact with each other. "You've got mics right over you," he'd say. "You don't need to project."

As the rehearsals progressed, some tension grew among the stars and producers as they tried to get the hang of this new approach. And in the case of Cloris Leachman and Gavin MacLeod, old friction returned. The two had worked together three years earlier in a TV show called *The Road West*. The opportunity had thrilled MacLeod, as he'd admired Leachman's work with Katharine Hepburn onstage in *As You Like It* and in the comedic play *Remains to Be Seen*.

In *The Road West*, MacLeod had played a saloon owner dumped by Leachman's character for another man. In their first scene together, MacLeod chased Leachman down on a white horse to confront her. He had to stage-slap her, but had no experience in hitting anyone, onstage or in real life. Something went wrong in the scene, and Leachman screamed out in pain. From then on, she avoided MacLeod; they didn't see each other until the *Mary Tyler Moore Show* pilot. The first days there, they shared no scenes, so there were no problems. But at dinner at the end of the first week on the set, MacLeod recalls Leachman declaring, "I won't sit next to Gavin MacLeod because I hate his guts."

Knight laughed as MacLeod simply muttered, "Oh, she's driving me crazy," without confronting her any further.

The cast arranged their dinner seating such that the two would not be near each other, but the incident did nothing to calm the actors' nerves.

As rehearsals for *The Mary Tyler Moore Show* got under way, CBS president Mike Dann was keeping a grueling schedule, spending two out of every four weeks living in rooms 176 and 177 at the Beverly Hills Hotel. The nearly eighty-year-old resort, discreetly tucked away amid the mansions above Sunset Boulevard, had been the temporary home to a number of stars and industry executives over the years, including Marilyn Monroe and Marlene Dietrich, who in the 1940s had forced the hotel's Polo Lounge to change its rule against women wearing slacks.

Dann was staying in town more often now to keep an eye on the growing Los Angeles production wing of CBS. His marriage was straining from his time away from home; he took the 4 p.m. flight out of New York every other Sunday to be in Los Angeles in time for dinner at Chasen's in West Hollywood. As the network's head of programming spent the summer of 1970 shuttling back and forth across the country, he still wasn't sold on the *Mary Tyler Moore Show* concept, despite the changes that producers James L. Brooks and Allan Burns had made to their proposal in hopes of courting favor with their network bosses. In all honesty, Dann didn't think about the show that much, period. He didn't have time to search the crevices of every pilot script for hidden potential as he tended to the more complicated and pressing matter of putting together the fall schedule. *The Mary Tyler Moore Show* did not make his top-priority list. He knew he wasn't crazy about the thing, he knew it wasn't shot yet, and he knew he'd committed to Moore that she'd get a slot on the schedule. As far as he was concerned, he didn't need to bother with it beyond that.

Besides, most of his colleagues didn't seem impressed with the script, either. Where were the jokes? Where was the comedy?

The day of *The Mary Tyler Moore Show*'s first chance to perform in front of a studio audience began with news of a bomb threat on the lot.

CBS had asked the producers to stage a preliminary taping, and a lot was riding on it. The network wanted the producers to test some new cameras, and the run-through would also allow them to prove that their pilot was better than executives thought it would be. It was *The Mary Tyler Moore Show*'s first major opportunity, and there was no room for mistakes.

And yet the problems mounted from the start. The bomb scare left a residue of agitation across the lot. Southern California had witnessed its share of bomb scares in the previous several months, as had every major metropolitan area across the country. Radical counterculture groups had taken to explosives to make their point and had targeted New York in spectacular fashion, hitting Wall Street, Macy's, Chase Manhattan Bank, the RCA Building, and General Motors among others, prompting scores of copycat threats. Just months before the taping, in March, the underground group the Weathermen had accidentally leveled an apartment building where they were constructing bombs in Manhattan's West Village. So a bomb on the set seemed all too plausible.

The threat was determined to be unfounded, and audience members were herded in. But the folks in the stands couldn't see the actors over the cameras, which were twice as bulky as the standard kind, so they were forced to try to catch the action on small monitors instead. The air-conditioning broke down, so the two-hundred-member audience and the actors were left to swelter in 90-degree July temperatures while watching a practice run of a series already being promoted to viewers as if it were a done deal. The microphones didn't work properly.

A nervous Brooks and Burns faced a cranky audience when they emerged on stage to do the warm-up. Getting the audiences ready for a good show was a job often taken by executive producers with a comedy background—but Brooks and Burns were merely great writers with nice personalities and zero stage presence. Brooks felt lucky, in a way, because he froze. Burns, on the other hand, just kept blathering.

When they got offstage, story editor Lorenzo Music offered to take over the job in the future. He had a dry wit and a distinctive, deadpan voice that sounded like a bored door hinge in need of oiling; he had written and performed on *The Smothers Brothers Comedy Hour* to great effect. "I could do that," he said of the emceeing duties, "and you guys wouldn't have to worry about it." They got the translation: They'd been shitty. Even the production manager, Lin Ephraim—a serious man who looked, Burns said, "like Mandrake the Magician"—told them he could do better. They realized they had been even worse than they had feared.

None of this struck the audience as funny. Neither, it seemed, did the script itself. Tinker recognized the pattern: Sometimes what works in rehearsal just doesn't connect with an audience. It was an old Hollywood story, but one he'd hoped to spare his wife from. Nary a chuckle escaped from the bleachers, and the less the audience reacted, the less sure the actors felt. Sandrich knew his actors weren't ready. He still needed time with them, and he hadn't worked with the camera crew at all yet. He recognized that putting the actors in front of an audience too soon was going to take a toll on their psyches, and it worried him.

Moore had replaced her signature Laurie Petrie flip hairstyle with a longer, straighter, more modern fall, but she couldn't seem to make audiences stop comparing her new character with her former persona. She could feel the audience's patience dwindling from the very first scene, in which Phyllis and her young daughter, Bess, show Mary an apartment that Rhoda claims as her own. Moore could tell the audience didn't like Rhoda. She could also tell they weren't sure what to make of her own character, Mary Richards. Where was Dick Van Dyke when you needed him?

Post-show polling indicated that Rhoda—who made her entrance from Mary's windowsill, threatening to take our heroine's new apartment from her—was indeed universally hated. Phyllis, also, was "too abrasive," according to audience feedback. Mr. Grant didn't fare better; he came off as humorless and bullying when he grilled Mary about her religion and marital status at her job interview, then ended by telling her, "I *hate* spunk."

The scene had given Asner trouble since his first audition. As a dramatic actor, he couldn't seem to dial down the anger. Asner knew it wasn't working as he was performing it. He felt miserable, and he could tell his costar did, too. He saw the looks on Brooks's and Burns's faces: They were not happy. Silence filled the studio. Brooks had never witnessed any of his work bombing before. No laughs. Some audience members left in the middle.

When the taping ended, Moore thanked the audience for sticking with her through it, then she fled the stage. Winant would remember it as the worst night she'd ever spent watching a sitcom taping.

Other cast members, however, didn't notice how horribly the night had gone, particularly Valerie Harper, who had never done a television show and was used to the long learning curve of the theater. She had no idea the audience hated her character. She hadn't expected laughs; after all, she hadn't heard them all week during rehearsals, so why should she get them now? In the theater, every show takes a while to gel. It's what previews were invented for—to figure out how to make a show better. Television, she started to realize, was rather punishing in comparison: first preview, opening night, and closing night all in one, and all on film.

After the disappointed audience left, Brooks and Burns returned to their offices, dejected, sweating, and confused, to find Price, Tinker, the crew, and, worse, all of the stars' managers and agents—about twenty people total—ready to point out everything that had gone wrong. Just as Brooks and Burns had choked onstage, they choked again here. Burns started babbling, while Brooks shut down. Burns talked to prevent everyone from leaving, as he had no idea what he and Brooks would do once the crowd dispersed and they faced their problematic script alone. Brooks was grateful Burns was at least saying something to the upset throng that filled their huge office. Everyone grew more depressed as they realized none of them knew what to do to fix whatever the problem was. They thought it was a good script.

Tinker hoped they were doing *something*. As he and Moore drove home from the disastrous taping, Moore had what Tinker calls "a fall-apart." She cried in the car, then pulled herself together to tuck her young son into bed and tell him the run-through had been fine. As she brushed her teeth, she fretted over her cracked stage makeup and her face, drooping with fatigue. She obsessed over plans for house renovations: What if they moved the bathroom sink to the opposite wall and put a closet in its place? Then the bedroom terrace could wrap around the wall with the bathtub.

She climbed into bed, leaving the bedroom lights on as she waited for Tinker to set the house alarm. The glare of the bulbs felt extreme. She mulled over the future of her precarious career. And her crying seemed far less cute in real life than it was when she did her famous sitcom cry on-screen. This project was supposed to redeem all of her dreams and hard work. Now it seemed hopeless.

Tinker heard her sob from the other room. For the first time since they'd signed the deal with CBS, Tinker wondered whether he'd made the right decisions for his wife's new show. He called his producers. When they answered—no one would remember later which one of them, and it hardly mattered—Tinker offered one suggestion: "Fix it." They had their work cut out for them. They'd never heard their heretofore supportive boss so testy. They had one more shot at a real taping of the pilot, but that would be it. If they lost the audience this time, the show was doomed.

Soon after Grant Tinker's ominous phone call, script supervisor Marge Mullen, who'd held the same job at *The Dick Van Dyke Show*, stopped by the producers' office. She had an idea—maybe not the biggest one, but it was something. "People don't seem to like Rhoda," they remember her saying. "There's this little girl who's Phyllis's daughter, and if the little girl likes Rhoda, it'll give the audience the opportunity to love her, too."

It was the only substantive idea for an improvement Brooks and Burns had heard all evening. They decided to take Mullen's suggestion, cut a few other lines, and call it a night, putting their faith in what they'd written and the cast they'd hired. Many things had gone wrong with that first taping, but the words and the talent, they believed, were there.

The next morning, Sandrich faced his dejected cast for another rehearsal. He said, simply, calmly, "This didn't work last night." But he reassured them that the air-conditioning and technical snafus were at least partly to blame for the problem. They would still need to focus on playing the script better, but the script itself, he told them, would get only minor rewrites: "We all believe in the show," he said, "and we're not going to change it."

As the official Friday pilot taping approached, the producers took all the practical steps they could to avoid another meltdown. They made sure the sound was working, the cameras weren't hindering the audience's view, and the air-conditioning was running. Brooks and Burns relinquished the audience warm-up: Lorenzo Music took over as promised, and charmed the audience. Sandrich reminded Asner to concentrate on delivering the "I *hate* spunk" line with "controlled anger," not all-out rage. The women sat in the makeup room's three chairs, chatting, practicing lines, getting primped with hair spray and amber eye shadow. The two hundred fresh audience members filed into the studio bleachers, ready for a show.

The only major change to the script was pigtailed twelve-year-old Lisa Gerritsen as Phyllis's daughter, Bess, saying, "Aunt Rhoda's really a lot of fun," as Mary opened the curtains in her new apartment to see a harried Rhoda on her balcony in the opening scene. Gerritsen was the granddaughter of child actor and later screenwriter True Eames Boardman, as well as the great-granddaughter of silent film actors, but she had now made her own showbiz history.

This time, the audience roared. Gerritsen's new line seemed to indeed be the magic bullet. The entire scene soared. Brooks and Burns avoided looking at each other, afraid to jinx the laughter they now heard. But they made delighted eye contact as the next scene began. The atmosphere lightened like it was filling with helium, taking the studio up higher and higher.

The audience's response this time gave Moore confidence that buoyed her right through the rest of the taping and spread to her fellow actors. In the next scene, Mary sat down for an interview with Mr. Grant. He asked her about her religion and marital status; the audience laughed this time. He offered her a drink. Asner's instincts told him to make an aggressive turn toward Moore as a windup to the scene's conclusion. His anger and mania finally came off the way it was supposed to: over-the-top funny. Dying was hard; comedy was harder. But it was awfully fun when you nailed it.

"You know what?" Asner finally said as Mr. Grant. "You've got spunk." Mary nodded in agreement, then he delivered the punch line: "I *hate* spunk!"

Asner saw the audience take off like a guided missile. He felt empowered, like King Kong. He could squeeze the entire crowd in his massive hands.

The audience laughed when Mr. Grant told Mary he'd fire her if he didn't like her *or* if she didn't like him. They laughed when Phyllis had the locks on Mary's apartment changed to keep "dumb, awful Rhoda" out. Moore pulled off a star-quality performance. She looked adorable while juggling high comedy and the weight of the more poignant moments when her ex pays her one final visit.

With the tiniest tweak to the script, the taping went down in television history as a smash.

As for that ex, and the originally disgruntled actor who played him, the producers had to admit he did a good job. But not quite good enough to make up for his earlier misbehavior. After the successful taping, Duncan asked them, "Could I be a recurring character on the show?"

"We don't think so," they replied, "but thanks for your offer."

Despite the triumphant pilot performance, *The Mary Tyler Moore Show* still faced a major hurdle: Test screenings, even of that second filming, were going poorly with sample viewers when they watched a taped version. The questionnaires that viewers completed showed they thought Mary was a loser. Why was she thirty and still single? Was Ed Asner's character Jewish? Why was Rhoda so mean? The network made Tinker and Moore an offer: They could negotiate a price to walk away from the contract, call the whole thing off.

Tinker still had faith in the show and stuck to it; he asked Dann to go ahead with it, taking his chances that it would become a hit with audiences and force CBS to continue with it. But Dann still got to choose the show's spot on the fall prime-time schedule, a decision that could make or break the series's future, and so far he had it set for a terrible slot. Dann knew the importance of a good time slot: "There's no such thing as a good show with a bad rating," he would say. "You always must win your time period." So the clearest statement of his true feelings for *The Mary Tyler Moore Show* came when his scheduling decisions were announced. Faced with intense competition from rival NBC in the previous TV season, Dann put the show on Tuesdays, between the very incompatible *Beverly Hillbillies* and *Hee Haw,* and opposite NBC's much-hyped *Don Knotts Show,* a variety hour starring the beloved Andy Griffith sidekick. *The Mary Tyler Moore Show* was scheduled, essentially, to be finished after its thirteen episodes.

And the negative audience testing hadn't changed CBS executives' minds about that scheduling. With CBS still short of confidence in the show, the executives listened to all of the test audiences' objections. They asked Tinker in for lots of meetings. He understood their trepidation: They had a thirteen-episode commitment, and that investment made them nervous. He tried to listen to their worries while letting his executive producers go about their business. But word was out in the industry: When Sandrich went to another studio to direct an episode of a different series, someone there told him CBS had a show called *Shane,* a Western series based on the movie, that it was preparing to put in *Mary Tyler Moore*'s slot when the latter inevitably failed. Even the producers, despite their general naïveté about the television business, knew they were dead in the time slot they'd been given.

Then things changed in the top ranks of CBS. Dann resigned to help launch the Children's Television Workshop in New York, where production was beginning on a new kids' show called *Sesame Street.* He'd been working in commercial broadcasting a long time, he told his colleagues, and he was rich enough to focus on doing something worthwhile with his career.

Of course, the move hadn't come without urging from his network bosses. After fourteen consecutive years of ratings wins, CBS had fallen behind NBC's new programs—most notably *Rowan & Martin's Laugh-In*—that packed, as industry parlance put it, "contemporary relevance" and were as glossy, sleek, and modern as Cher's hair. Big-money advertisers now wanted those audiences, who'd been suddenly flocking to NBC. Even if CBS caught up to NBC in overall ratings, it had a devastating disadvantage in the key demographic.

And when a network needs a change of direction, a change in programming leadership signals that intention to the industry.

Robert Wood had just taken over as the network's president after running its West Coast operations for a year; the often-frazzled executive defied the long tradition of network heads such as Jim Aubrey, Louis Cowan, and Merle Jones, who acted as if they came from nobility. Wood's energy spilled out all around him. One of his first major acts as president was to promote Fred Silverman, at just thirty-three, from vice president of program planning to Dann's old spot at the head of the programming department, and he started making changes. His mandate: Transform the network to attract cosmopolitan audiences in major cities. Television could no longer survive by appealing to rural viewers. Knockoffs of *The Beverly Hillbillies, Gilligan's Island,* and *Gomer Pyle* were over. It wouldn't be easy, of course. That was the nature of the business. Silverman joked, "I firmly believe that people do respond to different things. I just wish I knew what they were."

It turned out that, at least in this case, he did. Wood and Silverman would get credit for what became known as "the rural purge," the cancellation and marginalization of several still-successful, but demographically less desirable, comedies, starting with *Lassie, Hee Haw,* and *Mayberry RFD. Green Acres* star Pat Buttram, who found his show moved out of its desirable slot and then axed, would lament that CBS had "cancelled everything with a tree." The edgier creatives in the business hailed Wood for killing what they saw as stale, irrelevant programming.

The Mary Tyler Moore Show suddenly had some great advantages: its pronounced lack of trees and its air of sophistication. Perry Lafferty may not have supported Brooks and Burns as much as they would have liked at their big network pitch meeting, but the urbane CBS executive came to their aid now, urging Silverman to consider *Mary Tyler Moore* as just the sort of thing the network should nurture, and do more of. It felt current, positioned to capture the new, young demographics TV needed to expand its audience. Social awareness and challenges to traditional values were what the network needed now. It was time for TV to stop ignoring the world around it.

Just months earlier, in March 1970, a group of about one hundred feminists had made news by staging a sit-in at the office of *Ladies' Home Journal* editor John Mack Carter to protest the way the magazine depicted women's interests, and thus call attention to the importance of expanding women's perceived roles beyond the homemaker. The number of single women in their late twenties and thirties was on the rise as more women delayed marriage or got divorced. Women's lib was making headlines; it was cool and current. A show that demonstrated even a hint of women's liberation and genuine artistry screamed *young, affluent, and urban* at a time when most sitcoms were still using feminism as nothing but a punch line.

The Mary Tyler Moore Show went from dead-before-it-aired to potential network savior.

Fred Silverman flew to Los Angeles from his office in New York in the late summer of 1970, just a month before the new fall lineup would premiere, to screen some of the shows he'd inherited from Mike Dann's reign. He hadn't yet seen *The Mary Tyler Moore Show*. By that time, the entire East Coast office of CBS had written the show off, but he was intrigued by Lafferty's lobbying on its behalf. He wanted to see it for himself.

Silverman watched the pilot and a rough cut of the second and third episodes, with Ethel Winant and a few other executives by his side. He thought all three episodes were terrific. In fact, he thought you'd have to be a complete moron not to see that it was a great show. Now he had a problem, however: This show he loved sat in his schedule's worst time period, on its way to oblivion.

He called his boss, Bob Wood, back in New York, even though it was now Friday evening on the East Coast. Winant, in the room with Silverman at the time, held her breath, not knowing what her new boss was going to say about the show to his boss. "Bob, I just screened *The Mary Tyler Moore Show*," he told Wood. "You know where we've got it on the schedule? It's going to get killed there, and this is the kind of show we've got to support. We ought to think about moving this thing. We have a bunch of junk on Saturday night. We ought to move one of those hillbilly shows and put this there."

With that, *Green Acres* was packed off to Tuesday nights, and *The Mary Tyler Moore Show* was set to air at 9:30 p.m. on Saturdays, as part of a lineup that included two top-twenty shows, *My Three Sons* and *Mannix*, as well as *Mission: Impossible*. Instead of facing *Andy Griffith* favorite Don Knotts and *Mod Squad*, Mary would compete with the new (and destined to be short-lived) ABC drama *The Most Deadly Game* and NBC's movie night. These were much better odds. Fred Silverman had rescued *The Mary Tyler Moore Show* from a quiet Tuesday night death. When Wood announced his sweeping changes, which included the *Mary Tyler Moore* move, on July 21, 1970, the *Boston Globe* called it a "wholesale upheaval" of the network schedule, "unprecedented for so late in the season." But, writer Percy Shain noted, "the strategy involved in these transfers is obscure." No one in the industry was entirely sure yet what CBS was up to.

In any case, *The Mary Tyler Moore Show* was now in prime position to become a hit. The problems threatening Brooks and Burns's show had so distracted them, however, that they hadn't even had time to think about hiring writers. Finding any writers who could handle the unique tone of the show would provide a challenge. But now they needed them, and fast. And they wanted at least a few of them to be women, ideally young and single like the show's main character, to lend the sense of realism both Brooks and Burns cherished. But in 1970, few shows had hired anyone but white men to write them, no matter who the shows' main characters were. As a result, there were hardly any female comedy writers with experience. Another challenge loomed before them.

PART TWO
PART TWO
PART TWO
PART TWO
PART TWO
PART TWO
PART TWO
PART TWO

"Rule number one: Never hire friends.
I hired a friend once and you know what happened?
Worked out great. But that's me.
You couldn't handle it."
—Lou Grant

six
six
six
six
six
six
six

THE WOMAN PROBLEM

(1970)

A statuesque brunette beauty in a sari mingled with women in mini-skirts, bearded men, suited TV executives, and the cast of *The Mary Tyler Moore Show*. Their mismatched duo of producers, Jim Brooks and Allan Burns, circulated among them, flitting from table to table across Burns's lawn, soaking up the admiration. It was the best kind of office party, the kind celebrating success, with congratulations and compliments sprinkled among the cocktail chatter. Stand-ins, crew-members, husbands, and wives praised everyone from the actors to the writers to theme song writer Sonny Curtis.

There at the *Mary Tyler Moore Show*'s premiere-night party, the show finally felt like the show it was meant to become—the smash it was about to become. Or at least it seemed that way to the producers, who had defied the network and endured a disastrous preliminary tap-ing to emerge triumphant with a not-half-bad pilot episode and a solid time slot for their star. That star, in turn, glowed among the crowd that night. She had to take in the moment and all of its success, while still hoping this wouldn't be her new show's last celebration. A good pilot episode didn't mean the momentum would continue.

Indeed, CBS executive Frank Barton still didn't seem to believe in the show whose production he was charged with overseeing. Brooks and Burns already considered him their nemesis, the constant thorn poking them from the executive offices across town. The normally hospitable Burns had even balked at inviting Barton, but Tinker and Brooks had convinced him to. They didn't want to make an enemy at the network. "He's already our enemy," Burns said. "Why invite him?"

Burns felt justified in his resistance when his wife, Joan, got up to take something to the kitchen and Barton plunked down into her seat. "Get your ass out of my wife's chair," Burns grumbled, but to no avail.

Barton continued the conversation he'd been having with some guests nearby. He was predicting the show's inevitable low ratings, as Burns remembers it. Burns couldn't believe Barton's nerve. The producer was winding up to confront Barton again when Joan returned and, to Barton's credit, he relinquished her chair. That wouldn't stop Burns from calling Barton the next day and giving him hell one more time for his rudeness.

Other than Barton and Burns's momentary clash, however, the evening proceeded like a dream—the beginning of a good dream. As everyone toasted to the show's survival, Brooks made his way over to Treva Silverman, a TV writer whose smooth, dark blond hair and oversize glasses lent her the look of the librarian everyone had a crush on. Brooks had hired her to write for the show; she was the only woman he'd found thus far who was qualified. "Ah, here's an honest face," he said. "Tell me the truth. Is this just another sitcom?"

"Another sitcom," she replied, "wouldn't have had a character say, 'I hate spunk.' Nope, this is *not* just another sitcom." Jim laughed, since he and Allan had put that line in specifically to satirize the corny movies where a man would congratulate a woman in a condescending way for being spunky. He loved that Treva got the joke.

Brooks appreciated the accolades, but he knew that to keep their creative momentum going, he and Burns had to hire more writers they could trust. They had both thought of Treva Silverman right away. They loved working with her, and admired the work she'd done for them on a few scripts for *Room 222*. She had, as they often described it, a "wicked" take on writing, a unique voice that stood out from other comedy writers at the time. Her zingers threw curveballs and her plots took funny twists. She made audiences laugh by giving them what they didn't expect. Jim Brooks also harbored a nostalgic fondness for her. She'd once helped to inspire him to go into TV writing.

To entice her into the job, Brooks sent Silverman two scripts: the pilot and another episode he and Burns had written about Rhoda's mother coming to visit. Silverman fell in love with them right away. As she read them, she thought, *How did this happen? There are real characters here.* She told her agent she wanted to work only on *The Mary Tyler Moore Show* from now on. The agent warned against hedging her bets on a show that had yet to air, but Silverman didn't care. From then on, she wanted to devote all of her time to putting words in Mary Richards's and Rhoda Morgenstern's mouths.

That would suit her old friend Jim Brooks just fine. He wanted not only good writers for his new show, but women who could write comedy and lend insight into his single female character's point of view. Silverman could provide all of that and more.

But Brooks and Burns needed more than just Treva Silverman. While they felt confident in their ability to write female characters, the more they talked about the show with women, the more they realized there were certain story lines they'd never think of themselves, certain nuances they'd never get without female writers. Mary's workplace, in particular, was rife with story possibilities: How might it feel to be the only woman in a room? What was it like not to be paid the same as men in your position? How might you handle sexist talk and unwanted come-ons? The office, and women's place in it, could be the focus of this series, a revolutionary concept, but Brooks and Burns wanted to get their portrayal of Ms. Richards, associate producer, just right.

Treva Silverman had toiled for three years now in Hollywood, leaving behind writing sketches for the stage and playing piano in New York City bars to become a sought-after sitcom writer. After coming to Los Angeles, she'd written scripts for *That Girl, The Monkees, Get Smart,* and *Room 222,* all while outnumbered by male colleagues. And she was having a great time as a single young woman in Hollywood, though still maintaining faith that her dream would ultimately come true: She *would* one day find herself giving an Emmy acceptance speech while her sexy, smart husband waited in the wings whispering, "Hurry up, darling, finish your speech, because we're going to take the next boat to Europe." She was just working on the Emmy part for now; the dream guy would show up later.

Instead of worrying about meeting a husband, she threw herself into her work. She had gotten to the point where she was working regularly on sitcom episodes and pilots and was building a reputation. Although most of the time she worked alone, at one point she had a writing partner, Peter Meyerson (who went on to be the show runner of *Welcome Back, Kotter*). In those years, nothing had changed concerning the status of women writing comedy. It was still a boys' club. One time Peter and Treva were called in to meet with a major TV producer. When they met with him at his house—actually, at his pool—he looked at Treva, startled. "Oh. I thought Treva was a man's name." Before she could respond, he applied another coat of suntan lotion and said, "So, what is it, Treva writes the story and, Peter, you write the jokes?"

Few in Hollywood believed women could be funny. One of the exceptions was when Treva worked with Jim and Allan on *Room 222.* She had an easy rapport with both of them, and found that their senses of humor jibed beautifully. In one of her episodes, she used her latent songwriting abilities to make up the anthem for the fictional school,

Walt Whitman High. She grew to be close friends with Jim and Allan. They kept each other up to date with what was happening with their careers, and more than anything, she appreciated the feeling that they saw her as their equal.

In the late 1960s, a handful of women were in the same situation as Treva, but in different places. Each was the only woman most places she went—writers' rooms, meetings with producers, gatherings of other comedy-world folk. None of them had met each other yet. None of them had been given any reason to believe there were others like her out there. Each of them felt like the only smart, funny woman in the world, and each of them were proud of that fact—and yet it was lonely. That was, until they heard about Mary Richards.

As Susan Silver drove between the palm trees and gray, boxy buildings that led to General Service Studios at 6633 Romaine Street in Hollywood, where fans had once lined up to attend tapings of *I Love Lucy*, she went over her routine in her head one more time. She had the joke about her Realtor's name and the story about a wedding she didn't want to stand up for. Those were her two best bits, for sure. But that didn't make her any less nervous about this meeting—this job interview, essentially.

Silver's mentor, Garry Marshall, had gotten her a meeting with James L. Brooks and Allan Burns just after *The Mary Tyler Moore Show* started airing and Silver fell in love with it. Marshall warned her: Brooks and Burns needed good writers, particularly women, but they also had high standards for their brand of comedy. To prepare, Silver scoured her life for comedy. It started when she and her husband went to look at houses and a real estate agent gave them his card. She saw the agent's name, Arnold Tvedt, and there she found her first gag: "God, you can't kill this name with a stick," she said to her husband. "If you take out the *e* you still say it the same way, and if you take out the *d* it's still the same." That went on her list of jokes for the meeting. She wasn't sure what exactly a "pitch meeting," as Marshall called it, entailed, but she practiced talking in a mirror, honing her facial expressions while she told a few funny stories.

When the real thing came, she stood before them in her sensible dress and heels, knowing the ensemble was a better choice than the hot pants she'd naïvely worn to another meeting Marshall had arranged for her. She had realized her mistake the second she saw the ogles on those executives' faces. But now she had to wow Brooks and Burns based on her material, not her short shorts. It was a trade-off.

Brooks and Burns wanted to like her, were primed to like her, if only to start filling out their sparse writing staff. But they were surprised by how much they liked her. So was she: She was a sometimes-blond (depending on her hair-dyeing whims) bombshell used to having men's attention, but not this kind of attention—attention paid to her brain and her sense of humor. Brooks and Burns thought she was clever, even though she just told them stories from her life. They hadn't heard real stories from real women's lives pitched as comedy scripts before. They had never been forced to stand up for the wedding of someone they didn't like while wearing an ugly dress, for instance. It sounded hilarious to them.

The producers chose the bridal-party story as Silver's first assignment. She calmly accepted, then went outside to the parking lot and screamed with glee. When she returned home, she announced to her skeptical husband that she was quitting her job in casting at *Laugh-In* to make a go of being a freelance sitcom writer. She promised him she'd make at least twenty thousand dollars a year writing, and if she didn't, she would stop and go back to a practical job that would pay the bills instead of fulfilling her dreams. She was sure she could do it.

Silver had grown up in Whitefish Bay, Wisconsin, a suburb of Milwaukee, dreaming of being a writer. Her father kept everything she wrote, dating back to her first poems when she was five. She enrolled at Northwestern University in the Chicago suburbs to seek a degree in journalism, just to get away from her overprotective parents. An only child, she wasn't allowed to cross the street alone until she was twelve. So for college, her parents wouldn't let her go to California like she'd wanted to. Northwestern, eighty-five miles south of her hometown, was as far as she was allowed to go. Her sophomore year, she transferred from journalism to theater arts. She performed in the school's *Waa-Muu* variety show and wrote a sketch for it about an astronaut returning home (decades after Leachman appeared in the same annual revue). She was blown away by the fact that some of the audience members were from Chicago's famed Second City comedy troupe, even though nothing ever came of them seeing it.

The next year, she made a deal with her parents: She could go to Los Angeles if she lived with her uncle, Sy Howard, who worked in show business creating the radio programs *My Boy Luigi* and *My Friend Irma.* Silver transferred to the University of California, Los Angeles, and finally made it to the city of dreams and boundless freeway traffic jams. Once there, she spent her summers working as an extra in movies, meeting the likes of Steve McQueen. She knew she had to be in Los Angeles to break into show business. She knew that was where she belonged.

She met her future husband, stockbroker Arthur Silver, on her last day at UCLA. She was heading out to her graduation ceremony with her parents, and she ran into him on her apartment building's stairs. Arthur was carrying a trunk up the stairs, and her mother said, "There's a nice boy."

"Oh, Mother, *please,*" Susan said with an eye roll. But she married him within three years.

After graduating, Susan got a job as an associate producer for comedian Mort Sahl's talk show. She figured she got hired because he wanted to sleep with her, but that didn't bother her much. She got along with him just the same. In the first six months she was there, Sahl fired five producers. She became a producer by default. But soon afterward, she found herself fired as well: She looked out the window, saw her car being towed, and ran outside to try to stop it, even though

Sahl had a rule against leaving the building without asking him. She proved to be no exception to his strict edicts; she, too, was gone by the end of the day.

Despite the shock of her first firing, she got another job casting for an advertising agency until she saw *Laugh-In* on TV and decided to apply there. Soon she became the assistant casting director; she took over as the head of casting when her boss died.

She knew she was funny, as funny as the writers on *Laugh-In*. She didn't, however, know how to turn that into a real job. It all came together when Silver ran into an old boyfriend, who introduced her to his new girlfriend, another funny chick named Iris Rainer. The boyfriend suggested the girls work together on a script—he knew a guy named Garry Marshall who helped some other TV writer friends get their start, many of them funny women with limited writing experience. Silver and Rainer first conspired on a spec script for a new show called *Lancelot Link: Secret Chimp,* which featured live chimpanzees as *Get Smart*-style secret agents. The two wrote the spec hunkered over a typewriter together, on fresh onionskin paper. They would later thank God the episode was never made.

But the two also hammered out an episode of Marshall's *Love, American Style*—a romantic comedy series featuring a different story every week—that *was* filmed. Marshall got them a shot at a *That Girl,* too, on an episode in which the main character, aspiring actress Ann Marie, was to get engaged to her boyfriend, Donald. But then the show's producers decided not to let her get betrothed just yet—they'd end up saving that for the final season, in 1971. Iris and Susan's episode was never shot, and Iris decided to take a break to have children. The partnership dissolved (though Rainer, who worked as an actress as well, would later go on to write for variety shows such as *The Osmonds* and *Sonny & Cher*). Silver was a newlywed, but she was on the market, professionally speaking. That's when she landed the *Mary Tyler Moore* gig.

She and the other new *Mary Tyler Moore* writers—recruited via friends of friends, lured from off-Broadway, snatched from the male-dominated writing staffs like those Treva Silverman had endured—would make Mary one of the most authentic, and emulated, female characters to ever hit television. Getting to that point, however, wouldn't be any easier than it had been to get the show on the air to begin with.

SEVEN
SEVEN
SEVEN
SEVEN
SEVEN
SEVEN
SEVEN

pulling through

(1970–71)

Allan Burns drove down Melrose Avenue on his way to work at *The Mary Tyler Moore Show*'s lot in Hollywood on a late September morning in 1970, as the television season officially got under way. He was having a hard time concentrating, still distracted by what he'd read in *Time* magazine the night before. Amid stories about heavier issues—President Nixon's approval rating plummeting below 50 percent, worries that a new school year would bring new waves of campus violence—came this slap in the face: "*The Mary Tyler Moore Show*, on opening night at least, was a disaster for the old co-star of the *Dick Van Dyke Show*," the reviewer had written. "She plays an inadvertent career girl, jilted by the rounder she put through medical school, and working as a 'gofer' at a Minneapolis TV station. Her bosses, a drunken clown of a news director and a narcissistic nincompoop of an anchorman, do an injustice to even the worst of local TV news."

As Burns pulled up to a stoplight, something pulled him out of his sour reverie: the Jaguar idling next to him, driven by Moore herself. He caught her eye, and her expressive face fell. He knew from her look that she'd read it, too. The *Time* critic had even gone so far as to compare Moore's career—unfavorably—with that of Andy Griffith, who was also returning to his sitcom roots that season with a show set in a prep school, called *Headmaster*. Both huge TV stars were back on the small screen, "but only for Andy," the magazine said, "does it seem like a halfway happy return."

The "disaster" charge felt particularly hurtful in light of the calamitous first taping and the seeming victory of the second. The cast was now falling in love with each other, their jobs, their characters, and their leading lady, and they wanted very much for their show to last. Burns ached for everyone to think the show was as terrific as he did, for Moore's sake and his own. But *Time* wasn't the only publication to dismiss the show. *TV Guide*—the industry's most vital resource and frequent Pepsi coaster—grumbled that Mary Richards was "unmarried and getting a little desperate about it," and called Rhoda a "man-crazy klutz." The *New York Times,* meanwhile, had called the show "preposterous."

The best reviews only revved up to lukewarm; the *St. Petersburg Times,* for instance, hailed "the return of a delightful and talented actress" in Moore but summarized the show as about "the life of a 30-year-old spinster." The newspaper also named a show called *Arnie,* about a working-class couple with money troubles (months before *All in the Family* premiered with a similar premise), as the real show to watch for the new season, a common refrain among TV critics that year. The character of Lou Grant, another newspaper said, "may take getting used to," while Rhoda Morgenstern "is almost a cliché." For Moore, an actress who remembered every bad review she'd ever had, these pans in major publications stung. She struggled to maintain her famous smile as her blood sugar levels surged and plummeted.

Those bad reviews stung Burns as well. He had pushed himself to his limits coming up with stories and writing scripts for this show. The live audiences laughed at the tapings, but there was no way to be sure the material was good. The silly photo the cast had taken of all of them crossing their eyes—which they'd snapped with the intention of sending it out to critics who gave them bad reviews—suddenly seemed less funny. Brooks and Burns would soon tell their secretary, Pat Nardo, to throw out all the prints. But Nardo kept one copy in case it was worth something someday. At the time, such a show of faith seemed like a long shot.

Brooks and some of the other staffers took the bad reviews more lightly, at least outwardly. They bitched and joked about them, citing the studio audience's laughter. Brooks's braying guffaw stood out from the crowd on any given show night, audible even on air, but he wasn't the only one laughing. That was all they *could* be sure about, he felt. The rest was beyond their control.

Still, Moore wasn't yet convinced that the show would avoid joining her growing list of failures. She had faith in the series and the people behind it, but there was mounting evidence that it was not meant to be; it was stymied at every turn, from the network's rejection of the divorce premise to CBS executives' lack of enthusiasm for the project to these reviews. Hit status was getting harder and harder to imagine. CBS was at least promoting the show now, with spots featuring Moore's face mugging for the camera—nothing about the show or its plots or characters—and the tagline "We've Got It All Together." The network clearly hoped viewers would like the idea of watching Dick Van Dyke's former TV wife on a new show, comforted by her cuteness and former-housewifeliness, and would tune in just for that. Despite Fred Silverman's scheduling move, which saved the show in the short term, many at CBS still weren't sure what to make of the series.

When *The Mary Tyler Moore Show* finally premiered, the ratings bore out this ambivalence. They hovered just out of the top twenty—hardly an achievement in the '70s, when only three networks were vying for viewers. The new Saturday time slot was better than the show's original spot would have been, but it was still date night.

Sandrich continued to hear from friends at other shows that CBS was preparing another series to take its place if it failed. Jim and Allan could have panicked and begun altering their vision for the show to attract more viewers. But instead they chose to maintain their faith in their own talent, and that of their cast, determined to make sure everyone—even the critics at *Time* and *TV Guide*—saw it.

That meant, however, more pressure on everyone involved to perform. Though they were becoming a workplace family like the one they portrayed on television every week, it wasn't always easy to maintain that. Sandrich was constantly fighting Brooks on directorial choices and asking Asner to take his booming voice down several notches. Asner's dramatic skill often got the better of him. When his character was mad, he seemed *really* mad. For the first several episodes, he and Sandrich had to learn to trust each other. They both sensed they might get there, but they weren't there yet.

Sandrich and Brooks, meanwhile, often fought over Brooks's penchant for yelling out his suggestions to actors during rehearsals. Brooks just wanted to make his show better the minute he thought of an idea, but this interfered with Sandrich's process. Sandrich wanted the producers and writers to give their notes to the actors through him to protect his cast from being assailed with critiques from every corner. But Brooks couldn't help shouting out, "Oh, oh, oh, try this!" in the middle of rehearsals. The producer wasn't trying to circumvent the director's power. It just kept happening. He would apologize, but then he would do it again.

And Brooks and Sandrich often differed over how scenes should be played. Brooks thought like a director, even though that wasn't his job. The two sometimes found compromises, but not without occasional screaming matches. Sandrich frequently tensed up at the point in the week when the writers would come down from their offices to watch rehearsal. The actors hadn't quite learned the script yet and were generally still carrying pages. Things weren't working yet.

Sandrich felt outnumbered and outmatched by Brooks, Burns,

and several of their other talented, intelligent writers as they watched from the bleachers. Sandrich wanted to serve as the buffer between the actors and the producers, and this direct contact from the writers and producers threatened that. Sandrich didn't like the writers getting mad at the actors and vice versa, but the days when the writers watched rehearsal, it was out of his hands.

The negative buzz continuing to build in Hollywood about *The Mary Tyler Moore Show* didn't transfer to the audience, though. Even if the viewership wasn't as large as the network had hoped, many of those who did watch saw something in the pilot—the spark of something special.

Joe Rainone was one of those viewers. An intense nineteen-year-old student with a mop of brown hair parted in a left swoop across his black-framed glasses, he tuned in for that first September 1970 episode with only casual interest. He decided to watch with his parents at their Rhode Island home, where he lived while studying accounting at nearby Bryant College, mainly because he thought Mary Tyler Moore was pretty. He sort of remembered that she'd been on something called *The Dick Van Dyke Show*, but he had never seen it. The show had aired at 9:30 p.m., which was too late for him at that time—he was just ten then. More recently, he'd caught a TV movie she starred in called *Run a Crooked Mile*. She'd played the wife of a guy who got amnesia. Rainone thought she was very good in it; in other words, he thought she was sexy. When he saw promos for her new TV show, she also looked, you know, *good*. He made a mental note to see it.

Rainone liked the pilot enough to tune in for the second episode. That's when he got hooked. He was entranced when Richard Schaal—Harper's real-life husband—as Mary's overenthusiastic suitor, Howard Arnell, gave a hilariously overwrought speech about how he couldn't tie himself down to one woman. The words, and their performance, played like a master class in comedy. "Mary, if you say another word to me, I won't go," Schaal announces. She makes a show of zipping her lip. As he heads out the door, he hits her with another histrionic pronouncement: "Mary, no goodbyes." Then he turns and says, "Goodbye."

Rainone knew then that the show, as he says, had "revolutionary aspects." It was self-aware, multilayered, and very funny. He wanted to meet the people who made it. He especially wanted to meet Moore, for obvious reasons. But he was in Rhode Island, and she was in Los Angeles. His accountant's mind went to work.

Letters. That was the key. One of his favorite writers, fantasy master H. P. Lovecraft, wrote voluminous letters, as Rainone knew from the bound volumes of Lovecraft correspondence that he owned. Rainone would write to Moore about her show, the one thing they had in common, and would throw in references to his own life where appropriate. Then she would get to know him, get to like him. And then who knew what might happen?

The second episode now over, Rainone climbed the stairs to the office where his family ran a printing business. He sat at the typewriter and pecked out five double-spaced pages of his thoughts regarding the episode. Satisfied with his five pages, he sealed them in an envelope. The next day, he visited the local library, hauled a Los Angeles phone book off the shelf, and looked up "CBS Television City," a phrase he'd remembered from watching *The Carol Burnett Show*. He took his chances that *Mary Tyler Moore* was filmed there, too.

This would become his standard weekly ritual: five pages minimum, double spaced, full of scene-by-scene critical analysis of what he'd just watched on television. Addressed to Television City and dropped into the mail the next day. Through his letters, he would eventually develop elaborate theories about the show: His Theory of Parallel Characters posited that Mary's home and office worlds mirrored each other—Phyllis was to Ted as Rhoda was to Murray. His Theory of Anti-Mary held that the power of the humor in an episode was directly proportional to how far from Mary's central axis of goodness a featured supporting character pivoted.

Every week, he would send off his analysis, and await a reply. His letters did, miraculously, make their way from CBS Television City, up through the Hollywood Hills, and down again into Studio City, where the show was actually filmed, more than six miles away. But secretary Pat Nardo received all of the correspondence for the show, and she didn't think such obsession should be encouraged. So his letters piled up for months, unread and unanswered. He just kept sending them anyway.

The order came through the phone lines, spiraling around the curlicued cord and hitting Allan Burns's ear with brute force: "I'm giving you orders," Frank Barton, the network programming liaison and Burns's nemesis, told him. "You cannot shoot this episode."

"Why not?" Burns asked.

"The way Rhoda treats her mother? That's supposed to be funny? And this scene at the beginning, the sadism scene?"

The network still wasn't making life easy for Brooks and Burns. Even as some of the suits began to see the show's potential, many of them still couldn't stifle the urge to meddle. Somehow, the *Mary Tyler Moore* episode about Rhoda's mother coming to visit, titled "Support Your Local Mother," seemed radical to CBS executives, so much so that Barton called Burns to forbid shooting it. In the episode in question, the second that Brooks and Burns had written (it would be the sixth to air), Rhoda's mother, Ida, would come to visit, and her passive-aggressive tendencies would drive Rhoda to refuse to speak to her. The first scene of the script featured Mary distressing a table to make it look "antique" by hitting it with a chain, per Phyllis's suggestion, and laughing every time she did it. Burns had recently learned about the furniture refinishing technique from his wife, since they couldn't afford real antique furniture. It had little to do with S&M, unless, apparently, you had the imagination of a network executive.

Brooks walked into their shared office while Burns was on the phone with Barton. As Brooks listened in, he could tell it was a CBS suit on the other side of the line and he could tell the executive was telling Burns how unfunny the show was.

Frustrated by CBS's demands, they called Tinker, who was known for running interference with the network. "I just read that episode—it's funny!" he told them. "Shoot it." The network had committed to thirteen episodes with Moore, so contractually they couldn't stop Brooks and Burns from shooting whatever they wanted. The network could, of course, choose to air the episode at a time when no one would see it, but Tinker was determined to back his producers.

Besides, the producers had booked Nancy Walker to play Ida, and Walker was a sure thing, performance-wise. The tiny redhead, a Broadway mainstay, would make a funny episode even funnier. Sandrich was directing another show that week, so Brooks and Burns went ahead and hired a director—Alan Rafkin, who'd worked on *Andy Griffith* and *Dick Van Dyke*—and got to work. Rafkin was immediately impressed with Moore's leadership on the set, having worked with her years earlier on *Van Dyke*. He later wrote in his autobiography, "she seemed to act from behind a shield of thick plastic. Like her former co-star Dick Van Dyke, she would be great with an audience, while at the same time she didn't give anything of herself backstage. First and foremost Mary was a businesswoman and she ran her series beautifully. She was the boss, and although you weren't always wedded to doing things exactly her way, you never forgot for a second that she was in charge."

The episode would ultimately get Rafkin his first Emmy nomination and would win Emmys for Brooks and Burns's script—but for now all the producers had won for themselves was a bad reputation with CBS executives. The word around the network offices was that they were "asking for trouble."

They refused to do big, traditional "block-comedy" sequences, which were considered the essential ingredient in sitcoms at the time, thanks to *I Love Lucy*. Think of Lucy's most famous scenes, the kind of ha-ha funny clip that plays well in a promo without context: getting drunk on Vitameatavegamin, stuffing her mouth with chocolates from the conveyor belt at her candy factory job, battling overwhelming soap suds filling her kitchen. Why couldn't Mary Richards just get into those sorts of scrapes instead of worrying about why her new best friend wouldn't talk to her mother? The network fired off a warning memo that explained the basics of situation comedy to Brooks and Burns: "Mary should be presented with a problem. Toward the end she should solve that problem in a surprising and comical manner." Maybe, it also suggested, she could date someone fun, like a visiting prince, just to spice things up.

Brooks and Burns chose to ignore this. They instead pursued a loftier idea of what a sitcom could be. They resisted Mary engaging in zany antics just for a laugh. She would not stomp grapes or get mixed up in the chorus line at the Copacabana. They would start with a relatable premise and assume reasonable intelligence on the part of Mary as well as most of her supporting characters. They wanted to present plausible people who reacted in believable ways. Sometimes, they hoped, they would also make viewers laugh.

Relations with CBS executives lightened up a few months later as the show settled into solid, if not spectacular, ratings. Wood decided to take a chance on nurturing *Mary Tyler Moore* as the network's foray into programming for that demographically desirable creature known as the sophisticated urbanite. He signed off on a full season; the show had outlived the thirteen-episode commitment that so many in the industry predicted would be its entire life span. He called Moore, who was in the middle of a read-through, to deliver the news. The cast sat, silent, waiting for her to get off the phone. "Gang, we can hang out the laundry," she announced when she returned. "They picked us up."

Joe Rainone was growing depressed. He'd spent the entire first half of *Mary Tyler Moore*'s first season writing letters to its cast and crew every week, but he'd heard nothing. He started to wonder if he had the right address, but wasn't sure where to find a different one. He kept typing, five pages every week, just in case they were going somewhere. But his mood was growing darker with the winter months in cold, snowy Rhode Island.

On Saturday, January 2, 1971, he watched, as usual. He trudged upstairs to type his letter, as usual. It was a good episode, as usual, with one of his favorite characters—Howard Arnell, Mary's sad-sack admirer. The character had inspired Rainone's first letter to the show. That fact, coupled with Rainone's upcoming twentieth birthday later that week, put him in a reflective mood as he typed. "Here I am, I've probably lived a third of my life," his letter began. He went on to bemoan the lack of response to his letters and to mention his upcoming birthday. He put it in the mailbox, expecting no result, then went to bed.

The next week, the mailbox produced an unthinkable treasure: an oversize envelope with a Los Angeles return address, bearing his name. He ripped it open to find a birthday card signed by every member of the *Mary Tyler Moore* cast and the production staff. A letter inside, on stationery featuring a cartoon drawing of Moore, was signed by a woman named Mimi Kirk, who, she explained, was Moore's assistant. "The producers want you to know that as soon as they finish producing this season they're going to write to you themselves," she assured him. Soon, in fact, he did get notes back from Burns and Music, as well as another letter from Kirk. They sent him newspaper clippings about the show and production schedules, souvenirs they thought he might enjoy.

That spring, as more envelopes arrived from the *Mary Tyler Moore* offices, Rainone's parents started to ask questions. He explained the correspondence to them and his older brother, Eddy, a twenty-one-year-old who also helped run the family business. "Are you ever going to meet these people?" Eddy asked.

The thought hadn't occurred to Joe beyond his abstract hopes—spending his summers at the business and the rest of the year in school didn't give him much extra money. Eddy was already working full-time and drawing a paycheck from the business, though, so he offered to pay if Joe wanted to go to Los Angeles and take his brother with him. Joe dashed off a letter to Burns: If he came out west for a week, could he possibly visit the set?

Burns responded: Well, yes. But a week was a bit much. New York governor Nelson Rockefeller only got to watch one scene and shake hands with the cast when he visited recently.

The Rainone boys planned to go to Los Angeles for a week anyway. They'd find other things to do.

Halfway through the show's first season, fate, with an assist from CBS president Bob Wood, threw *The Mary Tyler Moore Show* another bit of luck. It came in the form of a similarly progressive new show called *All in the Family*. After ABC had rejected two pilots for Norman Lear's comedy about a blue-collar family, Wood bought the show for CBS and decided to premiere it in January 1971 during what was known as TV's "second season," the second half of the traditional September-through-May broadcast schedule. The time when "replacements" were rolled out to take the place of failing fall shows was becoming increasingly important as networks grew more obsessed with playing the "ratings game," as they called it. Wood, Fred Silverman, and their fellow executives loved the *All in the Family* pilot, though their boss, William Paley—the cantankerous chief executive who'd been with CBS since its radio days—hated it. He would allow Wood to put it on only if he buried it in a deadly time slot on Tuesday, the same wasteland *Mary Tyler Moore* was once rescued from. (Paley was perhaps even more obsessed with the bottom line than his colleagues at other television networks; he once grumbled to a shareholders' meeting that covering unexpected news—space launches, Churchill's death—had reduced earnings by six cents a share.) But soon the show would get the chance to team up with Mary and company, once Wood had the ammunition to stand up to Paley.

Lear had started writing for television in the early days of variety shows—Jack Haley's *Ford Star Revue* and Jerry Lewis and Dean Martin's *Colgate Comedy Hour*. He'd long since found his own comedic voice in films, however, and was nominated for an Oscar in 1967 for his script for *Divorce American Style*. Around the same time, he heard about the British sitcom *'Till Death Do Us Part*—about the tension between a middle-aged conservative at odds with his new, liberal son-in-law—and wished he could get the same sort of topical satire on U.S. television.

In January 1971, four years later, Lear finally got his remake onto American airwaves, and critics quickly agreed that *All in the Family* reached new heights for television comedy. CBS premiered the show with a careful disclaimer: "The program you are about to see is *All in the Family*. It seeks to throw a humorous spotlight on our frailties, prejudices, and concerns. By making them a source of laughter, we hope to show—in a mature fashion—just how absurd they are." The show tackled race relations, sex, politics, women's rights, and every other issue facing the country—and it did so forcefully, directly, and with loads of ethnic slurs, like no show on television ever had. Its spot-on casting helped it go down smoothly, with Carroll O'Connor playing the cigar-chomping Archie Bunker, balanced by the over-the-top antics of Rob Reiner as his son-in-law, Mike, Sally Struthers as daddy's girl, Gloria, and Jean Stapleton as daffy wife, Edith.

Lear attributed his show's artistic triumph to the network's "patient capital." After all, ABC wouldn't even take a chance on him. As Lear would later recount in a speech: "If CBS, in the person of Bob Wood, hadn't understood that a fresh entertainment menu was needed at CBS for success in the long term . . . if the network hadn't dropped all the constraints of numbers-driven management just long enough for *All in the Family* to get in the door . . . if they hadn't taken a leap of faith by ignoring the 'hard' numerical data of the research which said that America would not find Archie Bunker entertaining—the test results were the absolute lowest—they would have effectively squelched whatever innovation we were fortunate enough to bring to television comedy."

A month after *All in the Family*'s premiere, however, viewers weren't interested yet; the show placed last in its time slot in the Nielsen ratings. And yet it was one of the seventeen shows CBS kept on its schedule when, inspired by the new direction *Mary Tyler Moore* and *All in the Family* represented, Wood killed more programs than any other president in the history of the network. His schedule overhaul, announced in March 1971, was even bolder than his changes the year before. He dropped thirteen shows, including what was then TV's longest-running series ever, the twenty-three-year-old *Ed Sullivan Show*. Only *Medical Center*, the *Thursday Night Movie*, Doris Day's show, and *Mary Tyler Moore* would stay in their time slots for the following fall. New shows featuring Dick Van Dyke, Glenn Ford, and Sandy Duncan would be among the new crop.

It wasn't until the 1971 Emmys, given out in May, that both *All in the Family* and *Mary Tyler Moore* started to gain traction with larger audiences. The *All in the Family* cast appeared in a popular skit during the Emmy broadcast, and the sitcom won three major awards, including Outstanding Comedy and Outstanding New Series—beating *Mary Tyler Moore* for both. *Mary Tyler Moore* won four—Asner and Harper for acting, Brooks and Burns for writing, Sandrich for directing. Rafkin was nominated for his work on the "Support Your Local Mother" episode, but lost to Sandrich. Rafkin had a hard time feeling bad about losing though: He was sitting next to Asner when Sandrich's name was announced; Asner squeezed Rafkin's arm and said, "You know there'll be other times." After Sandrich accepted the award, he told Rafkin, "I just want you to know that the only reason I won was because I directed more episodes than you."

In their acceptance speeches, Asner and Harper referred to the cast as a "family," Sandrich paid tribute to Brooks and Burns, and Burns gave the credit right back to the actors: "The best scripts in the world are nothing without the kind of cast we have."

✦ ✦ ✦

After the Emmys, both shows, particularly *All in the Family,* shot up the ratings charts as viewers sought out their summer reruns. Wood could make his case to Paley: *All in the Family* was a phenomenon. Paley had to agree; Wood got the go-ahead to swap *All in the Family* into the Saturday night schedule. Silverman started to envision his network as ruled by two basic schools of equally classy, but distinct, comedy. One would be the *Mary Tyler Moore* style, with character-driven plots and film production values; the other would be the *All in the Family* style, with politically charged, edgier plots and a gritty, taped feel. He felt there was room for both, and he was right: *All in the Family* shot to No. 1 on the Nielsen ratings charts and stayed there; it both benefited from and helped boost *The Mary Tyler Moore Show.*

After that Emmy push, *All in the Family* topped the Nielsen ratings charts for its first five seasons and created TV-to-talk-about almost every week. It also helped lift *The Mary Tyler Moore Show* from No. 22 in its first season to No. 10 in its second. The combination of the two shows elevated the night to become one of the best lineups in television history. From start to finish, Saturday night on CBS looked smart and funny and sophisticated. With the help of other hits throughout the week like *The Waltons,* CBS now dominated the network rankings again.

All in the Family also challenged the *Mary Tyler Moore* producers to make every episode the best it could be. Producer David Davis would come over to Jim Brooks's apartment to watch *All in the Family* and analyze its every move. They felt like they were watching history from the first episode. "Man, they're so great," they'd always say to each other, "and we feel a little inferior." Then, just like the rest of America, they'd watch *The Mary Tyler Moore Show.* They'd have to admit, that one wasn't so bad, either.

EIGHT
EIGHT
EIGHT
EIGHT
EIGHT
EIGHT
EIGHT

SUCCESS

(1971–72)

Ed Asner realized he finally felt good about his new job late in the summer of 1971. He was waiting, along with Ted Knight and Gavin MacLeod, backstage for the first studio audience taping of the second season, listening to the familiar theme song play as they awaited their introductions. Peeking out at the cheering crowd, confident in the show's upward trajectory, Asner sighed. "Man, I can die happy now."

"Hold on, sweetheart," MacLeod cracked. "We haven't won *our* Emmys yet." Knight, silent, *wanted* that Emmy, too, and he was determined to get it.

The good news: It was starting to look like they'd have their shot. *The Mary Tyler Moore Show* was growing into a full-fledged phenomenon. As the women's lib movement went mainstream—*Ms.* magazine, Gloria Steinem, the Equal Rights Amendment, and Title IX—and *All in the Family* shocked audiences far more than a single lady could, people stopped worrying so much about Mary slipping into oldmaidhood. Even *TV Guide,* which had once described her as "unmarried and getting a little desperate about it," encapsulated the change in attitude she'd helped perpetuate when it later declared that she was "thirty-three, unmarried, and unworried—Mary is the liberated woman's ideal." The magazine put Moore on its cover three times in the show's first two years on the air.

The stars—and even the writers—became the subjects of incessant publicity in the likes of the *Hollywood Reporter, TV Guide,* and *Mademoiselle,* rivaled in coverage only by the stars of *All in the Family.* They were recognized everywhere they went. They were besieged by fans desperate to talk to their favorite stars but lacking in anything to say besides telling Harper she looked much prettier in person (a good sport, she took it as a compliment) or asking Asner stuff like, "Why are you so mean to Mary?" He had a stock answer, grumbling, "Yeah, yeah, every boss in the world should be so mean to his Mary." It was a pain in the ass and tiresome, but, they felt, a fair price for being on a hit show.

Shockingly famous people were now not only consenting to appear on the show, but requesting to. Walter Cronkite, watched by more than 20 million viewers every night, played himself and told the stars he was a fan of the show. When he spent his weekends sailing, he'd bring his boat into port every Saturday night, he said, in time to watch. He also took a particular interest in Leachman; MacLeod was certain that America's most trusted newsman had a crush on the flighty actress. Singer Carole King also appeared on the show, playing a family member of Mary's boyfriend, whose son Mary doesn't like. The woman whose plaintive songs—"So Far Away" and "It's Too Late"—had crackled through the cast's and writers' stereo speakers had volunteered herself for a low-key appearance on their show, just to be with them for a week. She was credited as Carole Larkey, using her married name, and the network didn't promote it as a huge pop star's guest appearance; they played it like just another episode.

The writers, meanwhile, collected praise and attention like few TV writers had ever enjoyed. Everyone from critics to Emmy voters to the actors themselves heaped praise on the artful writing, a concept still rare in television. After all, just nine years earlier, Federal Communications Commission chairman Newton N. Minow famously chastised broadcasters for their perpetuation of a "vast wasteland." Now viewers planned their Saturday nights around *The Mary Tyler Moore Show* and *All in the Family,* and felt no guilt in the pleasure.

The network executives were now leaving the *Mary Tyler Moore Show* scripts alone as ratings climbed and Emmys piled up. At last, Brooks and Burns got to run their own show without interference. The production moved into a permanent home, Soundstage 2 at CBS Studio Center, the same stage that had housed the hit show *Gilligan's Island.* This meant Brooks and Burns had to relinquish the office once used by Desi Arnaz, including the steam room, but it was worth giving up the chance to sauna with the ghosts of the greatest sitcom of all time for their show to have a real home. And they didn't have much time for steam rooms anyway. They were soaking in the experience of running their *own* successful sitcom. Brooks considered the entire experience his version of college. He learned everything he'd ever wanted to know. Leachman taught him about theater, Harper about improv, Asner about drama, Knight about his own vaudevillian approach. They would all discuss craft between rehearsals, while Brooks took in every word.

Even Mike Dann, the prickly executive who'd originally buried the show in a terrible time slot on the network schedule, had to admit: "They were the classiest situation comedy to be developed, and everybody after that modeled themselves after it."

If there was any doubt remaining that *The Mary Tyler Moore Show* had made it, two unmistakable signs of success proved the point: By the second year, Mary Richards's popularity was secure enough that Moore could ditch her wig. No one was about to mistake Mary for Laura Petrie any longer. At the same time, Burns called Sonny Curtis and asked him to record new lyrics to the theme song: "She's obviously made it," he told the musician, "so we've got to update it." Now, instead of worrying about how Mary would make it on her own, the new lyrics asked, "Who can turn the world on with her smile? Who can take a nothing day and suddenly make it all seem worthwhile?"

Soon berets became a universal symbol of independence. Lou, Rhoda, Mary, Ted, Murray, and Phyllis all became recognizable personality types. Single women everywhere longed for a cozy, $130-a-month studio apartment like Mary's, complete with their initials on the wall. Her home became so well known that the location, 2104 Kenwood Parkway in Minneapolis, turned into a popular tourist destination even though only her fictional address—119 North Weatherly—was ever mentioned on the air. The tourist traffic at the house got so bad that the owners put an "Impeach Nixon" sign in the window in hopes of preventing producers from filming the new 1973 opening-title sequence there. Given that Mary Richards admirers would still be visiting the house decades after the show aired, the effort's ultimate goal—stifling gawkers—was futile.

As the show reached new heights, a 747 carrying Joe and Eddy Rainone from Rhode Island to California—their first flight ever—touched down in Los Angeles. The airsick boys stumbled into their Riverside Drive motel, weary and uncertain of what would happen to them in the coming week. Would the *Mary Tyler Moore* people even remember that they'd given the go-ahead for a set visit? Would they know who the Rainones were? At the check-in desk, their questions were answered: The clerk handed them a package from the *Mary Tyler Moore* staff. Inside was a script for the episode being shot that week, titled "Thoroughly Unmilitant Mary," about a strike at WJM. With it was a stack of comic books, which Rainone had mentioned liking. A note signed from Lorenzo Music said the producer would pick them up at their hotel at nine the following morning.

As promised, their phone rang just before nine. Music's laconic voice was on the other end. "I'll be there soon," he told them, "driving a brown station wagon."

Rainone couldn't believe he was about to meet someone from MTM Enterprises! Who was driving an unassuming station wagon! His greatest dream was coming true. On the ten-minute drive to the lot, Music told the brothers that the producers had come to look forward to Joe's letters because of their detailed critiques. Once, when Brooks was out of town, he even had Music photocopy that week's letter and send it to him on the road.

Soon Joe found himself, wonder of wonders, plopped down in Allan Burns's office, awed by the shelves full of bound *Room 222* and *He & She* scripts. He felt a jolt when a lanky, gorgeous brunette passed by: Mary Tyler Moore, right there! When she peeked into the office, though, he could see that it wasn't the star: Instead, it was his first pen pal on the set, Mimi Kirk, who also worked as Moore's double during lighting setups. Eddy and Joe met her, then went across the hall to meet production manager Lin Ephraim. When they were whisked back to Allan's office, it had been transformed: A semicircle of chairs had materialized, filled with the cast members. Mary Tyler Moore, for real this time, along with Valerie Harper, Ed Asner, John Amos (who played WJM weatherman Gordy), Ted Knight, and Gavin MacLeod. Joe lost his footing when he caught sight of them, then recovered in time for Music to introduce him and his brother to everyone.

He took a seat and stared at his heroes. Harper barely looked like Rhoda, she was so luminous—like so many fans told her, he wouldn't have recognized her out on the street. Moore glowed from the couch, tanned deeply, her endless legs crossed, her smile overwhelming. Then, something even more overwhelming: She spoke to him. She knew who he was. "When I heard you were coming," she said, "I took your letters home with me over the weekend and I read them." He had written nearly forty letters at that point.

After the read-through came lunch. The producers explained that they'd deemed this "Joe Day" and had made a reservation for the cast and producers to eat with Joe and his brother at Tail o' the Cock, a restaurant popular with Hollywood types and paneled with wood so dark it made the sunniest Los Angeles afternoon seem like last call inside. There Joe sat, sandwiched between Harper and Moore, chatting about whatever. He kept an eye on his brother on the opposite end of the table, who was talking with Amos and MacLeod. Joe was mortified to hear his brother detailing his own stomach problems, then relieved when the conversation turned to hockey instead.

Brooks and Burns, down on Joe's side of the table, awed their fan with behind-the-scenes tales, including one about the final episode of the first season. Rainone hadn't exactly loved it, and he told them so in his letter that week. It turned out the episode had been so problematic that the producers had kept rewriting and reshooting it in pieces throughout the first season's production. First, they'd conceived it as a showcase for comedian Richard Libertini's impression of a bird—they would dress him in a chicken suit, and he'd play a character at the station, maybe from a children's show, called Big Chicken. But nothing they did with him worked right. Eventually, his scenes were edited down to just one, a gathering in Lou's office, and a new story emerged: Lou nearly getting fired because at forty-five, he was now "too old" to connect with the youthful audience the station needed. Slim Pickens played the station owner in a performance that made Burns cringe—it wasn't the actor's fault, Burns just knew it wasn't funny. But the season was coming to an end and *something* had to go on the air, so the producers stopped fussing with the episode and shipped it to the network. Every show has a worst episode, and this would be theirs.

Hilariously, *Los Angeles Times* critic Cecil Smith raved about it when it aired. He called it "of singular value to connoisseurs of comedy, if only for the portrait wrought by Slim Pickens of a TV tycoon who was once a cowboy star and who conducted business in the living room of his home astride the stuffed carcass of the horse he rode in movies." Brooks and Burns got a far more accurate reading of the episode's effectiveness when Joe's letter arrived the next week. By this time, Joe had developed an intricate "rating" system that he used to evaluate every episode. In short, he counted what he called "jollies" (times he laughed out loud), grins (times he smiled at a joke), and sobs (any tears would do). It was a weighted system, with jollies receiving two points to every one instance. This episode barely rated at all. "You picked up on something Cecil Smith didn't," the producers said of Joe's evaluation. "Here's this guy who's supposed to know TV, and you picked up that it was bad."

Brooks proceeded to probe Joe on his writing habits and aspirations. Had he ever thought of being a television writer? Joe demurred, saying he didn't think he had it in him to make up funny stuff like they did. He loved the idea of being able to work for his favorite show, of going to the set every day, but he didn't think writing was his way in.

Halfway through lunch, Tinker strode in and kissed Moore hello. "What are you doing here?" his wife asked.

"I'm here to meet this young man," he told the now-breathless Joe. "Before you guys leave this week," he said to Rainone, "I want to sit down and have a talk with you."

Tinker headed back to the office, Burns picked up the lunch check, and Rainone couldn't believe a thing that was happening to him. The rest of the day floated by, impossible to grasp, Joe's personal Land of Oz. He saw the set, Mary's apartment and the WJM newsroom laid out before him, Lou's office folded into the side. Right before him, his favorite cast rehearsed a scene in which a union representative bursts into the newsroom with word of a strike. And then Sandrich invited him, Joe Rainone, to step in and play the union representative. When he got tired of doing the scene over and over, and his delivery grew monotonous, Sandrich would have none of it. "What do you mean, coming onto my set and delivering that line like that?"

Joe Rainone put everything he had into that line for the rest of the afternoon.

✦ ✦ ✦

The remainder of the week swooshed by: an interview with syndicated TV columnist Charles Whitbeck, the beach in Santa Monica, the Wednesday run-through, Disneyland. Friday, the night of the taping, Rainone arrived to find the staff hyped up. Brooks—looking like a cross between Jim Morrison and John Lennon in wire-rimmed glasses and a skin-tight, chest-baring, lace-up shirt—was wearing a pin reading "It's a Girl!" His wife had just given birth to their first child. Rainone loved being there for such a significant event, chatting with Music near the cameras and posing for photos with Brooks, Moore, and Burns. Even better, Moore told him the producers wanted to let him be an extra in the episode's crowd scene. Joe had his long-awaited chat with Grant Tinker, in which the executive quizzed him on his interests and background. Rainone briefly wondered if this was a job interview of some kind; it sure felt like it. But soon it was time for filming to get under way.

Further investigation revealed that union regulations would prohibit Joe's appearance in the episode, but he was still happy to be there. After being ushered into the bleachers next to his brother with the rest of the studio audience, Rainone watched as the episode came together in its finished form. Music warmed up the audience, telling them about Brooks's new daughter. Music glanced at the note in his hand: "Amy Lorraine Brooks weighs . . . sixty-eight pounds?" The audience laughed. "Oh, wait a minute, that's six pounds, eight ounces."

Then Music introduced Joe and Eddy Rainone, fans who'd come all the way from Rhode Island for the taping. Joe stood up and waved. Two older women sitting in front of him turned and looked at him, he says, "like I was their favorite son." After the taping, Eddy and Joe stuck around as long as they could, watching the relatively boring process called "wild lines," lines from previous scripts that needed to be re-recorded for clarity. But eventually, it was time to go home.

Before Eddy and Joe headed back to their motel that night, Music told Joe, "There's been some talk of finding you something to do around here."

"Yeah, Mary told me about the crowd scene," Joe replied.

"No," Music said. "Something more permanent."

Brooks and Burns now felt more secure in their leadership role and projected that newfound confidence. In fact, they instilled awe in their cast, prompting the actors to work to meet their producers' expectations. Brooks and Burns were also, it must be said, getting wealthier than they'd ever been, though they barely had time to notice or enjoy it. They didn't even pay attention to the number on their paychecks; they just knew that it built up to a pretty terrific amount over time. Brooks didn't realize how much money he had until Burns and his wife bought their house on Mandeville Canyon Road in the tony Brentwood neighborhood for $260,000. The first time he walked into the plush, Spanish-style home, Brooks declared, "Oh, my God! I'm rich!"

Brooks and Burns now got to settle into their role as executive producers and hire additional producers. Music and Davis were preparing to leave the show to launch MTM Entertainment's second sitcom, which would star comedian Bob Newhart. Brooks and Burns were away from the clacking and dinging of their typewriters more now than they'd ever been, as they dealt with bigger production issues, so they needed help with day-to-day writing. Sandrich suggested a guy named Ed. Weinberger, a *Dean Martin Show* writer whose movie script draft he'd read. Brooks and Burns didn't know Weinberger, but they trusted Sandrich's recommendation and liked Weinberger's work samples. They took their chances on him even though he hadn't written a half-hour sitcom script before.

Being on the set amazed Weinberger, a Philadelphia native and Columbia grad who wrote for comedian Dick Gregory in the 1960s, almost as much as it had enthralled fan Joe Rainone. At first, when Weinberger critiqued the run-throughs with Brooks and Burns, he'd simply whisper his suggestions to Brooks, too scared to say them aloud. When he wrote his first script for the show, he gargled with his aftershave and patted his cheeks with Listerine the day he had to turn it in.

For another of his early episodes, he walked the streets of Los Angeles all night coming up with an ending because he didn't want to ask his new bosses for help. The script had Lou buying his favorite bar and trying to run the business. Lou's not sure what to do as it starts to falter. As Weinberger walked up and down Sunset Boulevard, he ran into some people he knew who were having a great time hitting the bars. Then he figured it out: Lou would *force* his bar patrons to have a great time. The episode scored; it became one of Burns's favorites of all time. "I've never heard laughs go on as long as that," Burns recalls. "It was wonderful."

The cast was now spending most of their waking hours on the set. Weeks took on a comfortable sameness. Leachman would come to the run-through before each Friday taping, even for episodes she wasn't in. She cackled like crazy as she watched her costars and said to the producers, "I love this! Put me in it!"

"This is a dress rehearsal, Cloris," they replied. "We are not putting you in it now."

Then three hundred audience members filled the powder-blue bleachers while three cameras recorded the actors' performances. On nights when Brooks's wife *hadn't* provided material by giving birth, Music developed some go-to routines for his audience warm-up. One of his typical shticks was asking the audience members to raise their hands if they hadn't seen the show before. "Uh-huh. About five or six. You, sir, will you please stand up? Now we don't want to embarrass anyone, but will you please take off your clothes and tell the reason you haven't seen the program?"

The filming would almost always go smoothly, with few retakes. After the taping, the actors thanked God for their ideal jobs and then went to dinner together, often at Tail o' the Cock—where Asner was a regular treated to doting service—or the Red Lantern Inn, a Laurel Canyon Boulevard mainstay owned by Frank Capra's son.

The scene that unfolded there followed a cozy, family-like routine as well. Asner chatted with, entertained, and befriended everyone in his orbit, "the king of the lot," as MacLeod called him. Harper made the rounds to ensure that all of her cast mates knew what a wonderful job they'd done, and the writers and producers, too. Harper and Moore played an opposites-attract pair—loud and quiet, loose and proper, free and buttoned-up—as did their producers, Brooks and Burns. Harper was a theater rat, a lapsed Catholic, a registered Democrat, and a proud women's libber who'd been inspired by reading Betty Friedan's *The Feminine Mystique*. Moore was a chorus-girl-turned-TV-star, a good Catholic, a registered Republican, and unwilling to declare herself a feminist. But they loved each other just the same, and fiercely.

Ethel Winant sometimes joined them, often with her young sons, who loved to come to tapings and sit next to their mom in director's chairs. Once, on a post-show excursion with the cast to the Aware Inn—one of the country's first natural-foods restaurants—a Mercedes painted in multicolored tie-dye patterns pulled up. Out came an Indian man with long, white hair, and a skinny guy with a dark mop and a brush of a mustache. When Ravi Shankar and George Harrison were seated at the table next to the MTM crew, Winant's teenage son, Bruce, was dumbstruck. Ethel rose and glided over to have a few quiet words with the former Beatle, then beckoned Bruce over to meet him. Bruce never knew if his mother had met the inconceivably famous musician before, but she certainly acted as if she had every right to be talking to him.

Knight and Leachman soaked up any attention they could, each in his or her own way. Knight demanded laughs with his over-the-top antics, preening for onlookers. Leachman could get even more outrageous. She told stories about working alongside a young Brando. She flirted playfully with Brooks, often teasing him about "thinking about the three of us girls when you lie in bed at night." Brooks rubbed

Leachman's back, fumbling and neurotic, overheated and nervous. "Jim," she told him once, "hands should never ask questions." He thought, *Holy shit. That's the coolest thing anybody's ever said.* She'd cross boundaries just to get a reaction, but if someone called her on it she'd retreat in childlike hurt.

Other times, she applied her maternal know-how with magical precision. Leachman returned Brooks's backrub once as they waited for the crew to change the set. Later, he told her, "I don't know what you did, but I went back to my office and burst into tears. I couldn't stop crying."

Leachman and MacLeod forgot their earlier differences. They now carpooled to work. In her autobiography, Leachman calls him "the person I had the most doubt about" when the show began, but, she adds, he "emerged new and splendid, [playing] his character with real sweetness."

During the week, Moore would sit on the stage in her canvas director's chair, dancer's posture in evidence, chewing gum as she concentrated while others rehearsed scenes that didn't feature her. Aside from the pack of Silva Thins in her hand and her hair pulled into a bun, she was almost indistinguishable from her character sometimes—were those *her* black boots and chic plaid knickers, or were those Mary Richards's? Surely, Moore had the meticulously cared-for skin and bright white teeth of someone who was beyond "regular," but she counteracted those factors with the way she acted. She rarely retired to her dressing room, as she preferred to know what was going on and to use her breaks to chat with her costars.

She didn't boss people around, but she did have exacting standards that perhaps contributed to the show's success more than we'll ever know. She simply didn't tolerate "when people don't do their work right," she once said. "That'll get me. But when I'm mad I don't take it out on anybody; I just like to sit down with whoever it is and talk things over, precisely and practically." Luckily, she didn't have to do that much on the set of *The Mary Tyler Moore Show*: "We have good, demanding people," she said. "I'm just part of the ensemble."

Moore did act like the boss on the set, in the sense that she exuded no-nonsense leadership, though she studiously avoided acting like "the star." She always insisted on being nothing but a fellow player. She almost never pulled executive rank on the writers, either, objecting to only one script idea: a plot in which Mary was to have a tattoo she was embarrassed about and wanted to get removed at the hospital. That pushed beyond the proper star's limits. "I can't play that," she said, calling herself a "good Catholic girl." The writers changed her cause of hospitalization to tonsillitis.

Harper had to demand her friend get star treatment because Moore wouldn't. Harper told Leachman over lunch, "You and I are going to have to make an effort to see to it that Mary is treated like a star because she isn't going to do it herself. She makes no demands on anybody and does what she's told. So every once in a while, you and I are going to have to say, 'No, Mary, what do *you* want?' "

Moore was also obsessed with being punctual. When her car broke down on her way to rehearsal, she almost broke down herself. She took a cab and scurried onto the stage, where everyone on set proceeded to ignore her as a joke, knowing she hated messing anything up. She knew their prank meant they understood and accepted her, flaws and all, like a family.

They all, in fact, accepted each other that way. As Brooks later said: "A television job that's working is the best job in the world. You get to do something you like. You get to do it with people you like. You have community of a sort that you're denied in movies, because shows can go on five, seven years, even decades. People meet, they get married, they have children. It's like a town. It's enormously secure—until it isn't. But as long as it is, it is, and it's great."

They would have to work extra hard now to keep their little work family grounded. By 1974, almost a quarter of total TV viewers in the country, or 43 million people, were watching their show every week.

Though *All in the Family* held on to the No. 1 spot with a full third of viewers, most of the major critics were now unanimous in their support of *Mary Tyler Moore* as a classic in the making: The *Wall Street Journal*'s Benjamin Stein called it "the best show on television, week in and week out, since its beginning four years ago. . . . [Viewers] are watching people much like themselves—doomed to live imperfect lives, often comically mixed-up lives, still stretching for a measure of dignity." Stein gushed, "It is these changes of mood, these swings from happy to sad, which parallel human life and make the show so rich. Mary is always being wrenched, as so many of us feel we are, and she always comes back for more, as all of us do. And she makes us laugh about it, as our best friends can and do. To do that on a continuing basis requires writing talent of a very high caliber fitted perfectly to the characters on the show."

Individual episodes didn't always spark immediate conversations across the country the way *All in the Family* did with its interracial sniping between Archie Bunker and neighbor George Jefferson or the Bunkers' handling of a swastika spray-painted on their door. But *Mary Tyler Moore*'s characters stuck in viewers' minds as if they were real—fans could find themselves genuinely depressed after watching Lou and his wife separate, elated when Rhoda won a beauty contest, or uncomfortable when Mary had another one of her lousy parties.

When the subject of TV came up, most erudite Americans would shrug and claim they didn't watch much. But *someone* was watching, because television viewership was growing every year, with the average home taking in six hours a day. And one of the few shows that even educated, upscale viewers often did admit to watching, along with perhaps the World Series or public television documentaries, was *The Mary Tyler Moore Show*. Even author Martin Mayer, who wrote the 1972 book *About Television* despairing about the state of TV—"Daddy only watches television when he's paid for it," he writes of telling his children—admitted to watching the occasional episode of *Mary Tyler Moore* of his own free will.

Television was gaining so much power that some, including Mayer, accused it of killing live entertainment and mainstream magazines, poisoning sports and news, and aiming to take down newspapers and political elections. Cable television *seemed* to simply be bringing broadcast television to far-flung rural areas that didn't have local stations, but Mayer saw something else. Those newfangled domestic communication satellites, beaming programs willy-nilly all over the United States, portended potential bedlam. Cable television, with its coaxials snaking their way underneath us all, weaving an invisible web whose force was yet unknown, would be the nation's next "impending disaster," he predicted.

NINE
NINE
NINE
NINE
NINE
NINE
NINE
NINE

girls' club

(1970–73)

Anyone who wondered where Mary Richards got her chic sense of style—and many young women across the country wanted very much to know—stopped wondering when they saw Leslie Hall. The former beauty queen kept the trunk of her Plymouth stocked with clothing, sewing kits, and other emergency fashion supplies, and she kept herself dressed in the kind of fitted pantsuits, trench coats, flared slacks, and tailored blouses Mary's character was becoming famous for.

Hall, who was married to an actor, grew up in Chicago and moved west as a young model to seek work as a showgirl. After her divorce in 1953, she went to work in live TV at CBS Television City. Though she'd hoped to be a set designer, she settled for costume design when she found the set world impenetrably sexist. Soon she was working on television shows such as *77 Sunset Strip* and in feature films such as *Bye Bye Birdie* and *The Music Man*. Her big break came when she dressed

Elizabeth Montgomery on *Bewitched,* which led to work on the fashionably influential *Get Smart.*

Hired as the *Mary Tyler Moore Show's* costume designer for the female cast members after the pilot episode, Hall constantly refined Mary's image, dressing Moore like her own life-sized Barbie doll. She would whisper her disapproval of the smallest details about Moore's outfits whenever she hadn't dressed the star. As she sat watching the Emmys on television with her young son, Gary, she'd scoff at how horrible Moore's taste was in her view. No one else did—Moore was a fashion idol dating back to *The Dick Van Dyke Show,* after all—but Hall had an impeccable eye. She couldn't tolerate anything outside the bounds of her own refined taste.

Hall felt at home on *The Mary Tyler Moore Show.* She was spirited and funny like the main character, and a trailblazer in her own industry. The costumers' guild awarded "cards" to members, rating them according to experience: 1–3 ratings had been reserved for men and 4–6 had been reserved for women until Hall made the first female 1.

Hall also brought an innovative idea to dressing Mary Richards: She decided to make a deal with one designer to provide all of the character's clothes for the season's twenty-plus episodes. This approach would expose the clothing to a wide audience and provide the character with a realistic, consistent, and stylish wardrobe. Evan-Picone, known for its ready-to-wear, career-oriented separates, would match Mary's character perfectly. Before that, costumers had simply gone to department stores and bought clothes that they would tailor to their actors. Hall's *Mary Tyler Moore* deal marked TV's first fashion product placement of sorts. It also marked one of the first instances of a character so realistic that she rewore the same pieces, mixing and matching from episode to episode. Mary's miniskirts and tasteful sweaters, tailored slacks and shirtdresses, would reappear throughout a season.

During the audience warm-up before every Friday night taping, so many questions came up about the clothes that Hall would routinely come out and answer fashion inquiries for twenty or thirty minutes.

And Hall's ideas made such an impression in the costuming world that the giant William Morris Agency offered to "package" her as they had the similarly talented Rita Riggs, a close friend of Hall who handled all of Norman Lear's shows. Riggs went on to handle several shows at a time with a team of assistants, but Hall declined. She didn't want to become a corporation.

Moore's stand-in, Mimi Kirk, contributed a key fashion element to the show, though she'd never get an official credit from the costuming department. The tall brunette with ice-blue eyes had assisted the star as her lighting double and secretary from the show's early days and always dressed in elaborate gypsy-style fashion. A widowed mother of four young children, Kirk began meditating after her husband died in a private-plane crash. And she took on many of the accoutrements of the health-food and self-help culture she'd adopted, including the flowy, hippie wardrobe. She loved clothes made out of scarves and tablecloths and even bedspreads. On a typical day at the set, she wore jeans and Frye boots, floaty tops and huge earrings, and the occasional headscarf.

While Harper spent the first episodes trying to look extra-chunky in baggy, store-bought clothes, she admired Moore's business girl wardrobe and wished her character could develop her own distinctive look. One day as she watched Kirk on the set, Harper asked Burns, "What would you think if I went that way?" Rhoda, she reasoned, thought of herself as an artist even though she was a window dresser, and dressing like Kirk would provide a nice contrast with Mary's tailored look.

Burns encouraged her to experiment with the idea, so she wore a cardigan and had Kirk tie it at the waist for her. She tweezed her eyebrows thinner and at Kirk's urging tried a headscarf, specially twisted and tied around her head by Kirk. Soon Kirk became Harper's assistant and Moore hired a new one. Kirk made clothes for Harper—scarf-like tops, a purse made out of an abalone shell. She coordinated with Hall, but brought in more and more clothing for Harper, eventually giving all of her scarves to the actress.

Kirk embroidered constantly, sitting with Moore and Harper

as they needlepointed on the set, and even embroidered a shirt for Brooks. Harper upgraded her own everyday wardrobe a bit to match her character's, having lacked any specific sense of style before that. Now, as more young women imitated Rhoda's headscarves, she, too, became a fashion icon. The headscarf—an idea Kirk had lifted from a photo spread she saw in *National Geographic*—had become a national trend. So much so that Harper suggested to Kirk, "Why don't you make these scarves and sell them?" But Kirk preferred helping her friend look great as Rhoda, nothing more.

As *Mary Tyler Moore*'s audience grew, advertisers, and thus TV networks, were scrambling to cater to the new consumer group known as "Life Stylers": women who embraced liberation in their everyday lives without necessarily identifying as feminists. These women *were* Mary Richards. And they needed fabulous clothes, beauty products, and furniture to feel like the independent women they wanted to be. The rise of the young, empowered woman on television had at least as much to do with marketing as with feminist ideals. Products such as Charlie perfume, Breck shampoo, and Aqua Net hair spray now had the perfect place to advertise their wares.

And *The Mary Tyler Moore Show*'s female stars were benefiting— their audience may not have been as big as *All in the Family*'s, but their target viewers were far more chic. Those viewers wanted to emulate their favorite characters, Mary and Rhoda.

Interviews became a regular burden, both on the set and off, during most of the women's downtime, particularly for Moore. Women's magazines hung on her every word. (*Ladies' Home Journal,* for instance, promised its readers: "Mary Tyler Moore, Ali MacGraw, and Others: Beauty secrets of the world's most glamorous women.") "I do interviews for the sake of the show, and that's about it," she told one reporter at the time. "Interviews are like set-pieces. I find that most of my life is doing set-pieces. At home, outside, and of course down here at work. Just one set-piece after another. Very rarely are there times when I can just be myself, be with my husband or a friend, and relax." Almost every interviewer who came her way mentioned in his or her story how proper Moore was—nice, but guarded. Her eye contact fluttered. Her most revelatory answers were about her own guardedness. "I'm cautious in my dealings," she said. "I'm a hang-back person when things get uncomfortable. I'm reserved, I guess. I'm precise; I'm never late to anything, always ahead of time and waiting. I tend to be moderate; some people think I'm very conservative, and sometimes I am."

But as the show became a phenomenon, Ed, Gavin, and Ted were keeping track of how much rehearsal time went into their camp—the newsroom—and the girls' camp—Mary's home. And they didn't like what they found.

The men could handle the fact that the women got more attention for their wardrobes and from the press—they loved their costars and didn't begrudge them the media spotlight. But the guys grew jealous of a slight they took personally: how much time the producers and directors spent on the girls' scenes. The guys hid their feelings; all three were experienced dramatic actors, after all. Sandrich never knew how they felt. He just knew they were efficient with their working style; they nailed their scenes and moved on. They also often had simpler staging to master in the office set than the women had in Mary's apartment. Sandrich didn't worry about the guys. But the guys worried about what they saw as a lack of support from their director, and they grew a little envious of their female costars.

Perhaps they also simply weren't used to playing second string to a bunch of women. Such was life on the set of TV's first truly female-dominated sitcom.

Asner, MacLeod, and Knight also grew close because of their separation from the women. They often sat together on the sidelines and watched Moore, Harper, and Leachman rehearse. They'd watch again from the wings during the women's scenes at tapings. Their beef wasn't with the women themselves, after all. The ladies appreciated the shows of support; they loved to come offstage and see the three guys lined up against the scrim in their director's chairs.

Other times, the guys took long lunches together, developing both deep friendships and tensions. Tellingly, Asner and Knight jockeyed for who would be the first man through the door whenever they entered a restaurant; MacLeod was always the third.

Asner and Knight had a bond MacLeod couldn't penetrate. Asner and Knight both knew what it was like to want to be the best, the biggest, the most. They bonded quickly and rushed into a brotherly level of closeness, often checking on each other throughout the day on the set whether or not they had scenes together. They shared an ambition the laid-back MacLeod lacked. He figured that what was meant to be would happen. Asner and Knight made things happen.

This instinct made for stellar performances, but it did no favors for their friendship.

Knight, it seemed, harbored more acute jealousies than his male costars did. He felt he was the lowest in the pecking order of all the regular cast members, period. It began in the first season, when he was the only one with an outdoor trailer for a dressing room, which he called his "pizza oven." More than a decade older than Moore, Knight felt he deserved his own show.

He envied the attention the women got, but he was most jealous of his best friend on the set, Asner. Asner felt that Knight was attacking him for winning some of the show's earliest Emmys. Knight would, Asner says, accuse him of "buying" his awards. Then Knight's mood would shift back from black, and the two would be the best of friends again.

One time, a particularly accusatory rant got under Asner's skin enough that he refused to talk to Knight all week. When the Friday night taping came, Asner was still fuming, and his mood wrecked his performance. He hated himself for not leaving his feelings at the stage door. Knight, however, didn't have such a problem. He floated onstage and nailed every laugh, irritating Asner but also making him smile. The two actors reconciled after the taping, even though Asner was still annoyed at himself for not keeping his personal feelings separate from his professionalism. They always made up in the end. MacLeod, as the peacemaker between them, had a theory as to why Asner and Knight loved each other so much and fought so much: "Ed and Ted both wanted to be No. 1 with Mary."

Asner didn't provide the only source of Knight's insecurity. Knight got sensitive about slights to his Polish heritage and chafed whenever anyone told a Polish joke at a table read—a common shtick in the '70s, just a few decades after the wave of immigrants from Poland to America following World War II, Knight's own parents among them. *All in the Family's* Archie Bunker, for instance, was prone to disparaging his son-in-law, Mike, as a "dumb Polack" to huge laughs.

Knight's sensitivity to Polish jokes reflected something deeper: his concern that fans thought he was as dim as his character. He was growing tired of being the butt of the joke, tired of people thinking he was dull-witted. The character revision that had gotten him hired to begin with—turning Ted Baxter from a love interest for Mary Richards into a shallow, aging, needy newscaster—now haunted him, even though he got some of the biggest laughs of anyone in the cast, most notably from the big boss, Tinker. Tinker loved to sit in the bleachers and watch rehearsals just to see what Ted Baxter was up to that week. No matter how much acclaim Ted's character got, however, MacLeod noticed Knight becoming increasingly possessed by his internal struggle with Baxter. "Why did they have to name him Ted?" Knight would complain to his friend as they dissected each episode over the phone on Saturday night. "Why did it have to be *my* name?"

Finally, Knight voiced his concerns about his character to Burns as he plopped down in the producer's office one day. He begged for changes to Ted Baxter's story lines, anything to humanize him, make him a decent person, make him smarter. Floundering, Burns called Weinberger to help him talk the actor down: "Ed., I need you. Get in here."

As Burns waited for Weinberger to arrive, he continued to try to soothe Knight. "Oh, come on, Ted. You're beloved! People love you. People know that Carroll O'Connor isn't that racist bastard, you know? On *All in the Family,* that bigoted guy? People know that he's not that. People know that you, Ted Knight, are not Ted Baxter."

Knight still wasn't buying it, but his mood started to turn around a little when Weinberger came in and talked about the history of the great clowns. Knight drank it in, though his insecurity continued to get the better of him. "I just . . . everybody thinks I'm stupid!" he cried.

"No, no, no, no," Weinberger countered. "You're an actor!"

"I know, but they think I'm stupid."

"No they don't!" Weinberger insisted. He amped up his talk of the great buffoons of theatrical history, going back to the masked comic character, Brighella, who was part of the sixteenth-century Italian tradition of Commedia dell'Arte. Andrew Aguecheek and Toby Belch from Shakespeare's *Twelfth Night* may have come up. These all, Weinberger contended, led directly to Ted Baxter, arguably TV's first such clown with dramatic purpose. Finally, Knight seemed to pull it together.

Then Brooks walked in. "Ted Knight!" he said, ignorant of the conversation's topic. "How does it feel to be one of the great schmucks of all time?" Knight collapsed all over again.

The producers did eventually manage to buck him up again, but they never knew when Knight might have another meltdown. And even on the days when he didn't fret dramatically about his character's mental shortcomings, Knight was always either basking in the glory of his fame or obsessing over his own inadequacies. He and his close friend Adam West (who played Batman on television) would meet for lunch at a deli in Pacific Palisades called Mort's, for instance, where Knight insisted on sitting outside so he could see fans notice him. "That's right," he'd tell them. "It's me!" Yet after every taping he begged his cast mates and producers to reassure him that he'd been funny enough: "Did I get them tonight?" he would ask. "I think I got 'em. Did I get 'em?"

Moore often reassured him by cracking up at his gags. "Never play a scene with animals, children, or Ted," she'd say.

The women in the cast, meanwhile, struggled to maintain their real-life relationships with men, given their growing fame and all-consuming jobs. Moore adored Tinker. Harper admired her talented husband, Dick Schaal, whom she regarded as her best friend and most trusted adviser. Leachman spoke of nothing but her husband, producer George Englund. "They were women who achieved a lot, but what they all had in common is that they weren't independent women," Brooks says. "They were women who lived, in large part, for the men they were with."

Still, Moore began to strain under the intertwined nature of her professional and personal lives; she and Tinker were together all the time, in a way, because of work, and yet they barely got the chance to spend time alone. Leachman broke up and reconciled with Englund a number of times during the show's run. Once she stood at Pat Nardo's desk in the producers' office, talking about her recent separation from Englund. She looked off in the distance, as if playing the most dramatic scene of her career, and said, ostensibly to Nardo, "George was the love of my life." Nardo was startled, since she barely knew the actress. But she understood: Leachman wanted to talk about her husband, and she didn't care to whom.

It was the men, including Brooks, who experienced the first official splinterings of relationships under the pressure of success. Brooks split up with his wife, despite the recent birth of their first child. MacLeod's marriage ended, too: He'd married his wife at twenty-five, when she was a Rockette and he was an usher. They'd had four children together, two boys and two girls, and had tried therapy for years, but couldn't hold things together anymore. He felt like a failure for letting it go, but he finally did.

Both men also recovered with new relationships quickly afterward. MacLeod joined a group dedicated to the preservation of the American musical, through which he met his soon-to-be-second wife, Patti Kendig, a stage actress with three children of her own. Brooks soon took up with a twenty-one-year-old flight attendant he had met on a plane trip from Minneapolis to Los Angeles for location scouting. He asked Holly Holmberg out on their first date over Memorial Day weekend in 1973, and she moved in with him in Malibu a year later.

More women on the set of a show meant, alas, that a particular obsession with weight permeated the atmosphere. Of course, the men weren't immune to the lure of the crash diet, either.

Perhaps it was Moore's own fixation on maintaining her svelte figure—she was five foot seven and 118 pounds—that prompted her costars to worry about their own. Several times a week, Moore ate a quick paper-bagged lunch and then changed into a leotard for an on-set dance class with her longtime instructor, Sallie Whalen. Moore had trained for decades in ballet—it most certainly contributed to her remarkable grace and posture—and she missed the toning effect it had on her lean body.

The actress had three portable ballet barres and a huge mirror on wheels brought to the soundstage on the days when Whalen visited. Harper and Moore would wear their workout clothes on Monday and Wednesday, Harper in her black leotard and Moore in pink, so they could squeeze in a class at lunchtime. Harper tried to pitch in for the cost of the teacher, but Mary insisted, "No, no, I need the company."

Sometimes guest actresses or crewmembers would participate as well. Beverly Sanders, a friend of Moore from Whalen's class at the American School of Dance in Los Angeles, played a waitress at the WJM crew's favorite restaurant, and she joined in the dance class whenever she appeared on the show. For all of the women, the class was more than a means for weight loss. It became a nostalgic reminder of their dancing days—they welcomed every groan-inducing stretch and new blister. They held ballet class as a sacred rite and bonding experience as much as a waistline-trimmer. "It's a discipline in itself and a lot more fun than just exercising," Moore said at the time. "And it makes dieting easier, too. Dancing for me is like a cheap form of therapy: When your muscles are in agony you can't think about your problems. Any psychiatrist will tell you that the greatest thing you can do when you're depressed about something is physical exercise." Afterward, they'd all get back to work, Moore wearing the muumuu and leggings that kept her body warm and supple after class.

Despite her willowy figure, dance class wasn't enough for Moore. She took up dieting and encasing her thighs in Saran Wrap in hopes of reducing them. Even though she knew she had good genes when it came to staying thin, she could be drawn into comparing herself to the models in *Vogue* and *Bazaar*. A typical lunch for her was a crab salad with diet cola.

Tinker would often chide her to lay off the calorie-counting and would cite the comedian Totie Fields, who based much of her humor on weight struggles. "It's all well and good," he would tell his wife, "but remember that somewhere along the line Totie Fields looked like you on the way up." His wife's general perfectionism troubled him as well. "I love her," he once told a *People* reporter, "but I sometimes find myself almost wishing she would do something wrong." Still, Moore worried about her body and her aging face—refusing, for instance, to watch old *Dick Van Dyke* episodes from just a decade earlier because, as she said, "it's like Dorian Gray in reverse." She wouldn't watch herself in movies, either. "On the big screen you don't *like* yourself," she told one reporter. "On the small screen you're not so bad."

Moore was hardly alone in her weight fixation. The more popular the show got, the more the cast became consumed with their fluctuating scale numbers. Harper's assistant and fashion muse, Mimi Kirk, requested the on-set breakfast be switched from sweet rolls to fruit, a move everyone in the cast appreciated. Asner took up jogging, horrified by what his two-hour lunches (often complete with vodka) did to his already-beefy build—especially given the on-screen comparison with Moore. He thought he looked like a pumpkin when he saw set photos of himself. He dropped from 250 pounds to 210, though he never totally gave up the lamb stew and double martinis he favored.

Leachman, meanwhile, gave Asner some extra incentive. She promised if he lost thirty pounds, she'd sleep with him. She liked to tease that he'd lost twenty-nine pounds then went right back up, for fear of having to make good on their deal. "I don't know who was more frightened," she would say.

MacLeod and Harper tried Weight Watchers together, inspiring Harper to give up her doughnut habit. "Isn't it wild?" Harper said to her diet mate. "All the potbellied guys are home drinking beer, looking at *Playboy*, while the wives are at Weight Watchers, sweating to be beautiful, so they can hold on to the fat guy!" MacLeod was not about to be one of those guys. He lost so much weight that the infamous episode in which Slim Pickens plays WJM's wacky cowboy owner looked even more ridiculous by the time it made it to the air: They reshot so many scenes throughout the season that MacLeod's weight appeared to fluctuate by up to twenty pounds from one scene to the next.

Still, the boys worried less about their weight than the girls did. The three male stars ate lunch regularly at Art's Deli, sometimes joined by Sandrich, while the girls went for health food across the street— salads, mostly, as Leachman was a vegetarian. "Look at our guys," Leachman would say, "trundling off to have pastrami." Avoiding the deli seemed to work for Harper. She shed the exact twenty pounds that had won her the role of Rhoda to begin with, thanks to Weight Watchers, dance class, and those salads with Leachman. Finally, Harper lost so much that she went to Moore, concerned for the sake of the show: Should she put the weight back on so as not to ruin her character's jokes? Moore assured her it would be fine.

The writers did, too, after some discussion. "Look, we're doing all these fat jokes and you aren't fat anymore," they teased her, "so what are we going to do?"

Harper offered, "You're absolutely right. How selfish it was of me to have lost all that weight. I'll eat Italian dinners for a few weeks and put it back on."

She actually did it, though the writers had thought she was joking, so they'd thought up "thin stories" for Rhoda instead. Harper took off thirty pounds this time, and stuck, at least for the moment, with her new weight. But she would never stop thinking of herself as fat.

Jay Sandrich, a focused director with a penchant for stuffy golf sweaters, had a problem in the uncontrollable free spirit known as Cloris Leachman.

Leachman was a brilliant improviser. From take to take, she never did the same thing twice. She was always messing with the script, then apologizing. Harper tried to soothe her: "You're the only one doing it right!" Leachman took the role seriously, and personally, often to her detriment. Sometimes when interviewers came to her house to write about her, she would find herself behaving as Phyllis instead of herself. She'd internalized the role, agonized over it, and analyzed her alter ego. On the surface, she felt, Phyllis might seem neurotic, but the fact was, she wanted badly to be perfect. Phyllis manifested the modern woman's dilemma: She aspired to the feminine ideal in the kitchen and the home as well as the bedroom, and she had no idea how to do it all. Even Leachman's mother had a theory about Phyllis; she summed up the character's personality as "the sure, firm touch on the wrong note."

All that analysis could lead to brilliance, but it made for tense moments on a sitcom set, which was meant to run on precision and routine, budget and schedule. While shooting scenes, Leachman often wandered off to a different part of the room than the script called for, so moved was she by Phyllis's impulses as they coursed through her. The problem with such method instinct on a sitcom: The cameras could film only certain parts of the set, as determined ahead of time by rehearsal blocking. If Leachman wandered off camera, it didn't matter how great she'd been; the audience at home wouldn't see it. Few rehearsals went by without Sandrich screaming, "Cloris!" at least once. At that, she would turn into "a pillar of salt," as Moore later recalled, but that didn't stop Leachman from doing the same thing again a week later.

In his calmer moments, Sandrich explained to Leachman that no matter how great her acting was, it meant nothing if she wasn't on her mark. Leachman put it another way: "I would always try to find some different way to do a thing and I suppose that Jay would then have to try to figure out how to get it on camera. I don't want to get into a pattern because patterns deaden. I see some actors go dutifully to their spots, cameras on them, being a good girl or boy, and that's not the stuff of greatness." Sandrich, however, dealt with the fallout, and often got notes from the producers that asked why he let Cloris do what she did. All he could say in reply: "I didn't. Cloris will do what Cloris wants to do."

Leachman often arrived late for rehearsal because she was so busy squeezing fresh juice for her five children in the morning, packing lunches, and dealing with other strife at home, which could set the entire week's production schedule back. She was juggling her large family and on-again, off-again marriage. She felt guilty and realized the others in the cast all knew their lines better than she knew hers. Ethel Winant, herself a mother, defended the actress to producers and CBS executives. "She has five children," Winant would say. "She needs to be at home. She'll get there when she can."

Harper, however, was Leachman's staunchest ally. Leachman loved that Harper was always saying, "That's my girlfriend!" when she saw Leachman. It meant more to Leachman at the time than Harper knew, the feeling that she had a fellow woman on her side. Finally, Leachman, inspired by the friendship and support she felt from Harper, stood her ground against Sandrich. During the second season, when she was on the phone with one of her kids and she heard Sandrich scream her name, she said to him, "Would you ask me nicely? Then I would be happy to come."

Now Leachman felt more secure asking for what she wanted from the crew, too; once, after she and Harper and Moore had blocked an entire scene, she protested. "Oh, my God," she said to Moore. "We have to switch sides. You girls have such cute noses, and this is my bad side."

"Oh, Cloris," Sandrich sighed, but the women obliged Leachman and did it all again.

"I don't know my bad side," Harper cracked. "I think they're equally not great."

Harper could relate to Leachman, as she had her own difficulties with TV production. She had to learn how to stand behind Moore in a shot without stepping on her heels or blocking her, a skill she hadn't learned in the theater. She was constantly refining her Bronx accent, often running up to the producers' office to ask their secretary, New Yorker Pat Nardo, to say a word or phrase for her. She also had to learn how to take feedback from the producers. Harper's actor husband, Dick Schaal, would counsel her when she came home to their new house in Westwood, distressed that the producers had criticized her: "Valerie, don't think of that. It's not us and them. They are Saint Bernards with brandy, and you are a stuck hiker. Help is on the way. They're coming to make the show better."

To assuage her anxiety, Harper grew obsessed with "keying" off furniture and props, always having something physical to do in a scene to make sure she was in the right place at the right time. She second-guessed her instincts and judged her own performances as they happened. In her theater days, she had been able to absorb the material slowly. Here on the set of *The Mary Tyler Moore Show,* she was often still struggling on Wednesdays, just two days before taping.

Once Harper calmed down, she was able to take the producers' advice and improve with every show. One particular bit of wisdom about her tendency to overact stuck with her: "If you're too presentational with a joke," Brooks advised her, "you're working without a net." If you let the audience know you think you're funny, and they don't laugh, he explained, you'll end up embarrassed; if you deliver the funny line like a throwaway, and they laugh, it's even funnier. Her casual laugh lines soon became one of her hallmarks as an actress.

Sandrich grew used to Harper's quirks over time, and his confidence in her grew despite her lack of confidence in herself. "She'll get there," he'd reassure the writers and crew. And she always did.

PART THREE

PART THREE
PART THREE
PART THREE
PART THREE
PART THREE
PART THREE

"I tell you, this is a great country.
You know what makes it great?
Because you don't have to be witty or clever
as long as you can hire someone who is."
—Ted Baxter

TEN
TEN
TEN
TEN
TEN
TEN
TEN
TEN

THE WRITERS WORE HOT PANTS

(1972–74)

When Ted Baxter—the show's resident chauvinist, with his penchant for calling women "chicks" and "broads"—made a joke about filing his dates as simply "blond, brunette, or redhead," Treva Silverman could not stand for the scene as it was written. Mary, she insisted, could not be part of it if she didn't pointedly object to Ted's behavior. "Either Mary can't be in the shot," she told Brooks and Burns, "or she's got to have a rejoinder."

The men were used to taking such corrections from the women they hired. In fact, they welcomed it. Silverman held the line on larger feminist issues, for the most part, while Susan Silver often set them straight on the minutiae of women's grooming habits. During a discussion about one particular scene, for instance, one of the guys said, "Then Mary will go get cleaned up." Silver objected: "No, women don't 'get cleaned up.' That's a guy thing."

By the end of the first season, Brooks and Burns went from having one woman on board—Treva Silverman—to having several on board, and several more on the way. Never before had so many women assembled to write one comedy series. Brooks and Burns went from being open to hiring women to being determined to disprove the long-standing belief that women weren't funny.

Word spread, and by the third season, female TV writers started to materialize in front of Brooks and Burns at every turn. They came at the producers through mutual dentists. They showed up in the bleachers at rehearsals and tapings. They called from across the country, lobbying for jobs harder than McGovern and Nixon were begging for votes. They sent in half-finished scripts. They came through Brooks's and Burns's producer friend Garry Marshall, a generous mentor who respected women's comedic talents. Marshall had a younger sister, Penny, who was very funny herself. (Brooks and Burns thanked Marshall by giving his sister a recurring part as Mary's new neighbor in the fourth season. But Penny would soon leave it behind to shoot a new show for her brother, *Laverne & Shirley*.) The question became how much time Brooks and Burns could spend shaping aspiring female writers' raw talent—few of them were as experienced as their male peers, because it hadn't been easy for them to get hired before *The Mary Tyler Moore Show*.

Advertising copywriter Charlotte Brown found her way to *The Mary Tyler Moore Show* via the dentist, who happened to mention during her checkup that Jim Brooks was his neighbor and patient. She ran home to put together a package with her commercial reels and her spec script, which the dentist passed on to Brooks. Eventually Brooks called her and told her he hadn't had time to look at any of it, but she was welcome to come to rehearsals and sit in the bleachers. She snuck out of her agency job by pleading a string of fake doctors' appointments—the dentist, emergency surgery, anything she could think of.

Every time, the same thing: Brooks gave her a friendly greeting, but nothing more. Frustrated, she wrote another spec script and gave it to him.

Just a few years out of UCLA, where she'd graduated Phi Beta Kappa with an English degree, she'd already made one career change, and the script, if successful, would mean a second. Brown had grown up in the sprawl of Los Angeles after moving there from Ohio as an infant, but she'd remained insulated in a middle-class world, knowing few people in Hollywood. She was at least three degrees of separation from anyone with a recognizable name. (The closest she got to a celebrity was going to college with the daughter of one of Bob Hope's writers.) Still, she'd longed for a career in television since junior high, the worst three years of her life. She'd spent her summers in a pink bathing suit, watching TV by herself. She'd enjoyed popularity in elementary school, but as high school approached, being smart lost its cool. She begged teachers to give her B's just so she could fit in with the others, but it didn't work. TV became her refuge.

By high school, she was already thinking *comedy writer* when anyone asked what she wanted to be when she grew up, but she didn't dare say it aloud. Instead, she went with one of the few acceptable answers for girls at the time: *teacher.* She earned her English degree at UCLA, and taught high school while her boyfriend finished up law school. For two years, she loved the kids, but hated everything else about the job. Seeking more intellectual stimulation, she volunteered for Bobby Kennedy's presidential campaign in 1968, just months before his assassination. There, she met a woman who was an advertising copywriter. Even though the advertising business in Los Angeles was nascent at best, Brown couldn't shake her fascination with this woman's profession. She put together a portfolio of pretend ads, and in a few months she had a job. She wrote copy for Thrifty drugstore ads: "Colgate Toothpaste, 89 cents," that sort of thing.

What came next was pure Hollywood. A few weeks into her new job, she wandered the halls of the ad agency office, bored, seeking the stimulation she'd believed she'd find there. The creative director invited her to help a group brainstorm ideas for a radio campaign for Bubble Up, a precursor to 7-Up. She suggested a character called "Bubbles

Upton," a takeoff on Goldie Hawn's popular dumb-blonde persona from *Laugh-In*. The client loved it, and Brown was catapulted out of the Thrifty account. The campaign proceeded until Hawn's lawyers served Bubble Up cease-and-desist letters for imitating their client, but Brown's course was set. She was a comedy writer.

And now she'd finally gotten Jim Brooks to read one of her scripts. He called to tell her. "God, this is awful."

But he added, "You do have a great ear for dialogue, and that can't be taught." The next time she came to rehearsal, he gave her a stack of scripts to study. She pitched him and Burns ideas every week from then on, and in January 1971, they bought one. She skipped out of the office, saying, to no one in particular, "I'm a comedy writer for television!"

The story she'd pitched had Mary dating a gorgeous guy she met at a ski slope who turned out to be less-than-smart. The script ultimately wasn't shot—though a later episode would have a similar story line— but Brown was now officially a *Mary Tyler Moore* writer. And she'd get her first episode on the air at the beginning of the following season with a story line about Mary's couple friends splitting up.

Brown's break illustrated the difference between Brooks and Burns and the many men who had run sitcoms before them: They were willing to foster the talent of any and all women who wanted to write for them, as long as they saw unique potential and a distinct point of view. At a time when the Writers Guild and the Screen Actors Guild were only just considering forming women's committees, Brooks and Burns were already hiring women left and right. In fact, they badly wanted these women's contributions.

After all, while Brooks and Burns knew how to write a great, character-driven comedy, they didn't know anything about being single, thirty-something women—the kind of women who were both their main characters and their most enthusiastic fans. "Allan and I, as straight guys, we don't do that pantyhose and nail polish stuff," Jim

The cast poses for
a publicity shot early
in the show's run.

Getty Images

Cast photo taken as a joke to
send to reviewers who didn't like
the show, then later dumped by
secretary Pat Nardo when bad
early reviews trickled in and
the joke didn't seem so funny
anymore. Nardo swiped one copy
for posterity. Top row: Harper,
Asner, Leachman; bottom row:
MacLeod, Moore, and Knight.

Courtesy of Pat Nardo.

Writer Treva Silverman at the typewriter where she perfected her scripts. *Courtesy of Treva Silverman.*

Silverman's more casual publicity shot. *Courtesy of Treva Silverman.*

Writer Susan Silver.
Courtesy of Susan Silver.

Susan Silver, right, with
then-husband, Arthur, at the
1972 Emmy Awards, where
Ed Asner won a statue for
his performance in the 1971
episode she wrote,
"The Square-Shaped Room."
Courtesy of Susan Silver.

Producer Lorenzo Music with fan Joe Rainone and his brother Eddy during their 1971 set visit. *Courtesy of Joe Rainone.*

Producer David Davis, Mary Tyler Moore, producer Allan Burns, fan Joe Rainone, and producer James L. Brooks in 1971. Note Brooks's "It's a Girl" button: His daughter was born that night. *Courtesy of Joe Rainone.*

Dear Susan,

By now I'm probably back to being just in the top ten, but let me say this — — — It's a plea- sure mentioning your name, it's a pleasure looking at you and it's a pleasure doing your words,

Thanks,
Ed

Ed Asner's note to Silver after the Emmys, where he thanked her in his speech for writing the episode for which he won: "It's a pleasure mentioning your name, it's a pleasure looking at you, and it's a pleasure doing your words." *Courtesy of Susan Silver.*

Mary and Rhoda chat
in Mary's apartment.
Corbis Images

Mary reacts to Phyllis
in a 1971 episode.
Corbis Images

Gavin, Ted, and Mary in the newsroom. *Corbis Images*

Lou, Mary, Ted, and Murray welcome guest star Walter Cronkite
to WJM in a 1974 episode. *Getty Images*

Nancy Walker, Treva Silverman, Mary Tyler Moore, Valerie Harper, and Georgia Engel discuss being "women in comedy" with reporters at a luncheon as the show reached the heights of its popularity. *Courtesy of Treva Silverman.*

Ted Knight, Mary Tyler Moore, Valerie Harper, and director Jay Sandrich at the 1973 Emmy Awards. *Corbis Images*

Mary Tyler Moore and Grant Tinker arrive at the 1973 Emmy Awards. *Corbis Images*

Valerie Harper and Ed Asner in their first Emmy wins for the show, 1971. *Corbis Images*

Rhoda weds Joe in a country-stopping 1974 episode of *Rhoda*. *Corbis Images*

Valerie Harper as Rhoda in one of her signature headscarves. *Getty Images*

Murray and Sue Ann banter
in the newsroom. *Getty Images*

Sue Ann and Phyllis confront
each other. *Getty Images*

Ted Knight and Mary Tyler Moore at a 1977 event where local newscasters "roasted" Knight. *Corbis Images*

The cast in 1975 with new additions Betty White and Georgia Engel— and minus Valerie Harper and Cloris Leachman, who'd left for their own spinoffs. *Getty Images*

Ted, Lou, and Mary get bad news in the 1977 series finale. *Corbis Images*

The cast celebrates the 1977 series finale, just after the famous group hug in the newsroom. *Getty Images*

Mary Tyler Moore and producer James L. Brooks, reunited in 1984. *Getty Images*

Moore, Ed Asner, Betty White, and Gavin MacLeod pose for a group shot in 2002. *Corbis Images*

Allan Burns, Grant Tinker, and writer-producer Stan Daniels (with Writers Guild Foundation President Barry Kemp) catch up at a 2005 event. *Getty Images*

Cloris Leachman, Mary Tyler Moore, Valerie Harper, Georgia Engel, and Ed Asner present together at the 2007 Screen Actors Guild Awards. *Corbis Images*

Grant Tinker in his office, taken by fan Joe Rainone during a 1977 visit. *Courtesy of Joe Rainone.*

Mary Tyler Moore and writer Susan Silver reunite, three decades after the show ended, at a diabetes-research benefit. *Courtesy of Susan Silver.*

Valerie Harper and Silver at a screening of Harper's film *Golda's Balcony* in 2007. *Courtesy of Susan Silver.*

was fond of saying. "I know there is a wealth of comedy in my wife's purse, but I can't access that."

Gail Parent, a thirty-year-old writer, was another woman who helped them do that. She showed up from *The Carol Burnett Show* to seek work with her partner Kenny Solms. Until coming to *Mary Tyler Moore*, Parent felt quite like Silverman did on *The Entertainers*, *The Monkees*, and everywhere else she had worked. Namely, alone. Parent didn't always mind, though; it was fun to be the only woman around. It made her feel special.

Parent had met Solms at NYU. He had memorized everything Mike Nichols had ever said, and she had memorized everything Elaine May had said, so they made a perfect pair. They started improvising together, and writing some of their bits down. They would sit in fancy New York apartment lobbies waiting for producers and comedians to come home so they could offer their writing services.

That didn't pan out. But they eventually found a less creepy route to success: They wrote a comedy album that did well enough to get the attention of Carol Burnett and her husband and producer, Joe Hamilton. The next thing Parent and Solms knew, they had a seven-week deal to come out to Los Angeles and try writing for *The Carol Burnett Show*. If they did well enough to stay on another thirteen weeks, their salary went down. Another thirteen, and it went down again. Still, they thought it sounded better than hounding people in their lobbies—they took the deal, and Parent made history as one of few women writing for Hollywood variety shows at the time. It turned out to be a smart move: Once the pair worked for Burnett, offers to write for other shows began to pour in, even as their base salary decreased. Just as Parent's role model Elaine May was producing and directing her first movie, *A New Leaf*—a film that would usher in a new era for female directors—it looked as if Parent was on her way to similar success.

Parent was also slaving away on a novel she hoped to publish, but in the meantime she needed a source of steady income. Parent couldn't wait to try her hand at *The Mary Tyler Moore Show*. She had never seen anything that dealt with women so realistically and relatably, so she was thrilled when she and Solms got hired. Once she got the chance to hang around the set, being around other funny women was also freeing for a woman whose mother used to tell her, "Try not to be so funny—men would rather be romantic on a date than laughing all night."

Pat Nardo, Brooks and Burns's secretary, also had loads of funny thoughts that Brooks and Burns encouraged her to put into scripts. At first, her main job was taking notes on their brainstorming sessions. As she shot down ideas she didn't think were good enough, they realized what a sharp comedic sensibility she had. "Come on," they'd chide her, "write it down." She refused unless she thought it was truly funny, and her high standards prompted them to try harder. Soon they knew a joke wasn't funny unless Nardo wrote it down.

The turning point in her career came when she read the guys parts of letters between her and her friend Gloria Banta, whom she'd met when she lived in New York in the early '60s. One day Brooks and Burns said, "You guys should try writing together." It didn't seem like such a crazy suggestion. Both women had worked in show business in New York. They always said they both had the "Gotta dance!" spirit Gene Kelly sang of in *Singin' in the Rain*. Nardo's overprotective mother wouldn't let her follow her original dream of being a ballerina, but she could no longer stop her daughter from putting on a show.

Nardo had been working for Brooks and Burns for a year and began considering going back to New York after the San Fernando earthquake shook Los Angeles in 1971. She and her bosses had grown quite fond of each other—Burns called her at home just after the quake struck at 6 a.m. to make sure she was okay. But things weren't working out with her boyfriend Chuck Barris. As aftershocks from the quake continued for weeks, Nardo thought, *What am I doing here?*

Around the same time, Burns walked her to her car after a late night at the office and said, "I think you can do it." He wanted her to seriously consider writing for the show. Nardo liked the idea, but she didn't want to do it alone. So she jetted back to New York to write with her best friend, happy to also return to her hometown.

Banta worked as an associate producer for media mogul David Susskind. She was in love with her city and her job, and she didn't mind working on this little side project with Nardo. But she had no interest in TV writing as a long-term career. She didn't want to move to Los Angeles, which just didn't have as much character as New York as far as she was concerned. She hated warm weather and the nonstop Hollywood haze that choked Los Angeles. She preferred New York's stage life to any other kind of show business, but writing with Nardo for *The Mary Tyler Moore Show,* one of her personal favorites, would be fun. Banta and Nardo called each other "Broadway Bess and TV Tilly."

For three weeks, they met every day under a tree in Central Park and hammered out an episode of *The Mary Tyler Moore Show.*

They based their script on a true story: New York mayor John Lindsay's assistant had asked Nardo out, back when she worked at Talent Associates and she was living with Banta. Nardo rarely dated, and she'd had a crush on this guy from afar for six months after seeing him in the paper, so the two women went all out to get her ready for her big date. After hours of dressing her up like a paper doll, they finally got a call from the doorman saying her date had arrived, and Banta pushed Nardo out the door.

He picked her up there in a limo, but said he'd have to get out of the car a block down on Fifty-sixth Street to use a pay phone and check on things at work. When he got back in from his call, he told her he was very sorry, but he had to go tend to the Students for a Democratic

Society riots at Columbia University. They were getting much worse than expected. He dropped her off after an approximately five-minute date, and they never saw each other again. Nardo laughed hysterically the whole ride back up to the apartment in the elevator, knowing how funny Banta would think it was. That became an episode called "The Five-Minute Dress," in which Mary dates a busy politician.

Nardo sent the script in to her bosses back in Los Angeles; they bought it and shot it. But Nardo decided to stay in New York. She got a job working for an executive in charge of daytime programming at ABC named Michael Eisner; she'd be heading up the network's new *After School Specials* series. She scored immediately, coming up with a movie about a girl who wanted to play Little League. Banta wrote the script for *Rookie of the Year* with her, and child actress Jodie Foster starred. The *Hollywood Reporter* ran a front-page story about Nardo's rise to the executive ranks, she recalls, under the headline, "It's a Woman's World at ABC." She was vastly underpaid at $265 a week for helping manage the daytime programming department, but she was still the only woman in programming.

She wore out her welcome with the network's other female employees, however, when she made a joke at the first women's group meeting that "any meeting announced in the toilet belongs in the toilet." She was trying to urge the ladies to stop posting meeting notices in the women's restroom and instead use interoffice mail, but they didn't appreciate her humor. She soon quit the women's group.

Treva Silverman had found heaven working for *The Mary Tyler Moore Show*. Brooks and Burns admired her work, which exceeded even their high standards, while many of the other young women writing for the show had to try and fail and try again in hopes of getting their scripts right. She displayed her uniqueness from her first episode, the second one to air in the series, in which Mary and Rhoda invite men they know over for an impromptu get-together, hoping to score dates. At Phyllis's urging, Mary invites an old boyfriend she hasn't spoken to in years named Howard Arnell (played by Harper's husband, Dick Schaal). He is so enamored of Mary from the second he walks in that he doesn't acknowledge Rhoda, Rhoda's "date," and her date's wife (oops). "Excuse me, I'd like to introduce myself," Rhoda says to Howard. "I'm another person in the room."

The line represented what Burns would call "pure Treva." Neither he nor Brooks would ever have come up with it. Silverman also particularly molded the Rhoda character, because she so strongly identified with her, and took Rhoda in directions Brooks and Burns had never anticipated when they created her.

She also helped mold the show's signature combination of comedy and drama, displaying a deft touch with the show's more dramatic episodes. Her script for the 1973 episode "The Lou and Edie Story" won an Emmy and brought divorce to the forefront of *The Mary Tyler Moore Show*. Better yet, it depicted a scenario typical of 1970s splits influenced by the growing women's movement: Lou's wife, Edie, played by character actress Priscilla Morrill, leaves him to find herself. "When I married you I was nineteen years old, and I thought you were the most wonderful man I ever met," she tells him. "I still think so. But I want to learn more about the rest of me. Not just the part that's your wife."

The *Los Angeles Times* called the episode a "breakthrough": "If you watch *The Mary Tyler Moore Show* Saturday on CBS, things will look the same, but you will probably feel differently," columnist Mary Murphy wrote the week before the episode aired. "You'll laugh, as you usually do between 9 and 9:30 p.m., but you may also notice a tight lumping in the throat or tears welling in the eyes as many in the audience did at a live taping."

The result was a vulnerable character arc for the tough Lou Grant. "That was pretty damn good, you know?" Burns says. The producers hadn't planned to divorce the couple, but when they thought of it, they went with it, and Treva was the perfect person to pull it off. "That was our way of doing divorce," Burns says, "which they had not wanted us to do." As *Time* magazine later said, "On MTM, characters developed, changed, sometimes in ways disconcerting to all those schooled in the inevitability of happy endings. Lou Grant (Edward Asner) and his wife Edie (Priscilla Morrill) separated; she felt stultified and wanted to try a different life. Ah well, the faithful said, they will get back together. They did not; they got divorced."

Though Silverman was great at what she did, she also appreciated her new bosses' patience with her process: She was slower than any of her colleagues, even if her work was worth the wait. Once her drafts arrived, they'd be near perfection. She spent all of her time at the studio office. MTM was *the* place to be for women in the TV business at the time, and Silverman wasn't going to relinquish her prime spot any time soon.

Susan Silver took pleasure in the chance to turn her life into sitcom scripts. The episode "Room 223," about Mary dating her journalism class teacher but getting a C on a paper anyway, counted among the many swiped from Silver's everyday existence. She relied so much on her life for plots that she barely realized she was allowed to make things up. If she was stumped for story ideas, she'd stare out her study window, watching the leaves in the gentle Southern California breeze. She'd even resort to pulling the dictionary off the shelf. If nothing had happened to her, she'd pick words at random hoping for inspiration: *Hmm, A: Maybe we could do something about airplanes . . .*

In fact, all of the women writing regularly for the show relied on their lives for inspiration. In the episode "Love Blooms at Hemple's," in which Rhoda falls for a guy so fast she starts planning their wedding, writer Sybil Adelman used the wording she'd always dreamed of having on her own wedding announcement: "Mr. and Mrs. Morgenstern are relieved to announce the wedding of their daughter. . . ."

Adelman couldn't believe her luck: As an aspiring TV writer, she'd once accepted a show assignment just because the office had air-conditioning and Los Angeles was caught in a hot spell. So to work on shows she loved, like *Mary Tyler Moore*, felt like a luxury even better than central air. Her former boss, Carl Reiner—she'd been his secretary—recommended her and writing partner Barbara Gallagher to Brooks and Burns. The producers hired the Mary-and-Rhoda–like pair. (Gallagher was the Mary, Adelman the Rhoda.) For Reiner, they'd written an episode of *The New Dick Van Dyke Show* in which Dick's daughter walks in on him and his wife having sex. CBS declined to air it, and Reiner quit the show in protest. But Adelman and Gallagher, with a real (if unaired) script to their credit, got a dream career.

In one of their *Mary Tyler Moore* episodes, the pair based the story on Adelman's relationship with Reiner: Lou worries Mary will get a better job and leave him. That had happened to Adelman, who just a few years before would thrill at the prospect of taking Friday afternoon off to walk over to the *Mary Tyler Moore* set from Reiner's office to watch the run-through. At the time, she'd thought it was better than the high school prom. Now those actors were saying her words, and she was no one's secretary anymore.

Karyl Geld, a thirty-year-old dress designer, had just moved to Los Angeles from New York with her husband and toddler son when she decided to be a TV writer. She was watching the Emmys at home, and when she saw Lily Tomlin come on the screen in a prom-like dress, she knew she should be critiquing the comedian's wardrobe, but instead she thought: *Maybe I should be a comedy writer.* She knew she was funny. So she started writing spec scripts.

Almost a dozen spec scripts later, none of them had sold. Then she wrote one for *The Mary Tyler Moore Show*, and her life changed. After becoming famous around the industry for *not* getting hired, she got a letter from Brooks and Burns saying they thought her script was terrific. Her first assignment: an episode in which Rhoda and Mary go to New York for Rhoda's sister's wedding. She thought that sounded perfect for her, since she was Jewish herself—she had a Jewish mother, too. And she had the perfect ending for the script: When Rhoda has a blowup with her mother, they make peace when her mother shows her a letter she wrote to Rhoda on the day of her birth. Geld copied the letter verbatim that her mother had written to her, to be opened on the occasion of her wedding—though she'd left it unsealed, and Geld had it at home in her garage.

So in a way, Geld's mother is responsible for one of the best jokes in the episode, a line from her letter to her newborn daughter: "God has been good to me. The nurses haven't been so nice, but God has been good to me." Geld had learned her first lesson of sitcom writing: Steal from real life.

Silverman's tenth episode, in October 1972 at the beginning of the second season, got even more personal: It tackled Rhoda's self-esteem and weight issues—and by extension, Silverman's own. In the episode, Rhoda has joined a Weight Watchers–like group, but she's also talked into competing in the beauty contest at the department store where she works. After the contest, she refuses to tell Mary and Phyllis how she placed; in fact, she won. Rhoda's self-deprecation reflected Silverman's own insecurities. The episode marked a turnaround in Rhoda's character, from the sweatshirt-clad schlub of the pilot to the fashion icon she became. Silverman loved writing about the "blossoming of someone's self-esteem. I was writing about Rhoda, but I was also writing about myself, about all women."

Brooks and Burns knew beauty pageants weren't exactly progressive, but they liked that the episode helped the character to evolve. They also liked that Rhoda finally admitted on-screen that she was beautiful, weight fluctuations or not.

Harper, who doesn't hesitate to call Silverman a "genius," won an Emmy for her work in the episode. The TV camera panned in for a close-up on the actress's striking face as she gave her acceptance speech: "I want to thank Treva Silverman for writing a perfect episode," she said. Silverman watched from, of all places, a health resort where she was trying to lose weight. The writer burst into tears at the public acknowledgment of her work, and the graciousness of Harper. She'd never forget it, she knew.

✦ ✦ ✦

Female TV writers became all the rage as *Mary Tyler Moore*'s popularity soared in its third season. The image of comedy writers was changing from swearing guys in alpaca sweaters and pinky rings to women in miniskirts with typewriters. When *Laugh-In* started in 1968, its writers worked in a hotel room across from the studio and thus claimed they "couldn't have a woman in that environment." The sketch comedy series was still on the air, but its male-centric writing staff suddenly looked like a relic. Executives across Hollywood were saying, as Treva Silverman put it, "We're going to do a story about women and we're going to have women writers and women producers and women actresses. It's women, women, women. Get Barbara, she's a woman! Get Linda, get Mary!"

Susan Silver soaked up the attention as one of the first women to write for *The Mary Tyler Moore Show*. As a newcomer to TV writing as well as a bombshell with a weakness for tight sweaters who made for a hell of a photo, she became a hot commodity. *Playgirl* sang her praises and described her "beautiful, tousled blond" hair and her "wry laugh." *TV Guide* nestled a career-defining piece about her among its orderly prime-time programming grids with a provocative headline: "The Writer Wore Hot Pants." She did, in fact, wear hot pants in the shoot for the story, which showed her posed at a typewriter while wearing short shorts, though she was embarrassed when she saw it in print. Every time she wore those damn things, she seemed to regret it.

In the interview, Silver painted an idyllic picture of being a groundbreaking woman in the industry: Being female and "presentable" helped her get work, she admitted. She wouldn't call herself a "militant feminist," she said, but she did attend a women's workshop at the Writers Guild. (In fact, she had to quit volunteering for the National Organization for Women because she was too busy writing scripts.) People often wondered why she worked when she had a husband, she said. She worried more about her own insecurity than about sexism. Getting a job just hadn't seemed that hard to her so far.

Silverman had gotten press a few years earlier when she broke barriers by writing for *The Monkees,* but she got plenty of attention within the industry now, especially when she became the show's executive story consultant—making her the first female comedy executive in television. Brooks and Burns had granted her the promotion by telling her, "We need another head. We don't care what your title is, whatever you want."

When she won an Emmy for her writing on the show, she became the first female writer to take home the comedy award solo, without a partner. She even won the TV academy's first (and only) "super-Emmy," a gimmick that pitted every winner of every category that year up against each other for a sort of ultimate award. She felt like she had the whole weight of womankind on her shoulders; if she failed, it seemed, all women would fail along with her. One might think that feeling would prove pretty daunting, but Treva Silverman found it exhilarating.

University of Michigan senior Marilyn Suzanne Miller spent the spring of 1972 watching every episode of *The Mary Tyler Moore Show*'s second season. The Rhoda clone—she was Jewish, with dark hair and a rebellious streak—was finishing her playwriting degree from home in the Pittsburgh suburbs. (She'd fallen one credit short and had to take a correspondence course in geography to graduate.) The accomplished eldest of four girls in her family, she was waiting around her "very middle-class" home to hear if she had been admitted to graduate school in the University of Iowa's prestigious creative writing program. She was worried about paying for it even if she did get in, and she got a job writing department store ads. Then she had an idea while she watched her favorite show: Maybe she could write a script for *The Mary Tyler Moore Show,* now at the height of its popularity, and sell it to pay for grad school. She sat down and wrote page after page of dialogue, oblivious to how TV plots were structured.

When she felt satisfied with her draft, she pored over the show's ending credits and spotted the name James L. Brooks. She called information in Los Angeles and got the number for his office. A secretary answered there, and Miller let loose with her practiced spiel: "Hi, I'm twenty-two, and I'm in Monroeville, Pennsylvania, and I'd like to send you a script." The secretary transferred her to Brooks, and Miller told him the same thing. He gave her the mailing address at the office, and she sent him her script.

Brooks read it when he received it, and was impressed enough to pass it around to colleagues, including producer Garry Marshall. Brooks also sent Miller a letter to tell her that she wrote better than most writers who worked in Hollywood—and that meant something, given that he rejected a fair number of sample scripts he received from aspiring writers. Brooks told her his writing staff was full, but he'd passed her sample on to some friends in the industry because she'd written some very funny dialogue. Eventually, Marshall's writing partner, Jerry Belson, called her at work and asked if she could be on a plane to Los Angeles in two weeks to write for *The Odd Couple*, one of television's more respected comedies.

Standing on a mezzanine in the office where she worked, she looked down on all the people in cubicles and knew her life was about to change. She had to overcome some minor resistance from her mother over the move, but Marshall called to reassure her. And Miller flew west. She felt like she was living a Hollywood story even as it happened. Jim Brooks had made her believe in happy endings.

When Miller got to Los Angeles, she worked as Marshall's apprentice, the only woman in the office at the time on *The Odd Couple*. Star Tony Randall would give her Neil Simon and Shakespeare plays to study for script structure. She was excited to shop in Beverly Hills at the Rodeo Drive designer boutique Theodore and carry her Louis Vuitton purse. She felt like a real Los Angeles girl.

Marshall and Belson paired her up with Belson's sister, Monica Johnson, and advised them to write scripts together. In the winter of 1973, Miller came back from lunch one day to the *Odd Couple* office to find a telephone message on her desk from Ed. Weinberger. She and Johnson had gotten their first assignment for *The Mary Tyler Moore Show*. Their episode, about Mary's very bad day as she prepares for the annual Teddy Awards banquet, was to air that February. Her first day on the set, Miller couldn't believe she was seeing the actors she'd adored, now here in the flesh before her, saying her words. She went to a store in Beverly Hills and bought the same jeans Mary Tyler Moore had. She copied Moore's haircut.

Miller felt that the show had changed her not just professionally, but personally. The show taught her to be who she was. Mary had left her ex and found herself a life and career on her own. As Miller started her own adult life, she longed to be independent like Mary. She had felt the character's impact in a way the older women writing for the show hadn't. She went right from resisting the Ann Arbor police at the University of Michigan to working for Jim Brooks, and Mary Richards was the reason.

Seeing the producers at work impressed Miller even more. As a young writer, she thought it was pure magic to watch the creative flow of Burns, Brooks, Weinberger, and Silverman. She loved to listen to them probe into the characters' psyches. As she witnessed them work, she says, she realized why *The Mary Tyler Moore Show* was different from *All in the Family*, or even *M*A*S*H*. The *Mary Tyler Moore* producers were doing something no one else was: "drilling into human beings," as she called it. That was why she and other fans felt so connected to the show.

Miller loved that Brooks and Burns asked her, Johnson, and Silverman, throughout their hours and hours of story meetings with the producers over chicken salad sandwiches, "Would she feel that way? Would she do that? Is that a girl joke?" Brooks *wanted* girl jokes, unlike many other producers. He and Burns *wanted* women around, and Miller could feel it.

Despite being nearly a decade younger than Mary and Rhoda, Miller and Johnson soon got a chance to work their own lives into a script in which Mary's twenty-something boyfriend invites her over for a party at his place with his friends. The girls got to write in all kinds of stuff about how people their own age acted, to represent hippies and other people they knew. Brooks and Burns wanted to use them as a source to get at the younger counterculture movement.

Miller and Johnson even got a friend of theirs hired for a bit part when they wrote that "a girl with red hair, white skin, and a big nose is sitting on the bed" at the party. The producers had to give the role to their friend because the stage direction was so specific. Their script also created a boutique for Mary and Rhoda to visit in search of "younger" clothes, the kind of place they regularly shopped. Miller and Johnson just knew that the girl behind the counter at a store like that would be reading *Siddhartha*. They put it in the script. "They wanted us to deliver what we knew of our world," Miller says. "They wanted the truth out of us girls. 'Let's get some girls together and see what they think and do and say'—that's the premise of *The Mary Tyler Moore Show*."

Of course, sexism hadn't magically dissolved overnight from television's airwaves to reveal a new egalitarian order. A 1973 TV viewer could still find talk show host Jack Paar needling guest Goldie Hawn about her flat chest, commercials declaring that "a woman should be soft all over," airline ads inviting customers to "come and fly" the stewardesses, and the *Dean Martin Show* featuring an all-girl singing group called the Ding-a-Lings. Only two women starred on network dramas at the time: Peggy Lipton on *Mod Squad* and Susan St. James on *McMillan and Wife*. And even though women were advancing at MTM, relatively few women worked in Hollywood overall—and fewer held a position as high as Silverman did. Of the Writers Guild's nearly three thousand members, just 411 were women. *The Mary Tyler Moore Show* had 25 female writers of 75 total freelancers and staffers, an astonishing percentage in 1973; *The Partridge Family* was considered progressive for having just 7 women among its 76 writers.

And even on the *Mary Tyler Moore* set, not every man felt as open-minded as Brooks and Burns did. Asner, for one, bristled in the show's early days every time he saw a female name as the author of a script. He still proudly identified as a chauvinist in the first and second seasons of the show. Once he argued for hours on the set with Harper about what he saw as the silliness of using "Ms." instead of "Mrs." Harper insisted on being called an "actor"—"you never hear people say 'doctresses' or 'writeresses,' " she explained. She would not back down on this point. Her progressive attitudes would later land her on the cover of *Ms.* magazine, which praised Rhoda as "one of the few realistic women on television" in an interview with Gloria Steinem. But Harper did not sway Asner's feelings toward women.

Something else did. When the Emmys for the second season were given out in September 1972, Asner won for his performance in an episode about Rhoda redecorating his place—written by Susan Silver. He thanked Silver and Silverman by name in his speech, and again via a personal note later. "Without them," he quipped to the Emmy audience, "I'd just be another pretty face." To top it off, Silver got to attend the Emmy ceremony that year with her husband as her date.

Miller, the show's youngest hire, was now using her new job to gain access to a rollicking social life in Hollywood. She hung out at the Comedy Store on the Sunset Strip. The club had just opened in 1972 in the space recently vacated by the nightclub Ciro's, where Marilyn Monroe, Humphrey Bogart, and Frank Sinatra had once frolicked. It had become the primary scene for aspiring comics; Jay Leno would soon meet David Letterman there. Miller lived in nearby West Hollywood, as did several aspiring standups, and was one of the few among her new friends who had a job. She paid a comedian named Al Franken to teach her tennis, just so she could give him some money without hurting his pride. She treated everyone to drinks and dinners.

At night she hung out with Garry Marshall's sister, Penny, and comedian Jay Leno at the coffee shop across the street from the Comedy Store, until 3 or 4 a.m., just hours before she'd have to get up for work.

As Marilyn and Penny sat across the street waiting for their friends to come off the stage, Marilyn ate chocolate chip cookies while Penny knitted. They gawked at Led Zeppelin, the Who, and the Rolling Stones as the groups smoked in the parking lot between the club and the Hyatt hotel next door (known in those days as "the Riot House"). Mel Brooks's cohorts Rudy De Luca—the club's co-owner with Sammy Shore—as well as Barry Levinson and Buck Henry, passed through.

To all of them, Miller seemed a fascinating enigma: a funny, attractive woman who had a job in comedy. She knew she was the queen of the hop. Her friends' whole lives depended on waiting to go onstage at the Comedy Store to try out their latest material, and they cared what *she* thought because she was a real, employed comedy writer. They all watched each other's acts, then went out and critiqued them. After hours of this, Miller retired to her sparse apartment to sleep on a mattress on the floor for a few hours before heading to work. She didn't have the time or inclination to buy a real bed.

Her days with her partner, Monica Johnson, turned out to be a different kind of crazy. Johnson had a wicked sense of humor, but no writing experience, so Miller was in charge of their collaborative efforts. At twenty-six, Johnson had already been married three times. Her most recent husband had been a clockmaker, so she had purged her home of all timepieces. Miller had to remember to bring a watch when they wrote at Johnson's place. Johnson would show up in meetings with her hair rolled around orange-juice cans—a low-budget version of curlers—still dressed in her nightgown because she'd locked herself out of her house. Because such things were commonplace in her life, Johnson simplified her writing approach: "I'll just think of funny things," she told Miller, "and you can put them in if you want."

Miller considered herself a serious writer, so if she was to be partnered with Johnson, this seemed the best method to her as well, since it gave her ultimate control. Miller made the rules of their partnership even though she was twenty-two and Johnson was twenty-six. And her rules were strict.

Miller refused to follow one common practice of comedy writing: typing "JTC"—meaning Joke to Come—when one can't think of a good gag and so resolves to do that later. "Marilyn Miller doesn't do Joke to Come," Miller would say. When the duo wrote their episode about Mary dating the younger guy, for instance, and Mary and Rhoda visit the youthful clothing shop, Rhoda asks the shopgirl, "What's the name of this store?" The writers wanted to think of a hilarious name for the kind of place that sold potpourri and books about how to find your inner soul. But they wouldn't settle for JTC on it. Miller turned to Johnson—this sort of thing was Johnson's department, for sure—and said, "Well, what is it?"

They sat for three hours in silence thinking of the name of the store. Finally, Johnson turned to Miller and said, calmly, as if it were completely obvious: "Shot Down in Ecuador, Junior." Miller bolted out of her chair, screaming and laughing and jumping up and down. Only Monica could think of that phrase. Miller would never understand what went on in her partner's head. (Years later, *Tonight Show* writer Herb Sargent would say, upon meeting Miller, "Shot Down in Ecuador, Junior, huh?" Miller treasured the compliment, even though it was for her partner's contribution.)

Despite her success, Miller resisted becoming a true Hollywood insider. She preferred staying a little outside the mainstream, like her comedian friends. She got an invitation to Chasen's, the famous Beverly Hills restaurant, for an industry Emmy-watching party thrown by the major studios. She and her friends thought it was dumb, and hatched a plan to go dressed in gorilla costumes. They didn't understand that the people at the gathering could make or break their careers.

Luckily, they abandoned their costume idea and Miller wore an evening gown, but still brought her petulant attitude. The West Coast head of the International Famous Agency, Frank Konigsberg, greeted her at the entrance saying, "Good evening, it's so good to see you."

Instead of returning the pleasantry, she snapped, "Really? What's my name?" Of course he didn't know. Part of her liked it better that way.

✦ ✦ ✦

Just as Miller was moving up in the TV industry while clinging to her independent spirit, so was MTM Enterprises. Though it had started out as a "production company" in name only, it was becoming more than the independent force behind *The Mary Tyler Moore Show*. Now, after a shaky start, the studio's *Bob Newhart Show* was a modest hit and there was talk of the company producing more programs in the upcoming seasons. Brooks and Burns were at the upper ranks of the expanding enterprise, whether or not they meant to be.

The writers they had plucked from inexperience and obscurity now had the chance to become major forces in the TV business, too, but that meant making some difficult choices. Susan Silver wrote two episodes of *Bob Newhart* but chose to take her chances on writing some pilot scripts for the next season in hopes of creating her new show. In essence, she declined to stop freelancing and join the *MTM* family full-time, with all of its attendant responsibilities, security, benefits, and clout. She entertained opportunities for producing and writing more, but she wanted to give more time to her husband. They were discussing having children. She didn't want to keep the brutal hours required to move up in the industry while starting a family.

As *Bob Newhart* soared into television's top-twenty ranks with a strong assist from its prime spot on the schedule, right after *The Mary Tyler Moore Show*, Silver would never stop wondering if she'd made the wrong choice.

ELEVEN
ELEVEN
ELEVEN
ELEVEN
ELEVEN
ELEVEN
ELEVEN

pot and the pill

(1972–73)

Treva Silverman liked to hang out in the *Mary Tyler Moore* offices on the lot, smoking grass with the boys after a day of sitting at her desk writing and revising. Amid the occasional clacks of typewriters working overtime and gales of laughter over shared joke ideas, she would puff on a pungent joint or eat one of her home-baked brownies. Lorenzo Music—a husky, dark, brilliant writer-producer—had great stuff, and it was the perfect way to unwind after another packed day on the set. She felt comfortable with Brooks and Burns, as well as Music. Once she'd been made story editor, she spent all of her time on the lot with them. They hung out wherever they could safely smoke joints, usually in their offices on the MTM lot. They all spent most of their after-hours stoned, except Burns. He loved to go home to his wife.

Silverman particularly enjoyed hanging out with Music and was knocked out by his warm-up performances. He was so subtle and silly and hilarious as the warm-up guy, entertaining the audience before the show and in between set changes, that she once whispered to him, "Don't be so funny. You're better than the show!" The workplace was becoming Treva's family, just as Mary's had become hers.

The MTM offices had turned out to be a dream come true, everything Silverman could have hoped for back when she was toiling away at piano bars. Silverman knew how lucky she was to have her job. The show was now part of what many have called the best lineup in network history, CBS's 1973–74 Saturday night: *All in the Family, M*A*S*H, Mary Tyler Moore, Bob Newhart,* and *Carol Burnett.* Silverman loved to sit on the steps to the offices reading a new script by one of her fellow writers almost as much as she enjoyed writing one of her own. It wasn't that everyone in the group had a lack of ego—in fact, she thought it just might be the opposite: Their egos were so strong, in the healthiest of ways, that it allowed them to not feel competitive. All they wanted was the best possible show. They rarely got jealous when another writer wrote something great. They just thought, *Wow. I want to do that, too.* It was a heady time to be a sitcom writer, particularly for *Mary Tyler Moore,* and not just because of Treva's brownies.

Brooks and Burns had instigated an unusual policy concerning a writer's credits, a policy that showed enormous respect for writers. No matter how many revisions were made on a script by others, the original writer's credit was kept intact. Even if a script was completely rewritten before it was shot, the producers would never adjust the credits. This policy ensured a level of collaboration rare on television shows. It also guaranteed that the original writer, once committed to an episode, would get all the royalties.

Silverman loved the work she was doing and felt herself growing as a writer. She learned to do the rewrites on someone else's scripts in that writer's voice. She learned to write on the fly. Although she longed for a situation akin to Proust's cork-lined room, she didn't always have the luxury of being in a quiet room with a typewriter. She did, however, love the group meetings where everybody contributed lines. Nothing is more wonderful, she thought, than being around first-rate writers who care. It always makes you better.

Silverman had almost everything she had ever wanted—the respect of her fellow producers, the other writers, and the cast; and the chance *Mary Tyler Moore* gave her to shape the image of women for a large, mainstream audience. She still dreamed of finding the man to complete her fantasy scenario: accepting her Emmy while her husband rushes her off on their trip to Paris. But she was racking up Emmys, so she hardly had time to find him. While she was self-conscious about her still-unmarried status—Mary and Rhoda's rise helped on this score, but didn't erase the stigma in less progressive minds overnight—she dated up a storm. Her hair was long and blond, and she wore lots of miniskirts. She was popular. She simply didn't find a keeper. Instead, she enjoyed what she thought was a wonderful time in America. She had what she calls " '70s kinds of experiences, Summer of Love experiences."

With so much freedom, and almost all of her dreams coming true, the key question in Silverman's life became: What do you do once you've gotten almost everything you wanted?

At the same time, there were much bigger battles to fight in television, and with television.

Norman Lear appeared before a U.S. Senate subcommittee on constitutional rights in 1972 to argue for greater artistic freedom for all involved in the arts, particularly TV. "As a writer and producer of *All in the Family,* I seem to be enjoying a rather singular experience insofar as network censorship is concerned," Lear said in his statement. "While I confer many times a week with the Program Practices Department of CBS, I am happy to report that we are not censored on *All in the Family.*" Indeed, later that year, *All in the Family* would feature prime time's first audible toilet flush, during a flashback to Mike and Gloria's wedding, and would make a point of often featuring commode noise in subsequent episodes.

This "Golden Age of Comedy" had happened thanks to a strange confluence of events: the rise of several talented writer-producers, namely Brooks and Burns and Lear, and a willingness at the television networks to run with anything that attracted younger audiences and watercooler buzz. Those who worked on these particular shows were having an exhilarating time of it. Their success earned them freedom.

Despite this freedom, these shows could not portray many key facets of the tumultuous '70s—and less successful shows could do even less. What happened in many young people's real lives and what happened on television did not necessarily correspond. As Silverman, Brooks, Burns, and the others sat writing *The Mary Tyler Moore Show*, their contemporaries around the country held key parties in suburban homes, experimented with group sex, and had a great time all around. Silverman thought it was a wonderful time, the way life should be and would be from then on. *We've finally found it*, she thought. *How nice*.

But *The Mary Tyler Moore Show* could only push so far, so fast. Those with less liberal minds than Treva Silverman weren't quite ready for all of that in prime time, and she knew it. It never even crossed the writers' minds to incorporate those more *realistic* aspects of their lives into the show. There would be no Mary Smokes Grass with the Guys After Work episode. (Mary rarely even got drunk.) Mary went on countless dates, and she may have spent the night with a few of them, but the writers weren't about to send her to a key party or an orgy. Mary, a good girl from the Midwest, might have a sexual affair or two, but, as Silverman says, "Mary Goes to the Playboy Mansion, I think, was an idea whose time had never come. 'Mary swims topless, as Hugh Hefner looks fondly on,' was not going to happen."

What the show could get away with, as it rose in popularity throughout its second season, remained to be seen. Brooks and Burns had instilled the ideal of authenticity in their writers and cast. But how much of single women's real sex lives would make it into the scripts, past network executives and censors? And how real could America take their fictional female characters, even those as now beloved as Mary and Rhoda, before they turned their dials? Was Mary Richards that kind of girl? And what kind, for that matter, was that kind?

Mary Richards may have summed up her own position on the matter best: "I'm hardly innocent. I've been around. Well, maybe not *around*, but I've been nearby." She did, however, grow more liberated over time. As the show hit its peak influence in the third season, one episode had Mary staying out all night with a man, though only by insinuation: We see Mary leave for a date at night, and in the next shot we see her arrive home in the morning wearing the same dress. Men across the country wrote to the show in despair over the betrayal of their trust and admiration. Just a few weeks later, an even bigger landmark in Mary's sex life came by quick, subtle suggestion: Mary's dad comes over for some father-daughter time, and as her mom leaves him there for dinner with Mary, she calls out, "Don't forget to take your pill!" Both father and daughter reply, "I won't!"

"The Pill!" Brooks says. "That was a *huge* landmark."

Birth control pills had first won approval by the Food and Drug Administration in 1960, and the Pill was credited for kicking off both the sexual revolution and the women's movement, as symbolized by a *Time* magazine cover story in 1967. But the Pill wasn't available to unmarried women in all states until the 1972 Supreme Court decision *Eisenstadt v. Baird.*

"Mary was a nice girl, in quotation marks," Silverman explains of the Pill moment's grand significance. "Had it had something to do with Rhoda it wouldn't have had that effect, because Rhoda was something of a rebel. If Mary was taking the Pill, it gave the stamp of approval for sexuality." In fact, several lines early in the show's run referred to Rhoda's active sex life, including a second-season episode when a fire in her apartment forces her to room with Mary briefly. As they get on each other's nerves, Rhoda threatens to go to a hotel; Phyllis cracks that it wouldn't be the first time. Rhoda—as a secondary character, a former New Yorker, and, perhaps, as a more "ethnic" woman—was accepted from the start as more worldly.

At last, in season three, Mary got to grow up, too. "Now she's aggressively feminine instead of passively feminine and has healthily accepted the modern-day concept that it's perfectly normal for a woman to be happy though she's 32 years old and unmarried," Weinberger told an interviewer at the time. "Instead of just reacting shyly to everyone else, the Mary character now yells at people and fights back."

The producers learned to skillfully walk a line between innuendo and explicitness that often allowed them to push boundaries while acting innocent—a reflection, perhaps, of their main character herself. It was a trick they'd learned by accident when they'd convinced CBS executives to accept the idea of Mary having once lived in sin instead of having gotten divorced. Now they used this kind of sleight-of-script—leaving out explicit information to imply a range of possibilities—to handle other complicated issues. An early draft of the script for the episode in which Mary stays out all night included an exchange with Rhoda about what had happened on her long date: She and her beau had talked until dawn. "In the romantic glow of sunrise, did he propose?" Rhoda asked. Mary replied, "Yes, but not marriage." The excision of the exchange in the final cut of the episode allowed viewers to imagine for themselves what happened: Likely, their thoughts were naughtier than anything the script could have contained.

Similarly, in the Pill episode, producers decided to nix a dialogue between Mary and her father about her sexual history, keeping the focus on their discussion about their own relationship. With that cut, they avoided any lines that implied judgment of Mary's Pill-popping and let viewers imagine how her father felt about the disclosure—or whether he noticed it at all.

By this time, *The Mary Tyler Moore Show* had made lady sitcoms hot commodities. CBS itself tried to duplicate its success with Sandy Duncan, first with a show called *Funny Face* in 1971, which lasted only half a season before *Mary Tyler Moore* was moved up an hour on Saturday nights, to 8:30 p.m., to replace it. The official word was that Duncan was undergoing eye surgery, but the show's format was scrapped when the star returned the next fall with a revamped version called *The Sandy Duncan Show*. Neither gelled with viewers or critics, who said Duncan's character was too traditional and innocent for '70s television. Its own executive producer admitted, "It was awfully old-fashioned in a year when *All in the Family* and *Mary Tyler Moore* were doing realistic comedy." ABC attempted to get in the game with *Shirley's World*, starring Shirley MacLaine, in 1971. *Diana,* starring Diana Rigg, hit the deteriorating NBC in 1973.

None lasted more than a season, but then came *Maude*. The show's star, Bea Arthur, made for a startling screen presence, the anti–Mary Richards. She didn't work, and she wasn't single, but she wasn't a standard housewife, either; she was a liberal activist on her fourth husband. Stately, imposing, and graying, Arthur had appeared onstage mostly in classical roles, such as Lysistrata, who famously led a protest against war in which women refused to have sex with their husbands, and Clytaemnestra, who betrayed and murdered her husband upon his triumphant return home from the Trojan War. As Maude says in one of the later episodes, she was a woman with "the innocent glow of Donna Reed . . . and the crisp features of George C. Scott."

When Mary Richards stayed out all night, the national debate that ensued played out on *Maude*. Like all of Lear's sitcoms, *Maude* took on the issues of the day, and it wasn't about to ignore those issues just because they came up on another sitcom. "Look what happened on *The Mary Tyler Moore Show* recently," Maude's stuffy next-door neighbor, Arthur (Conrad Bain), huffs. "She went out on a date and she stayed out all night."

"All night?" Maude responds, dripping with sarcasm. "Our little Mary?"

"You can sneer all you want, Maude," Arthur says, "but as Mary Tyler Moore goes, so goes America."

Maude had come into being as an adversary to Archie Bunker in a 1971 episode of *All in the Family*. Maude showed up to help her cousin, Edith Bunker, take care of the family when everyone in the house had the flu. But naturally, Maude had clashed with Archie quite spectacularly on political issues. After the episode was a hit, creator Norman Lear decided to give the character a spin-off.

From the beginning, *Maude* tore up traditional television social mores. Maude's twenty-something daughter, Carol, dated a succession of men and spent the night with them. Both Maude and Carol identified as feminists. Maude and her husband, Walter, often played in contrast to the traditional neighbors portrayed by Bain and Rue McClanahan. Maude took tranquilizers, Miltown and Valium. Her husband drank too much.

But nothing made bigger waves than the episode that in November 1972, just two months into the show—and perhaps not coincidentally, during the traditional "ratings sweeps" period, when Nielsen was tabulating viewership—addressed abortion. Maude, at forty-seven, had prime time's first legal abortion in an episode titled "Maude's Dilemma." Two CBS affiliates refused to show the episode, but the brouhaha just brought more attention to the show. "Maude is commercial TV's first striking manifestation of the frustrated housewife archetype," the *Los Angeles Times* said. "Her abrasiveness, while funny to viewers, is actually the expression of all her energy that has never left the home." Arthur called her character "the Joan of Arc of the middle-age woman." Fan letters poured in for her, gushing that she was "saying the things we've always wanted to say."

The Mary Tyler Moore Show suddenly had a sister in TV feminism, and even shared some of its female writers with *Maude*. But *Mary* also strove to define itself in opposition to the new hit. "We're not *Maude*," Moore told an interviewer at the time. "I feel strongly that sex is a private thing not to be shared with an audience—or even with friends."

Writer Sybil Adelman, who penned episodes of both *Mary Tyler*

Moore and *Maude,* noticed a difference between writing for the two camps. The *Mary Tyler Moore* producers constantly picked her brain for womanly experience; the *Maude* producers just gave her assignments. "Norman more than the others treated us as writers," she says, "and not *women* writers."

Brooks didn't worry much about *Maude,* and insisted his writers stay true to the original vision of *The Mary Tyler Moore Show.* They would not become an issue show just to keep up with the competition, even if the issue was feminism and the competition was directly referencing them. Moore agreed: "The show is opening up, widening its perimeters, developing with the times," she said at the time. "The characters are evolving. We're getting into things like divorce and affairs, but we'll never go where Maude and Archie Bunker have gone. That's not our show."

Some current social issues, however, couldn't help but sneak into *The Mary Tyler Moore Show*'s realistic, 1970s landscape. Most notably, a discussion of gay rights tiptoed into a 1973 episode in which Phyllis's brother, Ben, comes to town. Though Phyllis tries to set him up with Mary, he spends a great deal of time with Rhoda. By the end of the episode, a despondent Phyllis confronts Rhoda about her misgivings. "Ben and I aren't getting married!" Rhoda responds. "He's not my type!"

"What do you mean, not your type?" Phyllis says. "He's attractive. He's successful. He's single."

Rhoda concludes: "He's gay."

Phyllis hugs Rhoda. "I'm so relieved."

Silverman thought it was a great idea for the show to address the gay movement, which was still very much on the fringes of mainstream culture. But the gay issue itself found its way into the script by pure coincidence, and the rest of the episode was constantly evolving throughout the week of shooting, changed in some way by almost every major player involved. No one was sure until it was finished whether it would be a disaster or a triumph.

As written by Jenna McMahon and Dick Clair, the original script called for Ben to take up with Rhoda instead of Mary for the week and thus cause Phyllis great consternation, with no references to sexual orientation. When actor Bob Moore showed up to play the part, however, Sandrich saw an opportunity: The actor himself was gay. After the first rehearsal, Sandrich went up to the writers' office and argued for a rewrite. He wasn't seeing romantic chemistry between the actor and Harper.

Brooks liked the idea, but called Bob Moore to make sure it was okay with him. The actor happily agreed. It would become one of TV's first overt admissions that a character was gay, and that it was more than okay to be so—it was something to be appreciated, to laugh with, not at. The joke worked, but not at the gay character's expense.

The creative momentum built from there. When Harper read the line in which Rhoda tells Mary that Ben loves red, she thought of a fire-engine–colored Courrèges dress that she herself owned. She wore it in the episode without further comment—the implication being that *Rhoda* wanted to please Ben even though she acted otherwise—and the audience went crazy when they saw it.

When it came time to shoot the confrontation scene, Harper made a more meaningful suggestion that stuck. Sandrich directed her to break the big news to Phyllis lightly, but Harper said, "No, I think it should be factual, like he's a priest or he's married or he's going to Tibet for ten years."

It worked. When she delivered the killer line—"He's gay"—the show got one of its longest studio-audience laughs ever. Brooks said they'd have to cut the laugh in editing because it would be too much for the viewers at home—it went on for a good forty-five seconds or so. Harper and Leachman had to pause for that long while they stayed in character and kept the scene alive. Leachman's face went on registering shock, confusion, and then understanding. Harper took a sip of her drink. They waited out the laughs just as they'd been trained to do in the theater. They knew they had to let the audience members get it out of their system or no one would hear the next lines.

The controversial plotline didn't thrill the network, but by that time *All in the Family* was tackling such issues weekly, and burning up the ratings charts doing it. And *Mary Tyler Moore* had earned enough of a reputation that the executives simply warned the producers, "Be careful that the show does not go outside the bounds of its natural perimeters."

The next year, however, the show pushed those perimeters, just a little, yet again. A 1974 episode came the closest the show ever would to addressing Watergate by featuring our little Mary thrown into a jail cell full of hookers when she refused to reveal a journalistic source under court order. "What are you in here for?" one cracks. "Imitating a Barbie Doll?" A few episodes later, the hooker (played to memorable comedic effect by Barbara Colby), whom Mary befriends, gets out of jail, too, and wants to pal around on the outside. Mary encourages her to find ways to make a legal living, perhaps following her passion for fashion design. Her first project: a dress for Mary that clung to her every curve and completely bared her midsection. The joke was obvious even to those who didn't analyze it too deeply. Juxtaposing Mary's good-girl image with prostitutes was inherently hilarious.

The episode became a hit, with shockingly little backlash.

The producers had learned to be careful when they handled hot topics, but not because they worried about offending viewers—rather, because they had tried it before to disastrous creative effect. In a late second-season episode called "Some of My Best Friends Are Rhoda," which directly addressed anti-Semitism, their attempt played as nothing more than an *All in the Family* imitation. And not a particularly good one.

Rhoda's Jewishness, a huge part of her character, had never been the subject of a plot point before this episode. But viewers had certainly noticed the character's ethnicity. Harper received a letter from someone in Arkansas saying, "I really love your work but I want to know are you Jewish or a regular American?" Finally, the producers decided: Why not acknowledge that being Jewish came with difficulties?

The episode guest-starred Mary Frann as a new friend of Mary's who belongs to a country club that won't admit Jews. But putting Mary through the motions of learning about bigotry, and then giving a grand speech against it by the end of the half hour, looked silly in the context of the character-driven *Mary Tyler Moore Show*. The episode became a study in the difference between MTM and Lear. On *Mary Tyler Moore,* the plots were to grow from the characters, not to be giant social issues descending upon the characters as if from above, to prompt heated dialogue and then evaporate.

The *Mary Tyler Moore* producers would never attempt an *All in the Family* imitation again.

In fact, "Some of My Best Friends Are Rhoda" was the closest the show would ever get to explicitly making racial issues central to a plot. "That was just not our MO," Burns says. "There were maybe two or three times in the history of the show when we did something a little preachy, and it didn't really work." Only black-centric shows rivaled female-driven shows in trendiness as the decade progressed, but rarely did the twain meet; Brooks and Burns felt like they had their hands full with fighting for women's issues and Rhoda's Jewishness without taking on civil rights as well.

Mary Tyler Moore lost its sole black recurring character when John Amos, who played Gordy—WJM's smart, affable weatherman—left in 1973 to star in Norman Lear's *Good Times,* which chronicled the travails of a family living in the Chicago projects. Brooks and Burns had purposely cast a black actor as part of the WJM staff, seeing both the social responsibility of diversity and the potential for light humor. "We made him a weatherman, which seemed to us to be funny because every black guy you saw on the air in those days was the sports guy," Burns says. "Ted kept making the mistake, 'Here's Gordy with sports.' " Once Gordy had left, race rarely came up on *The Mary Tyler Moore Show* again.

Of course, the producers couldn't have kept one issue out of *Mary Tyler Moore* if they'd tried: women's lib. And though she'd ultimately be viewed in retrospect as a feminist heroine, Mary Richards had a fraught relationship with the women's libbers of her time. Moore was often asked about her own stance on women's issues, and she offered ambivalent answers at best: "I think women are okay. I mean, I like women, but I know a lot of people don't like them. That's partly women's fault: They allow themselves to be put down, put back in the kitchen when the men are talking. In my mind I can see a lot of the new thinking about the female role, but emotionally I'm not there: I tend to defer to my husband, to accept his dominant role. And there are certain things that I'd rather talk over only with another woman. Unisex looks like it's here, but I hope we never lose our sexuality. I wouldn't like that at all."

The feminist movement simply was not impressed with Ms. Richards, and Moore's lack of enthusiastic cheerleading on the cause's behalf likely didn't help. Brooks learned all of this in November 1975 when he was invited to speak on a panel at the Conference on Women in Public Life, held at the Lyndon Baines Johnson School of Public Affairs at the University of Texas in Austin. It would be a high-profile extravaganza at the height of the women's rights movement, a U.S. version of the United Nations' recent International Women's Year meeting in Mexico City. He would be part of a panel addressing women's progress in television and film. He could stay for the weekend at Lady Bird Johnson's nearby ranch, the organizers offered. Yes, of course he could bring his now-serious girlfriend, Holly Holmberg. The couple would just have to say they were already husband and wife so Lady Bird would let them stay in a room together. The former First Lady was a women's rights advocate, but she was very traditional. Surely he understood.

Brooks started to feel like he was in an episode of his own sitcom.

The morning before his appearance, women crammed the LBJ Library corridors to register for the event, making it the largest conference the facility had ever hosted and the largest in the United States for International Women's Year. Ambassador Anne Armstrong urged the women to "go public. Women are now in centerstage. You owe it to the movement not to shun that spotlight, that mic, that printed page, but to use it as a benchmark. Maybe to run for office, maybe to manage a campaign, maybe to press for an appointive position, maybe to get on a TV show or an op-ed page. In whatever way, go public."

At the Sunday night panel, before the packed thousand-seat auditorium—with another thousand participants overflowing into nearby hallways and rooms—Brooks filed onto the stage of the LBJ Library auditorium with the panel's moderator, *Ms.* magazine founder Gloria Steinem; Virginia Carter, who worked as Norman Lear's assistant; and Ann Hassett, the director of special projects at the NBC affiliate in Los Angeles. The crowd included young and old women, some in housedresses, some in business suits. Steinem—in wire-rimmed glasses, a floral print blouse, and long blond waves—leaned into the microphone to wild applause from the crowd.

Her opening remarks addressed the importance of TV and film in forming and reforming public attitudes toward women. "I'd like to ask each of us to consider how much television and films have shaped our dreams," she said. "Just consider what visitors from outer space might think if they were confronted with the last twelve years of television and films as the only evidence of what American women were like. First of all they would be convinced that there were twice as many American men as there were American women. It would be quite clear that we slept in false eyelashes and full makeup. Some of us would be taken to be a servant class of some sort. If we lived alone, we would almost have to be widows, at least until recently. That's begun to change, and we'll hear a little bit more about the change later."

To the continuous clicks of cameras documenting the event,

Steinem continued, considering the effect the women's movement had on pop culture—progress had been made, she said, but not enough. "We have begun to see women who are autonomous, who disagree, who argue, who have some identity of their own, who seek jobs and are sometimes even paid for those jobs," she said. "Mary Tyler Moore agitated for equal pay, and got half of what she asked for. It was a very pop cultural compromise."

When Steinem introduced Carter, she mentioned Lear's *Maude*. "Think of Maude!" she said. "Gives us hope." Brooks, she said, was "a person who has tried to be very sensitive to the changes that women are demanding."

During the question-and-answer period (which, unlike the introduction, was not recorded in Steinem's archives), Brooks recalls Steinem pointedly criticizing *The Mary Tyler Moore Show* for allowing Mary to call her boss "Mr. Grant" when all of the other characters called him "Lou." She got still more applause for this; the Mr. Grant Issue had become a major talking point for feminist activists. A terrified public speaker, Brooks was sure he even heard some boos from the audience when he was up to speak.

Mary Richards had officially become a polarizing figure, a fact that would have shocked the character herself.

On the one hand, she was continuing to bring issues specific to young, working women to the TV screen, and becoming even bolder about it. For instance, Mary's adventures in the local TV news ranks often mirrored those of the women in Hollywood—she complained of pressure to "represent women everywhere" and of the station manager "trotting in groups of people and saying, 'This is our woman executive.'" By 1974, *Variety* and the *Hollywood Reporter* were filled with announcements about groundbreaking promotions for women at movie studios and networks, including Ethel Winant, who was now officially vice president of casting at CBS. The moves were meant to publicly prove the Hollywood establishment was not sexist.

In the episode Steinem referenced, Mary fretted over the discovery that her salary was lower than that of the man who held her job before her; in the end, she did win a raise, though it was true it didn't bring her totally on par with her predecessor. Others had praised the show for addressing the issue of equal pay realistically: "This is hardly earthshaking," wrote the *Los Angeles Times*' Don Shirley. "But the cumulative effect of such statements, with more or less subtlety, in almost every episode of the series, is hard to ignore."

Mary's famously quavery voice made the demand for equal pay both funny and poignant, but it wasn't presented seriously enough for some critics. Mary also seemed to at least consider Mr. Grant's argument that the guy deserved the extra fifty dollars a week because he had a family to support. Moore personally admired this mark of what she saw as Mary Richards's reasonableness.

Many critics beyond Steinem complained that was exactly the problem with *The Mary Tyler Moore Show*. Now that feminist ideals were becoming mainstream, it didn't seem like enough simply to have a heroine who was over thirty and refusing to define herself by her search for a man. Mary Richards, some women's lib activists said, was not nearly liberated enough. Her celebrated theme song identified her as a "girl." She wasn't a feminist heroine; in fact, she was a pushover. Critics said Mary Richards offered a "compromised and contradictory feminism," with her empowerment tempered too much by "girl-next-door sweetness." The *New York Times* pointed out that "she hardly ever gets to write the news or report it on camera—even though she appears to be several times brighter than the men who do." Even the mainstream *TV Guide* complained in an editorial that characters like Mary Richards weren't "challenging the family system, demanding a new kind of sexual relationship or a new division of labor in the home."

The producers defended themselves, however: As for the Mr. Grant Issue, Mary was the kind of person who would address her boss properly. And while she was a bit of a people pleaser, she stood up for herself when necessary. They wanted to favor character over social statement, even as more women were entering the workplace, demanding equal pay just like Mary, and even reaching the upper echelons of the producers' very own industry. The producers wouldn't identify themselves or the heroine they'd created as feminist, per se, even if they were proud of the empowering figure she was becoming. Because she represented "good girls" and had a sense of vulnerability, they observed, no one could resent her as an icon.

That was, in fact, the secret to her unique power.

They even played her conflicted "Mr. Grant"-ing for laughs: In the 1973 episode when Lou confides in Mary about his divorce, he demands she call him by his first name if they're going to have such a personal conversation. "Would that be just for the purpose of this conversation, or for, you know, all time?" she asks. Then she tries it out, stammering an awkward "Mr. . . . Lou."

That changes his mind. "Call me Mr. Grant," he concludes.

TWELVE
TWELVE
TWELVE
TWELVE
TWELVE
TWELVE
TWELVE
TWELVE

THE GEORGIA AND BETTY STORY

(1972–74)

Among *The Mary Tyler Moore Show*'s biggest fans were actress Betty White and her game-show-host husband, Allen Ludden. Almost every Friday, the couple could be found in the bleachers of the sitcom's live tapings.

Moore had been friends with White for a decade now, since their husbands had introduced them. Both women were TV stars at the time, though White had been around since the medium's earliest days, hosting talk shows, producing and starring in the low-budget, traditional-couple sitcom *Life with Elizabeth* in the '50s, and becoming a fixture as a game-show guest in the '60s. She met her husband on his show *Password*. Their love was legendary: They attended each other's tapings every time they could, and drove matching Cadillacs. Ludden was also close to Tinker, and Mary and Grant were among the first friends Ludden had introduced to his new bride in 1963, the same year that they, too, had gotten married.

The Luddens had been cheering for the show from its beginning: Allen sent Mary a floral arrangement shaped like the number 1 for that first precarious taping, and continued the tradition at the beginning of each subsequent season, sending a 2 for the second year, and so on. Allen and Betty knew about every labored-over script revision and ratings point change from dinners with Mary and Grant. They loved watching the show from its initial struggles to its grand popularity.

When Allen and Betty returned from a trip to Ireland just in time to send the "4" flowers, White got a call from Burns, who asked her to play a one-episode character named Sue Ann Nivens, known as "The Happy Homemaker" at WJM. She would have the thankless job of trying to steal Phyllis's husband, Lars. Burns described the character as "cloyingly sweet on the surface and something of a dragon underneath, with a tinge of nymphomania."

White said yes, taking great glee in calling her old friend and taunting: "Guess who's doing your show next week!"

"Oh, no," Moore joked. "I may not butt into the show often, but I do have veto power."

In fact, writers Ed. Weinberger and Stan Daniels had, in their script, described the character as "a Betty White type"—that is, a seemingly pleasant lady with a warm smile and darling dimples—"but as vicious as a barracuda." Ethel Winant had suggested they go ahead and try White herself instead of searching for a replica. Because White had been around the stage so much to support Moore, the producers got to know the actress a bit, so they recognized that she was bawdier than some may have realized. They knew she could pull off the role; they simply worried about forcing Moore to mix business and friendship.

Weinberger and Daniels auditioned other actresses for the part but couldn't find the right one. Finally, they gave in and asked Burns to call White. Moore gave the go-ahead, saying, "I think she'd rather be asked than not given the chance because it might go badly."

White felt nervous at her first rehearsal because she was so friendly with the talented cast and wanted to live up to their expectations.

And despite having been on television since almost the moment of its invention—her first job was on an early Hollywood-based talk show in 1948, the very year network programming began—she felt, with this part, like she was starting her career all over again. But she settled right in once she saw the familiar set.

Leachman and White were facing off in front of a gaping oven on the fictional set of Sue Ann's *Happy Homemaker* program. Leachman, as Phyllis, was confronting Sue Ann after finding out WJM's helpful-hints guru had slept with her husband after meeting him at Mary's party. "This is a very critical time," Sue Ann cooed, referring to the state of her chocolate soufflé in the oven.

"I'm sorry, but this is a very critical time for me, too," Phyllis snapped, opening and slamming the door.

"Oh, my poor baby!" Sue Ann cried, rescuing the dessert from the oven.

Sandrich cut them off there. It was a brilliant scene, perfectly acted, except for one detail: The oven door gaped wide open after White removed the soufflé, and the women were stuck sniping in front of a distracting black hole.

With the same combination of crude and smooth that her character had, White—still holding the white ceramic soufflé dish—lifted her knee and smacked the door shut.

She'd meant it as a between-takes joke, but Sandrich fell in love with the move. "That's it!" he said. "No more problem." That one gesture would become the most memorable part of an indelible episode.

When the episode came together for show night, White awed everyone by making this dislikable character who stole Phyllis's husband watchable. Far more than watchable, in fact: She gave a transcendent performance that prompted viewers to ask: Where has *this* version of Betty White been, and how can we get more of her? As Sue Ann, she invented her own brilliant combination of manic and passive-aggressive, with a little bit of delusion thrown in. ("I cannot do a chocolate soufflé with only two cameras," she told her *Happy Homemaker* show crew through a clenched smile.) She was, in fact, the only person who could make Phyllis look sane by comparison.

When the taping of White's episode ended, there was no question about what to do next: Brooks and Burns asked her not to make any plans in the near future, and Moore happily signed off on bringing her friend back to the set more often. Moore couldn't wait to see what White would do next as Sue Ann, whom she called "everyone's delicious pixie." White, on the other hand, graciously attributes Sue Ann's instant success to Moore's subtle acting choices during the character's introductory episode. Rather than disliking her, White says, Moore's Mary Richards found the humor in Sue Ann so the audience could relax and laugh along with her a little. No matter who was responsible, the character was a hit. *Los Angeles Times* TV critic Cecil Smith wrote, "The happiest comic creation of the season for my money is the Happy Homemaker. Not surprisingly, she turned up on *The Mary Tyler Moore Show*. But what is surprising is that Betty White plays her. Because, as Betty so succinctly puts it, 'She's a bitch.' "

The morning after White's first appearance on the show, her doorbell rang. When she and her husband opened the door, they found Moore and Tinker holding the soufflé dish from the episode, filled with flowers. "We just read some more scripts they wrote for you," Moore told her, "and they're wonderful!"

As Sue Ann developed, she'd become a sly reversal of the sweet "Betty White type." Or, as White told Smith, "She's not only a bitch, but a nympho. She can't keep her hands off any man, not even Ted. I've been waiting all my life for a part like this." She could cook a soufflé like a nice housewife, but she didn't apologize for her sexual appetites or her bitchy bite. The best of her many great lines: "Mary, believe me, I'm proud that you haven't been disheartened by those who murmur that you've sacrificed your femininity to your ambition." White's personal favorite came when Sue Ann asked her coworkers, "Does this dress make me look cheap?" And when they said yes, she replied, "Oh, good!" The writers built the character so that audiences didn't turn against her even as she started out bad and got worse. White admired her alter ego's ability to even nearly murder her friends—when she poisoned everyone at work by knowingly giving them rolls full of custard that had gone bad—while still courting viewers. "Sheer genius," Smith raved.

Sue Ann's arrival began a new era marked by even greater freedom in addressing sex on the show. Seducing Lars without apology in her first episode was only the beginning. In a later episode she has a drunken one-night stand with Lou, and Lou is the only one who shows a hint of regret. In fact, he is mortified when Sue Ann shows up in his office the next day to return his socks—laundered, of course. He's devastated when he finds out that Mary, who witnessed the sock exchange, accidentally told Murray; one of the show's most dramatic moments comes when Lou confronts Mary in his office, telling her he won't fire her—but he doesn't like her anymore.

As further proof of Sue Ann's ability to court controversy, Brooks and Sandrich clashed on how to play the scene out. "My concept was instead of Lou yelling, the quieter it is, the more it hurts Mary," Sandrich recalls. "That's not how they had conceived it. It was a wonderful scene, and Jim and Allan came up with a brilliant end to the show to get Lou back to being friends with Mary again." They ended up shooting it Sandrich's way, and, Sandrich says, "I think that was a great collaboration between the stage and the office."

White would go on to win two straight Emmys for her performance as Sue Ann. Asner presented the award to her the first year she appeared on *The Mary Tyler Moore Show*, twenty-two years after she had gotten her first and only previous nomination; in 1951, the first year there was a category for women, she was recognized for her work as host of the variety show *Hollywood on Television*. In her acceptance speech, White thanked the "evil, wonderful, nasty" television industry for keeping her well-employed, even at the age of fifty-four. The next year, she found herself at the podium accepting her second straight

Emmy, this time wearing a black and white chiffon gown she got on *The Carol Burnett Show,* and this time with her beloved Allen winning one, too, for the hosting of *Password.* The two flew to Hawaii the next day for a week's vacation.

Treva Silverman was writing an episode about Rhoda considering a move back to New York, and she needed to cast a coworker of Rhoda's at Hemple's department store. She remembered a film called *Taking Off,* a movie from Czech director Milos Forman about a couple, played by Lynn Carlin and Buck Henry, searching for their missing daughter. It included an actress Silverman thought was named Georgette, who was soft-spoken and spacey, with blond curls and perpetually startled eyes, the anti-Rhoda.

Silverman went to Burns and described whom she wanted, and he knew the actress she was talking about: Georgia Engel. Silverman had now named her featherbrained character in her script Georgette, and she kept it. Burns called Engel's agent to offer her the part. The agent balked at how small the role was, but admitted he wanted his client, a summer stock veteran who had just appeared to great reviews in the surreal drama *The House of Blue Leaves* on Broadway as a deaf starlet, to branch out into TV.

Engel's show had just ended a run at a Hollywood venue, the Huntington Hartford, after its New York theater burned down, so she was in the market for work. She had acted onstage since she graduated from the University of Hawaii three years earlier; she'd finished a year early and skipped the ceremony to get to New York to audition for *Hello, Dolly!* She wasn't about to miss the final year of the company headed by Ethel Merman. She followed her instincts and got her first big break.

Her instincts kicked in again when she got the call from her agent suggesting she go out for that teeny part, hardly more than an extra part, on *The Mary Tyler Moore Show.* First of all, it felt a little like fate. During her run at the Huntington Hartford, Engel had already met

Moore, at a ballet class on Hollywood Boulevard. One day, an almost unrecognizable, makeup-free Moore, her hair back in a bun, told Engel she and Tinker, along with their friends Betty White and Allen Ludden, had seen her play, and they all loved it. Engel could hardly believe her luck—a woman as famous and talented as Moore had seen and liked her work! Now it was six months later, and Engel was back in her New York studio apartment with a Murphy bed, collecting unemployment and looking for acting work. How could she not try for even a small part on Moore's show?

Engel turned out to be just as Silverman had imagined her, such a little dumpling, a baby-voiced, wide-eyed actress. As the week of rehearsals progressed, Engel got more and more lines, as well as a clear indication that her character could return. The producers wanted to write something for this girl who fit in with their quirky cast. In particular, something magical was sparking between Georgette and the long-vacant character of Ted Baxter. Though Georgette fawns over Ted in the episode, asking him to read some of Rhoda's farewell cards aloud—"I just love his voice," she gushes—she also ignores his offer to take her home. She was the perfect combination of naïve, sweet, and inscrutable—a challenge for Ted Baxter, and his perfect match.

Engel so charmed the producers that by the time the Friday taping came, Burns told Silverman, "We decided we want her back for seven episodes, and we want you to tell her." It became one of the highlights of Silverman's life, giving the news to Engel that she'd acted her way into a bigger job. Engel's eyes went wide and teary when she heard the news.

Engel had to fly home to teach Sunday school that weekend, but she promised to return as soon as possible. Her agent, however, really had misgivings about the job this time. Though he'd supported her in pursuing the high-profile part, he worried that the return flights to Los Angeles from New York for the continuing gig would cost her more than she'd make doing it. "Sometimes you pay to work with the best," she reasoned. The following Monday morning, the buzzer rang at her

New York apartment. She opened the door to find a potted palm had been delivered, with a card that said, "Welcome to the MTM family." She knew then that she'd made the right choice.

The producers knew exactly what they wanted to do with her during her seven episodes: She'd become a legitimate love interest for Ted Baxter, which would particularly please Knight. He had long been complaining that he needed a story line that would make him seem more human, that went beyond his character's mindless gaffes. The producers agreed, and had been on the lookout for the right girlfriend to expand Ted's character in the same way that Lou's divorce had given him more substance. Georgette seemed immature but knew how to put the chauvinistic Ted in his place. For instance, in her first episode back, called "The Georgette Story," she learns, with the help of Mary and Rhoda, to refuse Ted's requests that she do his shopping and laundry.

As she got to know the cast, Engel learned one thing quickly: "With the exception of Betty, every single person on the show was like their character," she says. "The writers take a kernel of what the person's like and then shape it for however the drama needs to happen. Betty, her humor is that kind of sophisticated, almost lewd stuff she can do so well, but she's so unlike that." Engel had to admit she was a lot like Georgette—she seemed dippy but knew exactly what was going on, and could pull off a zinger when you least expected.

Knight, right in line with her observation, proved a bit of a challenge for her at times. She had difficulty connecting with him in a performance because, she says, his character was so self-absorbed. The two didn't connect much offstage, either, because of their large age gap. Knight, who was Engel's father's age, had a son her age. But she saw the good in Knight, too. Though she didn't feel close to him, she admired him, particularly his dedication to his family; she often thought of Knight's wife, Dottie, as "the real Georgette."

True enough, Leachman tells tales of Knight resisting beautiful, young female fans. "There was a girl, he'd have liked to have gone to bed with her," Leachman recalls. "He used to say, in that Ted voice, 'I can't . . . I could, you know. But I can't.'" Knight also turned on the kiddie-show-host charm he'd perfected early in his career whenever kids frequented the set, including Leachman's. Despite his better qualities, however, Engel says, "He was not my most fun one to work with. He worked in a vacuum, as opposed to Mary and Ed and Valerie and Gavin, who always connected with you with their eyes."

Engel also had to get used to life in Los Angeles, both on the set and off. Brooks and Sandrich's screaming matches alarmed her at first. Moore comforted her: "It's okay," she whispered during one. "They do like each other." Engel also had to adjust to the driving culture of Los Angeles—or, rather, the driving culture had to adjust to her. She stayed in a hotel down the street from the studio during her first year on the job, and she would walk to work. As a young woman with plenty of energy, and a New Yorker used to walking everywhere, she enjoyed it, but Los Angeles streets have never been pedestrian-friendly; sidewalks will disappear and reappear with no hint of logic or concern for safety. One of the crewmembers saw her walking and thought she was too shy to ask for a ride; many on the set then got the same impression. But she simply liked to be vehicle-free.

Eventually, when her contract was extended beyond her first seven shows, she gave in and got a furnished apartment in the Hollywood Hills near her dance studio, and her sister gave her a giant, old Buick for one dollar; she called it "the Booper."

She was thrilled to become a permanent addition to such a generous cast. She'd never get over how wonderfully they treated her. In one episode, for example, titled "Murray Can't Lose," Engel had to learn an entire dance sequence, which she worked on for weeks back home in New York. When it came time to shoot the show, the script ran eight minutes over time. Brooks and Burns contemplated cutting the dance scene, the easiest solution, but Asner and Moore asked the producers to cut their own scenes instead. The producers obliged. Engel knew Knight wouldn't have wanted any of his lines cut, so she was grateful for Asner and Moore's acknowledgment of how hard she'd worked.

She felt like part of the *Mary Tyler Moore* family for sure now. So much so, in fact, that when Asner and MacLeod vacationed with their wives in Hawaii together, Engel's parents, who lived on the Kona Coast, hosted them. Engel thought it was awfully cute that these big television stars went out of their way to find her parents in the middle of nowhere for a visit.

When the cast returned for the following season, Georgette and Ted married on-screen in a memorable, impromptu ceremony performed by a minister played by John Ritter, clad in tennis whites, at Mary's apartment. Their marriage, though tested by Georgette's unfounded suspicions of infidelity, would become one of the series's few enduring romantic pairings.

And Engel got to be part of the growing "women over thirty can actually be on TV, too!" media storm, even though she was six years too young. A magazine reporter called the MTM publicity department, wanting to meet with Engel, Harper, and Moore for a piece about actresses over thirty, and Engel happily went along, even though she was thinking, *I'm not even over twenty-five!* No one ever knew the difference, and no one ever asked her age.

The real-life marriages on the set weren't always as easy as Georgette and Ted's, particularly for the couple at the center of it all.

In a sense, *The Mary Tyler Moore Show* had begun back on the set of *The Dick Van Dyke Show,* during the shooting of the pilot in 1961. Grant Tinker, then an advertising executive with the New York–based firm of Benton & Bowles, flew out to Los Angeles to watch the filming of the first episode of the show that his client, Procter & Gamble, was sponsoring. The dashing businessman, known for his stylishly narrow ties and Protestant ethics, looked forward to watching Van Dyke work, though he didn't know anything about the lady who was cast to play the wife.

Then he met her: Mary Tyler Moore. Tinker admired her ability to not come across as "actressy"—she seemed to him as real off camera as on, and he fell in love with her genuineness. He didn't believe in love at first sight, but he fell deeply in love with her over time, and knew from that first meeting that something special could grow between them.

He asked her out the day they met, which happened to be the same day her separation from her first husband was announced in the Hollywood papers. "I don't think I should," she told him. "I think some time should elapse before I start to see people."

Tinker nodded in agreement and turned to leave, then doubled back. "Look, a friend of mine just gave me his house in Palm Springs," he said. "Would you like to join me there for the weekend?"

"No!" she replied with a laugh. "You don't get it, do you?"

A month later, though, Tinker—recently divorced himself—arranged for Moore to come to New York on a publicity tour. They spent time together and found they shared a serious attraction and admiration of each other's professional drive. The match was made in overachiever heaven; they supported each other in their complementary careers. One time early in their relationship, for instance, Tinker returned to Los Angeles after a meeting in New York with advertisers about *The Dick Van Dyke Show*. He brought Moore a huge bouquet of red roses, but his message was at least as much business as romance: "Take these and put them at Sheldon Leonard's feet," he told her of the show's legendary executive producer, "because he just gave the most wonderful pitch to Kent cigarettes and Procter & Gamble."

Just a year after meeting, the two married and settled into a fairly regular life, not terrifically Hollywood. They had a nice house in the Hills and a cook to handle dinner, but they spent most of their downtime listening to music—opera, rock, pop—and reading—*Time, Newsweek,* Book-of-the-Month. Of course, they didn't have much downtime. The longer their relationship went on, the more work they had to attend to and the emptier it became.

Now, five years after launching *The Mary Tyler Moore Show* and MTM Enterprises together, and twelve years after getting married, their relationship had hit a kind of autopilot: It hummed along at high gear, feeding off their shared energy, mutual appreciation, and business interests. But it seemed their business interests were all they had in common these days. They kept their marriage so private, however— even from the *Mary Tyler Moore* cast and producers—that it came as a shock to everyone who knew them when they announced their separation.

Moore and Tinker never spoke in specifics to anyone about the temporary breakup, even on the close-knit set. They didn't have a huge fight, they explained; that wasn't their way. They just felt that their marriage had fallen below their high standards. Moore had suddenly become aware of her great dependence on Tinker, as her best friend and business partner. She felt she leaned on him too much. She was trying to figure out how to balance her independence with her ingrained habit of deferring to her husband's dominant role. She admired the way her friend Valerie Harper maintained such effortlessly equal status with her own husband, Dick Schaal, though Moore wasn't sure she could ever achieve that herself. Maybe it just wasn't in her nature. "I allowed myself to be treated like his student," she later wrote, "taking every one of his lessons on people, places, and driving very, very seriously."

As that realization weighed upon her, she finally snapped at him one night after a silent dinner in front of the evening news: "Can't you remember to put your knife and fork together on the dish when you finish?"

Tinker calmly suggested they separate, saying they had "poisoned the marriage." He proposed waiting until the May hiatus in shooting so as not to upset everyone at the studio. She countered that she didn't want to pretend, and asked him to have his things out of the house in two days.

Moore and Tinker spent their months apart in dignified management of an uncomfortable situation. They still worked on the same lot, and Tinker ran the company whose signature production was her show. His presence at her show's run-throughs and filmings felt awkward, but they handled it with characteristic dignity. Most afternoons, as Moore left the lot, she'd wave to Tinker as he sat in his fourth-floor office. The two remained civilized, above all.

Their separation shocked no one more than their double-date partners, Betty White and Allen Ludden. The four went to dinner so that Moore and Tinker could explain their split to their closest friends. Moore confided in White about how much it hurt, and Ludden and White had their own kind of grieving period.

Five months later, something magical happened. Tinker called the Luddens and asked to take them to dinner, adding, "Would you mind if I brought a date?" They reluctantly agreed. They'd have to move on sooner or later.

The couple met Tinker at Chasen's, where he said his date would be coming a little late from work. Then she showed up: It was Moore, and they had reconciled. Ludden and White delighted in watching Moore and Tinker drive home that night together up Benedict Canyon Road.

The following day at the lot, Harper lamented to Moore and White that it was her last on the set. She'd gotten her own spin-off show, *Rhoda*. As the three women sat together on the bleachers, Harper mused, "It's so hard for me to leave this show. It's a sad day."

Moore took Harper's hand and smiled. "You can't ask me to feel very sad today," she said. It was a good thing she had something to be so happy about; she would miss Harper dearly. Harper was one of the few people Moore had felt comfortable opening up to.

Soon after reconciling, Moore and Tinker moved into a new Bel

Air home. They felt that briefly separating had been beneficial, and recommended it to anyone they knew who had marital problems. They thought they were stronger for it.

Treva Silverman loved bringing Mary and Rhoda to life every week, and she loved breaking down barriers for women on the screen and behind the scenes. But the stability of her television industry jobs, starting with *The Entertainers*—the first time in her adult life that she'd had a regular paycheck and security and an office—gave her time to reevaluate. She realized that since being deemed a musical prodigy at five, she had done nothing but give of her creative capital. She played, she wrote music, she wrote scripts, she played some more, she wrote some more scripts. The thought struck her: She had to take in some of the world, or her creativity would just dry up.

But all the women writers—on the show, and even in the industry—looked up to Silverman. She had come before most of them. She had gotten promoted from freelance writer to story consultant, the first female with an executive title on a network sitcom. She also maintained an air of unassailable coolness. All of the other female writers wanted to hang around her, even though she was closer to the guys than anyone. She provided a laugh a minute. Gail Parent's writing partner, Kenny Solms, would throw parties stocked full of comedy writers, where Kenny and Treva would make up musicals on the spot. Gail wasn't such a great improviser; Kenny would call her the next day to tell her how terrible she had been at it. But Silverman was always at the center of the party. Could she walk away from that?

If it saved her sanity, if it inspired her, she thought, maybe she could.

She remembered an illuminating moment from a brief vacation she'd taken to Athens the year before. A taxi driver had offered to show her the sights. She told him she couldn't afford that, but he said, "I'll do it as a friend." She trusted the older, kindly gentleman. As she waited for him to pick her up the next day among the Greek parliament buildings, an elderly, English-speaking couple asked her if she was lost, and she explained that she was waiting for this cabdriver.

"I'm a little concerned," the man said. "You don't know this person."

"Honey, let her be," the woman countered. "You're only young and pretty once!" It struck Silverman then: She *would be* young and pretty only once. She had to spend that time doing more than hanging out in the MTM offices, eating pot brownies and writing scripts. She went home to America and made a list of things she wanted to do before she died, and living in Europe was number one.

She had accomplished one part of her Emmy-speech fantasy scene: the part where she wins an Emmy. She'd done that twice, and yet the other part—going to Europe with the dream guy—had yet to materialize. Figuring she'd be hard-pressed to will a dream guy to appear, she decided to make the other part true. She would catch the next plane to a new life in Europe.

In June 1974, she left the show. It now rested in good hands with Brooks and Burns getting help from Weinberger and his writing partner, Stan Daniels. It had amassed a deep well of regular writers, too, like the prolific David Lloyd. With a clear conscience and a sense of freedom, Silverman booked passage on the SS *France* and headed for Paris, the city where many expat writers had gone before. The day she left, a dozen friends came to see her off at the dock, smiling and waving. As the gangplank was pulled up, the last voice she heard was her father's, calling out to her, "Don't talk to any strangers."

By the time President Richard Nixon resigned in a live television broadcast in August, she was renting "the world's most incredible apartment" in Paris's artistic Sixth Arrondissement. Solms, knowing how involved she was in politics, sent her some taped clips of Nixon flashing a "victory" sign at the cameras as he boarded the helicopter that would take him home to California after his resignation. She and some American friends in Paris watched them and howled. She took French classes and forgot all about deadlines and agents and Emmys.

She only briefly dipped back into her American life a year later when *Ladies' Home Journal* honored her and fellow MTM writer Charlotte Brown in a televised "Woman of the Year" celebration along with the likes of Lady Bird Johnson and Congresswoman Barbara Jordan. The magazine sent her first-class airfare and put her up in a New York hotel to attend the ceremony. While she was there, producer Lorne Michaels told her he was launching a show called *Saturday Night Live* and he wanted to hire her for his writing staff. But she didn't want to get sucked back in. She told him: No, thanks. Then she flew back to her new European life. She was living the dream. She was more than five thousand miles away from Los Angeles when the Screen Actors Guild elected its first female president, Kathleen Nolan.

Brooks and Burns, meanwhile, prepared to lose Harper and Leachman as well, to their own spin-offs. Like Treva, the actresses had grown restless to try new ventures.

PART four

PART four
PART four
PART four
PART four
PART four
PART four

"I really miss Phyllis.
Of course, I never knew her very well.
Maybe that helps."
—GEORGETTE FRANKLIN

THIRTEEN
THIRTEEN
THIRTEEN
THIRTEEN
THIRTEEN
THIRTEEN
THIRTEEN

Girl, This Time You're All Alone

(1974)

Back in the first season of *The Mary Tyler Moore Show*, Fred Silverman—the owlish executive heading CBS's programming—visited a Friday night taping and asked to see Valerie Harper afterward. She thought she was getting fired. "That was a great show tonight," he told the actress. "What would you think if we spun you off?"

For a second, she still believed she was getting fired. "Spinning off" sounded like a bad thing. At the time, in 1970, spin-offs weren't all that common in television. She considered it a few more seconds before responding. "Oh, *spun me off*! Like my own show?" she said in the familiar, exuberant cadence of Rhoda Morgenstern. Silverman nodded. But Harper still had her doubts. "I think it's a little soon," she concluded.

The prospect scared her. Being on *this* show still scared her. First, she talked to her husband about it, and he encouraged her to consider the idea. It would give her a chance to play Rhoda's life on her own terms instead of just relating to Mary, he said. She wouldn't have to worry about blocking Mary's shot; the shot would be hers.

Harper also confided in Mary Tyler Moore about the idea. Moore's heart sank at the prospect of losing her friend as her costar, but she put aside her own feelings and told Harper it seemed like a natural progression. "Do you want to be my sidekick all your life?" Moore asked her.

"What if it bombs?" Harper replied. She and her character shared the same self-confidence, or lack thereof.

"Then you move back to Minneapolis!" Moore said, painting on a smile.

That helped. When Harper's fan mail continued to increase, talks about a Rhoda show grew more serious. Three years into *The Mary Tyler Moore Show,* Harper felt better about it, even though she was still nervous. She went to her on-screen mother, Nancy Walker, a show-biz veteran, for advice. "Stop obsessing, Val," Walker said. "It's a job. Take it."

Harper agreed to do it, and the producers went to work figuring out what the concept behind Rhoda's show would be.

The "spin-off" had existed since at least 1941, when the character Throckmorton P. Gildersleeve, from the radio comedy show *Fibber McGee and Molly,* got his own show, *The Great Gildersleeve.* Television, however, was only just beginning back then and there was no need to recycle characters. Now, in the early '70s (and a few years after Silverman first mentioned the idea to Harper), the spin-off was booming thanks to the character-driven comedies of MTM and Lear, which produced intriguing roles faster than they could get their own shows. *All in the Family* alone would eventually beget *Maude, The Jeffersons,* and *Good Times.*

The *Mary Tyler Moore* producers resisted the idea of spinning Rhoda off this early, even now as the show's fourth season approached. They were interested more in quality than a spike in ad revenue. Fred Silverman assured them, "I think she's so strong a character that she should have her own show." Brooks and Burns didn't want to fight the network president who'd been their savior, nor did they want to risk losing the in-demand Harper to another production company or network. That would be worse than spinning her off prematurely.

The problem: Rhoda was hardly your typical main character on television. Though Harper was a striking beauty, she had a good ten- to fifteen-pound advantage over most of her contemporaries. She had the kind of hips you didn't always see on actresses, and she had a self-deprecating way of putting on another ten pounds just by joking about her own weight. The fact was, Harper loved to be perceived as "dumpy and frumpy." She enjoyed having the distinctive job of lobbing all the zinger lines without having to worry about how she looked.

She also delighted in her character's attitude, her outsider status as a witty Jewish girl from the East Coast. Harper realized early on that the only way Rhoda could hold her own with the too-perfect-to-be-true Mary was with her New York confidence: *I'm gonna straighten this shiksa out.* She asked Brooks and Burns, "Can I call her 'kid'?" They loved the idea and used it from then on.

Rhoda always had a joke to hide her insecurity. Rhoda to Phyllis on what single people do to have fun: "Same as you—sit around and wonder what it would be like to have a happy marriage." Rhoda on accidentally using Mary's makeup mirror: "Mary, why didn't you warn me? I thought it was a relief map of the moon. When they sell those magnifying mirrors they should include a printed suicide note." Rhoda on candy: "I don't know why I'm putting this in my mouth. I should just apply it directly to my hips." (That oft-quoted line was an off-the-cuff addition from writer Treva Silverman, directly from Harper's own mouth, during a run-through.) On Mary's assertion that chocolate doesn't solve anything: "No, Mare, cottage cheese solves nothing; chocolate can do it all!"

Rhoda's accent had its own odyssey. Harper was born in Suffern, New York, and after moving around the country as a child had spent her share of time in New York City, performing in theaters. But she was neither from the Bronx nor Jewish, like Rhoda was supposed to be—Harper's parents were Catholics of French and English ancestry. She picked up the accent itself quickly, thanks to her Bronx-raised stepmother and some Jewish friends back in New York, but she constantly pushed her Jewishness further than the producers wanted. Brooks's own Jewish heritage gave him the final authority on such matters, and he didn't want to overwhelm viewers with her ethnicity. Harper was always asking: Could she say "schlep"? "Shiksa"? "Schmuck"? No, no, and no, Brooks answered. The revelation of Rhoda's Jewishness to the network executives—in the first-season script featuring her mother, Ida—had come just months after the "audiences don't like mustaches, divorce, and Jews" speech from the CBS brass. Brooks didn't want to back down from the network, but he didn't want to go too far just to incite them, either.

By the fourth season of *Mary Tyler Moore,* in 1973–74, Rhoda had settled into everything unique about her character—her Jewish background, her New York street smarts, her body, her wardrobe. Harper even used the hiatus between *Mary Tyler Moore* and *Rhoda,* the summer of 1974, to play another Jewish woman, returning to New York to play a character named Sally Kramer in a Broadway domestic drama, *Thieves.* She enjoyed the change of pace that returning to the stage allowed her—and the easy entrée to Broadway that her stardom now afforded her—but as *Rhoda* prepped to premiere in the fall, Harper had anxiety dreams. In one, her three favorite actresses—Anna Magnani, Anne Bancroft, and Maureen Stapleton—invited her to appear with them in a play, but she stood onstage confused, mute, and scriptless while they performed perfectly.

Harper worried about the more practical changes that having her own show brought to her life as well; after years of handling her household tasks herself, she was forced to hire help with the shopping, cooking, and cleaning. Mimi Kirk, Rhoda's fashion muse, came with Harper to the new show as her assistant, jewelry-maker, headscarf-tier, and lunch-maker. She called Kirk "a friend, an alter ego whose taste I rely on in decisions I don't have time to make." Harper could afford the help—she was now making twenty-five thousand dollars a week, plus a cut of the show—but it felt unnatural to her. She still drove a 1968 Pontiac Firebird with two dented fenders, and hated talking or thinking about money. She did spend on travel and clothes, but the rest went to housekeeping—she believed strongly in paying well and giving raises.

More than anything, she loved sharing her newfound wealth. She bought her mother her first pair of real gold earrings, pledged five thousand dollars to the effort to pass the Equal Rights Amendment, and donated to the United Farm Workers. Schaal had supported her in the beginning of her acting career when she was making almost nothing, and she was thrilled to finally be able to reciprocate. "Now that I'm making more money than he is, even if we split up, half of everything should be his," she told *Ms*. "Friends advised me to get a sugar bowl, stash away money, keep everything for myself. It's interesting what money brings out in people: If a woman has *no* money, she's supposed to get a husband; if she has a lot, she's supposed to keep it from her husband."

Her darling *Mary Tyler Moore* costars sent her a gift to cheer her up, and cheer her on: a photo of them all with exaggerated sad faces, except for a laughing Ted, with the caption, "We Miss You."

As work began on *Rhoda*, Brooks and Burns refined its concept: Per Fred Silverman's wishes, Rhoda would meet the man of her dreams, at last, and get married, making the show about the travails of a modern marriage. The producers decided Rhoda would move back to New York City (which, of course, would be re-created on a soundstage a few doors down from *Mary Tyler Moore* in Los Angeles) after meeting said man on a two-week visit to the East Coast. They also settled on featuring Rhoda's parents as regular cast members—already played by Nancy Walker and Harold Gould on *The Mary Tyler Moore Show*—and giving her a sad-sack younger sister, Brenda. For that role, the producers found a nasal-voiced treasure in theater actress Julie Kavner (later to voice Marge on the Brooks-produced *The Simpsons*). Bob Moore, who'd played Phyllis's gay brother on *The Mary Tyler Moore Show,* would serve as *Rhoda*'s regular director. He set a tone for working on the show: It would be fun and laid-back, just like its leading lady.

But finding the love of Rhoda's life turned out to be as difficult for the producers as it had been for Rhoda. They had hoped to sign Judd Hirsch, a thirty-nine-year-old actor who'd appeared in a few TV movies and could provide an authentic Bronx-born, Jewish match for Rhoda. But he backed out of contention for the role because of scheduling conflicts, so the producers kept looking for Rhoda's man.

After seeing nearly 150 actors for the role, they settled on a tall, curly-haired hunk named David Groh, who'd played only a few small TV parts before but looked like he could sweep Rhoda off her feet. He had little comedy experience, but he had a great camera presence, and the pilot was set to shoot soon. So the producers tested their luck— they'd had so much luck with their *Mary Tyler Moore* cast—and hoped some of Harper's perfect timing and delivery would rub off on Groh. "He was a good actor," Burns says. "A very good actor. Great looking. Not much comedy. But he worked hard and he tried so hard, David." Groh also came off a little shy, but he was well liked by his costars. "You know what I liked about him? He was so appreciative," says Candice Azzara, who played Joe's secretary. "He was a humble loner."

Lorenzo Music, the writer-producer who'd been with *The Mary Tyler Moore Show* since the beginning, rounded out the regular cast. He'd come over to *Rhoda* to help write and produce it on a daily basis, but now he'd stumbled upon his first TV acting job. As the producers auditioned voice actors to play the often heard, never seen part of Carlton, Rhoda and Brenda's drunken doorman, no one quite nailed it the way Music read it. His distinctive drowsy, cracking voice would eventually become famous in the part as the guy always announcing himself on Rhoda's door buzzer as "Carlton your doorman."

With rehearsals for her show now under way, Harper often sneaked back over to her original television home, the *Mary Tyler Moore* set, three doors down from what was now her own set, just to rub the sofa where she'd sat dozens of times or to smell the Oreos and Lorna Doones kept in Mary's cookie jar. For some reason, despite Moore's diabetes and Harper's weight struggles, the stagehands thought it was a fine idea to use real cookies as props. Moore and Harper, good-natured about almost everything, sniffed but did not snack.

As *Rhoda* progressed, Harper continued to have an on-again, off-again relationship with various diets. Her size fluctuated enough that the wardrobe supervisor would hold up items, asking, "Are you going to attempt to get into these today?" Harper called them "attempt pants" and "attempt suits," some of which were never worn at all.

Grant Tinker was now worried about spreading his company too thin—it was launching *Rhoda* along with a sitcom starring *Hogan's Heroes'* Bob Crane called *Second Start* as well as its first two dramatic series. Tinker was so uncharacteristically anxious that he had migraines. And he was losing sleep fretting over what the loss of Rhoda, a major ingredient in *The Mary Tyler Moore Show*'s success, might do to his flagship series. Would the company, and his wife's show, survive these major moves that he'd approved?

Tinker hadn't planned to run his own production company. He'd worked as an executive at Fox and Universal, so he figured he'd go back to a network or major studio job after he helped launch *The Mary Tyler Moore Show*. But *The Bob Newhart Show* followed in 1972 as MTM's second production, and, as a witty take on a straightforward concept—a Chicago psychologist tends to his colorful patients and relationship with his smart wife—upheld *Mary Tyler Moore*'s high script standards. "It would have been very easy to do craziness," Newhart's TV wife, Suzanne Pleshette, said in an interview at the time. "But the show is not bizarre. There's no freaky hook. No one's mother is a car." She likely didn't realize that her production company's star writers, Jim Brooks and Allan Burns, had written for *My Mother the Car*, and she meant it as a compliment.

Newhart himself, however, knew the company's pedigree when he signed on for the show after turning down dozens of other pilots that he didn't think had much potential. "When I got the offer for this show, I knew the quality of the guys working on it," he said. "And it wasn't [about] a wife and a dog and three kids." His show would soon do for psychologists—and their patients—what *Mary Tyler Moore* had done for single women. Newhart was soon receiving letters thanking him for demystifying therapy. And MTM would develop a curious reputation in the TV business: It seemed the place only hired nice people, stars who didn't act much like stars, casts who all got along, and the best writers around.

In any case, soon Tinker found himself heading a company that bore his wife's name. Since this seemed to be where fate had placed him, he did his best to make it into the kind of company he'd always dreamed of working for. He didn't want a factory. They'd only make shows they wanted to make; they wouldn't chase ratings for the sake of ratings or lower standards just to make network executives happy. Why would he bother having an independent company otherwise? Why not just go back to work for Fox or Universal?

The *Rhoda* spin-off seemed like a natural. Few secondary characters break out as huge and as fast as she did. Young women who weren't too busy imitating Mary Richards's style tried to figure out how to twist and tie headscarves to look like Rhoda. Her zingers, often delivered during the characters' late-night, post-date girl talk in Mary's apartment, stuck with fans. A 1974 *Time* magazine story declared Moore and Harper "a neatly balanced show business cartel" for MTM Entertainment. "One is tranquil, the other seems to have been born with sand under her skin," the article said. "Doublehanded, they are bringing a new sophistication back to television entertainment." Even better, "Audiences in search of funny girls have learned to forsake the theater for Valerie and Mary on the smaller screen."

Rhoda was poised to take advantage of the barriers *Mary Tyler Moore* broke down. Feminism, *Ms.* magazine, and sexy singles life were referenced. From the first season, topical, edgy, and undeniably '70s references stuffed the show: "I'm not talking about a one-night stand," one swinging bachelor told Rhoda as he asked her out. "We're in town till Thursday." When Rhoda moved in with Joe, he jokingly asked her how she wanted to be listed on their mailbox: "What would you like, Ms. or Miss or what?"

Harper, a self-proclaimed feminist, made sure the show was as true to her beliefs as possible, just as she'd done on *The Mary Tyler Moore Show*. When Rhoda suspected she was pregnant, the original script had her say to the doctor, "I'm thirty-three—I've just got under the wire, huh?" Harper, however, would have none of that. She complained to producers, "Hey, people get married at thirty-three. What do we say to them?" They cut the line. In the episode in which Joe and Rhoda decide to get married, the script originally had Rhoda begging Joe to marry her, but Harper wouldn't play it, so the producers rewrote it to make the marriage mutual.

From its beginning, eight women wrote for *Rhoda,* many of whom had honed their skills on *The Mary Tyler Moore Show*. Several of them came back to MTM specifically to write for their favorite character—it was no coincidence that so many of them were Jewish girls from the East Coast.

Gail Parent had written an episode of *Mary Tyler Moore* with her longtime partner Kenny Solms, but when she tried her hand at a few *Rhoda*s, it was the first time she had worked solo. She got to write some of the show's most memorable early episodes, including Rhoda's bridal shower. Writing alone terrified Parent. It required a different process. She had written a novel, *Sheila Levine Is Dead and Living in New York,* in the time since working on *The Mary Tyler Moore Show*. The hilarious book-length suicide letter chronicled a single thirty-something woman caught between wanting traditional marriage and living it up on New York's singles scene. It became a bestseller in 1972. Though Parent was married and living in Los Angeles at the time, she based the book on the experiences of her then-single best friend, who was living in New York. She didn't expect her book to become such a huge sensation, but the reviewers raved, and the phenomenon grew from there. Between Mary Richards and Sheila Levine, no doubt remained that single, thirty-something women were the rage.

Now that she was working on *Rhoda* alone, however, Parent had a problem. She had written her book in longhand, then hired a typist. Kenny had always been the typist in their partnership. For *Rhoda,* she had to peck through her scripts alone.

Charlotte Brown, who'd struggled to sell a few scripts for *The Mary Tyler Moore Show* and then had written several *Bob Newhart* episodes for MTM, joined *Rhoda*'s stable of regular writers. Her first episode of *Rhoda* featured Joe and Rhoda meeting each other's parents. She loved to write anything that featured Ida Morgenstern because the character was so similar to Brown's own mother. She often gave Ida lines her mother had said, verbatim. Brown once told a *TV Guide* writer that her mother was the "prototype" for Ida. Her mother read the article, and while she didn't know what "prototype" meant, she was insulted.

Brown sat in the audience with her parents the night of one episode's taping, her eyes trained on her own mother's face as Rhoda noted that her mom had taken the plastic covers off the sofa. "What?" Brown's mother whispered, wondering why her daughter was staring at her. "I never had plastic on the furniture!" When Brown got home late that night, she called her brother to demand he confirm her memory. (He did.)

Brown soon became an executive script consultant, her first step up the chain of staff producers for *Rhoda.* The job demanded all of her time, but she couldn't imagine doing anything else. She worked fourteen to sixteen hours a day. Sometimes she drove home just as normal people were driving to work. But her efforts didn't go unnoticed. Later, she'd become the first female show runner on a sitcom when she took over *Rhoda*'s top post from Davis and Music. Harper took out an ad in *Variety* thanking Brown for all of her hard work and told Gloria

Steinem in an interview that Brown was "literally doing the work of four men who used to be there."

Gloria Banta and Pat Nardo finally gave in and moved back to Los Angeles from New York. Since writing their first script for *The Mary Tyler Moore Show,* they'd written a few more scripts, After School Specials that Nardo produced for her network, ABC. After they'd amassed a body of successful work, the recently formed ICM talent agency wanted to sign them for a pilot project starring Maureen Stapleton called *Ladies from Flatbush.* Nardo's boss at ABC, Michael Eisner, had gotten promoted from managing daytime programming to primetime, and he helped secure her the new gig. Banta and Nardo decided, reluctantly, to move back to Los Angeles. They knew that was where they needed to be if they wanted to keep working in the industry.

When the pilot didn't make it on the air, Brooks and Burns—who were fond of the women's work together—asked them to write for the *Rhoda* spin-off. They happily signed on. Nardo also started hanging out with Jim Brooks and Dave Davis more than ever. She often went to lunch with them, begging them like a pesky little sister to tell her what they were discussing when they referred to producer business she didn't know about. They became her best friends, her big brothers, and her closest advisers whenever she had trouble with men, which was fairly often. The three of them went out to Dave and Jim's beach house, taking care of Jim's baby daughter when he had her for the weekend. For Pat, at least, it was the best time of her life.

In fact, Nardo and Banta were both having a blast. They thought the people they worked with on the show were wonderful, and they loved having an office to go to every day. It felt, even in the moment, like a golden time in their lives. The women took refuge in the comforting world of MTM Entertainment, away from the still-sexist world that most of Hollywood was. They'd tried to write for some other shows, including one where they stood outside a meeting room while the male producers discussed their script. They could hear one of the guys saying, "Well, it's a piece of shit, but I'd sure like to fuck that Banta." They knew there were men like that in the business, but none of them was at MTM.

New writer Deborah Leschin also found her place among *Rhoda*'s young female staffers. The bubbly twenty-six-year-old started out at Garry Marshall's new project, *Laverne & Shirley,* but she dreamed of working with Valerie Harper or Dick Van Dyke. She was living back at her parents' place in Passaic, New Jersey, after a stint with Marshall, when she decided to write a few spec scripts for *Mary Tyler Moore*. She soon got a call from *Rhoda* producers asking her to come aboard, and she was breathless with excitement. She felt like Rhoda made the single woman in the '70s look like a "bright, shiny penny." She'd wanted to work for MTM Entertainment so badly that on a previous trip to Los Angeles, she'd driven by the studio on Radford Avenue and took a photo of the gate, determined to drive through it someday.

When she returned to Los Angeles for a job interview with Charlotte Brown, she didn't feel it went well, but she got the job anyway. The two didn't seem to mesh, but Brown needed another woman on her staff and chose Leschin.

Leschin couldn't believe her luck, regardless of her friction with Brown. She would drive home from work in her new little Mercedes and scream with joy. She had said she was going to be a writer for *Rhoda,* and, dammit, she had done it. Her parents had scoffed at her dreams. Her friends had said, "Do you know how many single Jewish girls in New Jersey want to write for this show?" But she did it. Dream after dream came true. Some of those old friends back in New Jersey were now getting married and having babies, but to that she said: *Feh.*

Brooks and Burns, meanwhile, along with Davis and Music, worked overtime now to crank out quality scripts for both *Mary Tyler Moore* and *Rhoda,* in addition to attending to *The Bob Newhart Show.* Music had audience warm-up duties at all the shows, with the tapings spread throughout the week. Brooks shocked his coworkers by getting only more brilliant the more he produced. The writers and producers would all sit in a room thinking, *What are we going to do? The second act is a mess.* Brooks would say, "What if . . . ?" And then he'd tear into an idea, complete with plot twists and killer lines. His colleagues would wonder, *What are we doing here?* They could see they were in a room with a genius, and they weren't sure their own contribution was even necessary. They knew their script would end up with five lines of their own and the rest Brooks's, but they didn't mind one bit.

The Radford Avenue studio became known as "Camelot" because of Tinker's insistence on giving his writer-producers autonomy and fighting network interference on their behalf. Brooks and Burns, encouraged by the Camelot philosophy, had just created yet another show for the MTM empire as well, *Friends and Lovers*. They raked in three hundred thousand dollars per year each at this time, though the work was endless. To keep themselves sane—or was it the opposite?— they developed a system to test jokes. Since Nardo was no longer their secretary, they didn't have her disapproval as a bellwether for bad lines. Now they had a buzzer at the office that they could hit to signify their lack of approval for a gag, while a unanimous winner was signaled with a music box that played "The Impossible Dream."

With *Rhoda*, however, the producers had one major concern beyond writing good jokes: forestalling her marriage as much as possible. Silverman pushed for a fall sweeps wedding. "I think it's going to be a number-one Nielsen show," he told them.

"Aww, come on!" they remember protesting. "We've got so much we want to do in the first year. Maybe at the *end* of the first year we get them married. Not this close to the beginning!"

But by the eighth episode, on October 28, 1974, Fred Silverman had his way. Rhoda and Joe walked down the aisle in a two-part special that brought Mary, Georgette, Phyllis, Murray, and Lou to New York for the nuptials. Silverman's prediction came true; the episode went through the roof. In fact, it broke several records. It became the highest-rated television episode of the decade thus far, and the second-

most-watched of all time, beat only by the birth of Little Ricky on
I Love Lucy in the '50s. More than 50 million Americans tuned in,
which represented more than half of the total audience watching television that night. *Monday Night Football* host Howard Cosell, as he
called a game on a different channel opposite the broadcast, cracked
that he hadn't been invited to the wedding. Fans held wedding parties
to watch together throughout the country and sent "wedding gifts" to
CBS. Harper—who, in the episode, famously ran through the streets
of Manhattan in her wedding dress after Phyllis forgot to pick her up
for the big day—won her fourth Emmy for the performance. Brooks
and Burns enjoyed notching a new accomplishment: They had produced their first country-stopper of an episode.

In fact, *Rhoda* even beat *Mary Tyler Moore* in the ratings during
its first season on the air, 1974–75, which solidified Rhoda Morgenstern as an icon. Mary and Rhoda made the October 1974 cover of
Time as "Funny Girls" when the magazine declared that year "the
Golden Age of comedy." Harper, the Jersey girl who'd dreamed of
being a ballerina, had turned her New York upbringing—and her impression of her stepmother, Angela—into one of TV's most memorable
characters. "A failed ballerina you have before you," she would say,
"but a successful actress."

When Grant Tinker asked Jim Brooks and Allan Burns about writing a spin-off script for Cloris Leachman, even his confident baritone
couldn't convince them. Both producers said a polite, "No, thanks."
They respectfully offered a litany of potential pitfalls they saw with
the project. They were both pretty busy by this point, overseeing *Mary
Tyler Moore,* helping with *Rhoda,* and launching *Friends and Lovers.*
So they had a perfectly good excuse not to get involved in *Phyllis,* but
their objections went beyond that.

For starters, there was the Cloris problem. Just because Phyllis
stood in a certain place or said a certain line at a certain time in a script
did not mean Cloris would perform it that way. In fact, it almost guar-

anteed she wouldn't. She wanted to live every last scene as Phyllis; she wanted to embody the essence of Phyllis, which was to be the most important person in the room. Onlookers had a hard time telling where Cloris ended and Phyllis began; even Cloris herself did. And that was despite the fact that she'd continued appearing in several of the era's most progressive films. In Peter Bogdanovich's adaptation of Henry James's *Daisy Miller*, she played Cybill Shepherd's mother. She stole the show as the terrifying Frau Blucher in Mel Brooks's *Young Frankenstein*. Yet, when she returned to the job of playing Phyllis, she *became* Phyllis, through and through, with all the difficulties that entailed.

This approach worked on the sets of Oscar-caliber films and it even worked on the set of *The Mary Tyler Moore Show* for a recurring secondary character once everyone got the hang of her. It remained to be seen, however, how her approach would transfer to her own spinoff. And yet the prospect of a show of her own grew likely as Leachman became a star in her own right. MTM would likely lose her to another production company if it didn't give her a bigger showcase.

In addition to the Cloris problem, however, there was the Phyllis problem. Phyllis was an even trickier character to turn into a leading lady than Rhoda had been, given that her main function on *The Mary Tyler Moore Show* was to be abrasive and self-absorbed. But Leachman, then forty-nine and reaching a new apex, wanted to follow in Harper's footsteps, and Weinberger and Daniels were up for the challenge of creating a show for her. Tinker put his faith in Leachman's performance and hoped for the best.

In an effort to soften Phyllis for her role as a main character, the writers lost many of the kooky elements that made her such a hit in a supporting role, though Leachman still tore into the part with her trademark scene-chewing force. The show explored new sitcom territory in featuring a middle-aged widow, with Phyllis's often-mentioned, never-seen husband, Lars, dying in the pilot episode. Phyllis is shown grieving and finding out that Lars left her no life insurance. (Perhaps befitting the invisible Lars, no one ever explains how he died.) The conceit was a clever way to start Phyllis on a brand-new life in San Francisco when she moves in with her in-laws, and it helped garner instant sympathy for the notoriously prickly character.

But the show suffered from comparison to *Mary Tyler Moore* and *Rhoda*. Even worse, it weathered a devastating loss to its cast early on. Barbara Colby, once a crowd favorite on *Mary Tyler Moore* as Mary's prostitute cell mate in the episode in which Mary is jailed, joined the spin-off cast as Phyllis's new boss at a photography studio. After she appeared in just three episodes, however, Colby and a colleague, James Kiernan, were both killed while walking to her car after an acting class in the Venice section of Los Angeles. They were shot by two men in the parking lot the night of July 24, 1975. Kiernan lived long enough afterward to describe the murder to police, but it was never solved; authorities classified it as a random "thrill killing" since the victims weren't robbed and the perpetrators didn't seem to have another motive. Liz Torres took over Colby's role on *Phyllis,* but the show never found its footing afterward.

Leachman proved the ideal star to lend her cast emotional support after the tragedy—she was nothing if not a mother. She would tell "Barbara stories" to cheer everyone up, recounting funny incidents in which Colby had ad-libbed off camera. Leachman herself had more trouble coping, but she kept it to herself. "It was the worst death I've ever experienced," she said at the time. "With my mother and father, at least it was fair."

Then, two more cast members died during the show's run: eighty-six-year-old Judith Lowry, who played Mother Dexter, died in 1976, and just two months later, her ninety-two-year-old on-screen boyfriend (whom she'd just married on the show), Burt Mustin, died as well.

There were, however, other problems with the show. Leachman's perfectionism ate at everyone's patience, and it was harder to handle when she was the dominant force on the set. She could spend hours debating the optimal heights of stools she and her boss would sit on for a scene or demonstrating how a supporting character should deliver a line. She came on strong with her fellow actors, who could get defensive if they didn't know her well. Besides which, if they did do what she'd asked, often the result was for her character to be in the spotlight, all others fading out.

The series also suffered from a sudden increase in scrutiny of sex on network television, even on the groundbreaking shows that had been enjoying great artistic freedoms. In one episode, Phyllis's daughter, Bess, now a teenager, goes on an overnight ski trip with friends and Phyllis believes she's spent the night with a boy. Phyllis frets to her boss, Julie, about her fears that Bess might "become a woman" on the trip, and Julie suggests Phyllis initiate a mother-daughter sex talk. First Phyllis insists she'll know if her daughter has "matured" just by looking at her. But when Bess arrives home, Phyllis isn't sure. She eventually takes Julie's advice and confronts Bess about her concerns, only to learn from Bess that she didn't do it. The script called for Phyllis to do a double take afterward and say, "unless she lied," which would leave the matter open to interpretation—a tactic that would have fit right into the glory days of *The Mary Tyler Moore Show*. But *Phyllis* was no *Mary Tyler Moore*.

CBS originally refused to air the episode and backed down only after Brooks and Burns, who now had serious clout at the network, stepped in. They compromised with the network in the end, agreeing to cut the last line; there would be no ambiguity about whether the teenager had sex. The conflict, as it turned out, was a harbinger of a more conservative era in television to come, the "family hour" initiative that would soon burn some of the biggest hits of the '70s. Times were changing. Antifeminist crusader Phyllis Schlafly now had a regular commentary spot on the *CBS Morning News*. The Equal Rights Amendment no longer seemed like a sure thing. Single women facing relevant, realistic issues were on their way out. And surely no proper lady talked openly about sex.

The episode would hardly be the most difficult trial that *Phyllis* faced, but it would be among the last. Though *Phyllis* ran for two seasons, from 1975 to 1977, it never gained traction with audiences, who were already moving on to lighter TV fare such as *Happy Days* and *Charlie's Angels*. No one blamed Leachman. Tinker knew the scripts never quite got up to par.

Then, shocking news came for *Rhoda*: The woman whose long-awaited wedding had brought the country to a standstill was heading for divorce.

Rhoda hadn't quite made it on her own, despite her show's record-breaking early achievements. After the big wedding, the show was noticeably less funny—and less interesting. Soon it became clear: The audacious Rhoda had married kind of a dud. "When Rhoda got married, it was a disaster," Banta says. "It just changed everything. It changed her personality. Suddenly the show was hard to write."

Furthermore, it turned out that many fans hadn't wanted Rhoda to get married in the first place—her appeal as a character came from her outsider status, her valiant battles in singlehood. " 'Sadie Sadie married lady' was what went wrong with *Rhoda*," Harper says. "Success is equated with marriage. The base of her character was this victorious loser, and she was perceived to have won—she had this hunky husband." Rhoda had excelled on *The Mary Tyler Moore Show* at sniping from the sidelines, and now here she was representing mainstream married women. Adds *Rhoda* writer Deborah Leschin, "I wanted it so much to be a women's show about women, and her being married took that spin off of it for me." Now Rhoda had become thinner and more fashionable than ever, married, and settled. Parent says, "I learned early on that it was a bad idea to pitch the 'bop-on-the-head' show, where something happened to a character and they changed. It never worked because characters have to stay the same."

CBS's Standards & Practices department, fearing conservative backlash, added to the trouble, allowing so little sex that it was difficult to portray a fun, modern marriage: Groh, as Rhoda's on-screen husband, always had to have a pajama top on if the two were in bed together. And any talk of sex had to walk a fine line.

After two seasons of fighting Rhoda's fate, the producers made the historic decision to break up their central married couple. Harper's favorite quip became, "This is the first divorce where the charge is lack of comedy." And the producers faced the unfortunate task of telling Groh, whom everyone on set liked, that he was out of a job. The chemistry between Harper and Groh had never developed the way they'd hoped, the producers explained to Groh. He took the news well, and appeared periodically throughout the third season so the show could portray the split. "I don't think we ever cast the guy great," Brooks says. "The right person has to walk through the door, and it just didn't happen in this case." The good news: Six years after they pitched a show about a divorced woman on her own to CBS, the MTM producers had one. And one about a Jew in New York, no less.

The divorce idea still made the network nervous, but Silverman and his executives also saw that it had to be done. Viewers, on the other hand, were less easy to please. Even though many had hated that Rhoda was no longer single, at least as many now wrote in to complain about Rhoda getting divorced. CBS's early edicts against divorce proved at least partially true; women in particular felt panicked by the idea that Rhoda could get divorced. If Rhoda could get divorced, anyone could get divorced.

With Rhoda on the dating market again, however, there was room for creative renewal. The show could add new characters, most notably a swinging-single neighbor played hilariously by Ron Silver. Still, Brooks never felt like the show reached its potential the way *Mary Tyler Moore* did. "I feel like the divorce was a mistake," Brooks says, even though he also felt the marriage was a mistake. Leschin, too, couldn't warm to the divorce even though she'd hated the marriage. "That made it even worse," she says. "It left us no place to go. We had no stories."

✦ ✦ ✦

Despite the setbacks on *Rhoda* and *Phyllis,* MTM Enterprises had become a major force in the industry. By 1974, MTM was grossing more than $20 million and had eight comedies in the works or on air: *Mary Tyler Moore, Bob Newhart, Rhoda,* and *Paul Sand in Friends and Lovers* on CBS; *The Texas Wheelers* on ABC; and *Doc, Three for the Road,* and *Phyllis* being prepped for the following season. Although movies steered the national conversation like never before—the sequel *Godfather Part II* was released in 1974 and grossed $193 million—television still permeated life across the nation. Americans talked about the Corleones at a cocktail party or two, but they invited Mary and Rhoda into their living rooms every week. Since *The Mary Tyler Moore Show* had premiered, CBS had remained atop the ratings, with NBC and ABC fighting it out for second place every year, thanks in large part to MTM. And women were proliferating on TV as strong main characters, even beyond the sitcom—*Police Woman* and *Wonder Woman* were now hits, and that was at least partly thanks to MTM as well.

Only Norman Lear and Garry Marshall rivaled MTM's output and clout. "It was a phenomenon," says composer Pat Williams, who went from scoring *The Mary Tyler Moore Show* to orchestrating most of MTM's series. "That whole period of time where Mary's show went into *The Bob Newhart Show* and so forth, the way Grant Tinker ran that place was with such class."

Now Moore's dream of a hit show had come true, and Tinker's of an independent studio had as well. "On Mary's shows, nothing is sacred and few things are profane," *Time* gushed. "Sex, inflation, urban miseries and small-time office politics are alive and laughing on prime time." Tinker put it more simply: "On Friday nights," he said, "I used to make my rounds to all the different shows, and witnessed a hell of a lot of good television being made." No laugh tracks allowed, or necessary.

FOURTEEN
fourteen
fourteen
fourteen
fourteen
fourteen
fourteen
fourteen

the best job of their lives

(1975–77)

Actress Lee Grant, a high-cheekboned beauty with a wheat-colored bob and blue eyes, was on the rise after winning a best supporting actress Oscar for her portrayal of a flirty wife in *Shampoo*. As she got ready to hit the stage for a 1975 appearance on Johnny Carson's *To-night Show* to promote her new television show, *Fay,* she got some bad news: *Fay* had been canceled.

This moment was, arguably, the beginning of the end for *Mary Tyler Moore*.

NBC had attempted to match CBS's edgy programming with Grant's show, a sitcom about a divorcée with two children, created by *Maude* writer Susan Harris. (Typical Fay line about her unhappily married friend: "Marian starts the day with Cocoa Puffs and vodka. By nine she's forgotten her name.") But after *Fay* had aired for just three weeks, the network caved to public protests. Grant went through with the Carson interview, calling NBC vice president Marvin Antonowsky a "mad programmer" and punctuating the pronouncement with her middle finger. (Thereafter, she left her TV acting career for directing.) Harris felt frustrated by the cancellation as well and complained in the press, "I don't like having to write down, which is what I have to do now."

TV's evolution in the early '70s had created, it turned out, a backlash. Thought-provoking television like *All in the Family, The Mary Tyler Moore Show,* and *Good Times* had begun to give way to fluffier fare like *Happy Days, Charlie's Angels,* and *What's Happening!!* Every bit of progress that *Mary Tyler Moore* and its cohorts had helped the industry make was now facing reversal. Skyrocketing inflation, the oil crisis, and the Cold War were providing enough real-life anxiety for viewers, sending them to their TVs looking for escapism, as many critical analyses opined. Or perhaps, as some said, the bounce back from issues shows to *Happy Days* represented an endless cycle in television: Producers had worn out the realistic, gritty sitcom, and networks looking for something fresh alighted upon whatever looked like its opposite—anything shiny and mindless.

Fay counted among that movement's first victims, but soon even *Mary Tyler Moore* would fall prey, to some extent, as well.

"*The Mary Tyler Moore Show?* Oh, how interesting. Is Mary as pretty in real life?" It was Treva's first dinner aboard the SS *France.* She had been seated at a table with eleven Americans who were traveling in a group, all of whom were nervous about eating food they weren't familiar with, so all of them ordered steak. Well done. "*The Mary Tyler Moore Show?* So what is Valerie Harper really like?"

No, Treva thought. *I'm not going to go to Europe to get the same questions and give the same answers about myself.* From now on, she decided, she was going to keep her U.S. life vague. She would tell the next person who asked that she worked "in an office." Keep it blank. She wouldn't even tell people she was a writer: There would be an automatic assumption about what they thought writers were like. No, let them have no preconceptions. She would just be another anonymous American.

She would be whoever she was, maybe even whoever she wasn't. She would test her fears, test her limits. Be and do things she never would be and do in Real Life. Because this would be Experimental Life.

She had always been careful about decision making, planning in advance. When she went on a trip, she would pore over schedules, hotel ratings, guidebooks, checking out each detail. Her first week in Paris, however, she packed an overnight bag, went to the nearest train station, and got on the first train that was leaving. She stayed on until it had reached its final destination, which was Lyon, walked into the first hotel that had a vacancy, explored the town, and spent the night. The next day, the same thing. The first train leaving Lyon. She got on, and then got off at the last stop. Grenoble, then Milan. The trip lasted six days.

While she was living in Copenhagen she joined an improvisation group for English-speaking actors. She had always been terrified of acting, and thought a little private improv group might help. (Her singing and piano playing didn't count—there was always a piano between her and the audience.) The director of the group liked her acting and asked her if she would star in a production he was mounting at an English-speaking theater, the Mermaid. *Not for nothing was I voted Best Actress at Lawrence High School,* she thought to herself at the first preview, as she stood behind the curtain trembling and praying she wouldn't pass out.

At a hotel in Mykonos there was a handwritten list of places to go, among them, a nude beach. A nude beach? Exactly what she would never ever do. So she decided to do it. The first bus left at 8:30 a.m. She delayed and delayed until 4 p.m., then, determined, hopped on the bus. When the bus dropped her off, she walked resolutely onto the beach, not looking left or right, put down her towel, and then, with a flushed face and clenched teeth, took off all her clothes—standing, even!—and sat down, nude, on the towel. She thought she would die. Then she noticed that a lot of the people were looking at her. What? Was her body that good? Or—*uh-oh*—that bad? When she got up enough nerve to look around her, she saw that everyone was dressed. Fully clothed. It was so late that they had gotten dressed to take the last bus back.

She lived in Amsterdam in a hotel that had no closets. She lived in Copenhagen with a Danish family who had a parrot who kept talking back to the television during the pauses. (During the film of *Hamlet*: Laurence Olivier: "To be—" Parrot: "TEW BEEE." Olivier: "Or not to be." Parrot: "AW NOT TEW BEE.") In Yugoslavian restaurants, she arbitrarily pointed to items on the menu, not having a clue what kind of food would appear on her plate. She rode a motorcycle on a winding coastal road, clutching the back of a waiter she met in a fishing village in Portugal.

Friends wrote to her from home—when was she coming back? She felt she would know when it was time to go back home: when she got tired of living in Europe.

She was walking along a street in Copenhagen, and was mesmerized by a photo in the window of a travel agency. Wherever that photo was taken, she wanted to go there next. She went into the store. "That photo—where is that?" "Oh, that's Lucca. In Italy." Treva gasped. She had been to Lucca. Two weeks before. She realized then that she would never get tired of living in Europe. It was time to go home. She had ended up staying two and a half years.

When she returned, she would find a television business radically different from the one in which she'd started her career nearly a decade earlier.

There was no doubt that female protagonists had come a long way thanks in large part to Mary Richards. They'd come so far, in fact, that they were no longer seen as unique, as was apparent with *Fay*'s cancellation. Reflecting this change, many of the writers who had helped build *The Mary Tyler Moore Show* into a phenomenon had dispersed around the world—like Treva Silverman—and across the country to test their cachet on other shows and in other genres.

Marilyn Suzanne Miller moved to New York when producer Lorne Michaels asked her to be on the writing staff of his new late-night sketch show for NBC, *Saturday Night Live* (the job Treva had turned down to return to Europe after the *Ladies' Home Journal* luncheon). Miller was one of only three women on the original team. It felt far different from working for *The Mary Tyler Moore Show,* the land of orderly desks and regular schedules. Hard drugs were everywhere, far beyond the occasional after-hours pot haze at *Mary Tyler Moore.* Her old friends from the Comedy Store had moved up the showbiz ranks, gotten jobs at *The Tonight Show* and sitcoms, and had enough money to buy cocaine.

When Michaels called to offer her the job, she was planning to marry the boyfriend she lived with and write sitcoms forever. "There were so many great sitcoms to be written," she says. "It just never ended. *Barney Miller, Welcome Back, Kotter.* You would just do it and do it and do it. The need for material was endless then." She also got an offer to be a story consultant on *Maude* while she weighed the *Saturday Night Live* opportunity. *Maude* was a guaranteed six-figure deal versus *Saturday Night Live*'s $750 per week, and no assurance that the show wouldn't be canceled. She took *Saturday Night Live* anyway. She won an Emmy for her efforts.

Writer Susan Silver, who'd gotten her start in the first season of *Mary Tyler Moore* but turned down MTM's offer to produce *The Bob Newhart Show,* had escaped the suffocating Hollywood scene altogether. And even though she'd once abandoned her career with MTM to focus on starting a family with her husband, they'd since split up. She was now thirty-two and living the Mary Richards life in a two-room sublet on New York City's East Fifty-eighth Street. She traded on her looks, personality, and pedigree with TV's most respected comedy to make connections and score media attention. She charmed her way into a lunch at the old-school media haven '21' with a writer from *Esquire,* who penned an entire column that, she says, "made" her. Robert Alan Aurthur anointed her "the most beautiful, talented, beautiful, talented writer in television."

She even got to be featured in her own "Dewar's Profile," an ad campaign for the whisky that told the world of her love for *The Diary of Anaïs Nin* and tennis and declared her "honest, determined, and intelligent." She got a case of Dewar's for her trouble. She handed the bottles out to friends as Christmas gifts, as she had developed an ulcer that prohibited her drinking. Seven years into her career, she still got so nervous at pitch meetings that her stomach was disintegrating. She had to swig Maalox before each pitch, though she didn't mind letting the producers and executives see the bottle of antacid. She figured it engendered sympathy.

There was a much bigger reason for Silver's anxiety: As the *Fay* cancellation indicated, the TV industry had become a confusing beast to serve. Did it want edgy or safe? Did it want to please those young viewers who loved controversial shows, or did it want to please the protesters who were vocal about hating them? The industry itself, as a whole, clearly had no idea. In one 1975 TV column, for instance, *Washington Post* critic Benjamin Stein complained about the aimlessness of the current lineup. NBC's *The Family Holvak* made that wholesome Walton family "look like the Gestapo." A *Hogan's Heroes* copycat, ABC's *On the Rocks* glorified prison life but wasn't funny. And even MTM's own *Doc,* about an older doctor in a poor New York neighborhood, was deemed "syrupy and cloying."

A game of executive musical chairs ensued as the networks panicked over their conflicted priorities. And *The Mary Tyler Moore Show's* network savior, Fred Silverman, was among the first to grab a new spot: He abandoned CBS just as it faltered, taking a job at struggling ABC instead. He would program against the schedule he'd assembled, the schedule with which CBS had dominated the early '70s. He felt his work at CBS was done and was looking for a new challenge. One of the ironies of success in television is that it leaves executives little to do once they've achieved it. It also means that anything that doesn't go perfectly will be deemed a failure. ABC was younger and scrappier and could use his help—it offered him a chance to be a savior all over again.

Silverman knew he needed to take ABC in the opposite direction he'd once taken CBS. His new network simply couldn't compete with what CBS did best: those urbane, topical comedies. He tried something else instead: sex and escapism. He figured he'd just try a few shows and see how it went. Television programming is an inexact science—trying out a bunch of stuff, seeing what sticks, and throwing out the rest. The law of averages, as Silverman said, meant something had to work eventually—when it did, the network, and the entire industry, would follow.

His new schedule delivered sooner than he would have dared hope. He promptly boosted ABC to number one with shows such as *The Six Million Dollar Man*, *The Captain and Tennille*, and *Three's Company*, quite a feat after CBS's years of domination. The other networks scrambled to catch up, to please viewers, advertisers, politicians, and activists—and ended up pleasing few with their unmemorable fare. "I think of commercial television like Times Square," former CBS News president Fred Friendly said in a *Newsweek* article titled "Why Is TV So Bad?" "In trying to make more money, the lowest common denominator was catered to. And now TV entertainment, like Times Square, is nothing more than a slum." CBS president Robert Wood, the onetime champion of *The Mary Tyler Moore Show*, offered this as an explanation: "You sure don't start out to make a bad show. But safer and on the air is preferable to different and off the air." The loss of one ratings point in a network's seasonal average could cost $20 million in advertising.

Pressure came from outside the business, too. Conservative groups amplified their criticism of TV's edgy content, and discovered the power of the Federal Communications Commission complaint. The bureaucratic organ received two thousand complaints in 1972; it received twenty-five thousand in 1974. So the FCC—charged with licensing stations, and therefore with policing their commitments to the public interest—stopped short of outright censorship, but pressured the networks into agreeing to a "family viewing" period for the first hour of prime time: Between 8 and 9 p.m. Eastern Standard Time, programming was to be free of sex and violence, a broad order. The networks, wary of censorship accusations as well, presented the idea as their own: In a December 1974 letter, CBS executive Arthur Taylor told the National Association of Broadcasters' Television Code Review Board that he was concerned about a recent surgeon general's report that found a link between TV violence and children's violent urges. "What I'm hoping for is that we can discover new creative devices that can sustain action, adventure, jeopardy, and threat without using cruelty and brutality," he told the *New York Times* amid the controversy.

The change, however it came about, sparked an outcry among producers and writers, who felt their creative freedom (and, some claimed, their First Amendment rights) slip away. No one seemed to doubt that violence was not the only element of drama that would be curtailed during the forbidden hour. Public reports about a meeting a month before Taylor's letter, between the FCC and the networks, indicated that FCC chairman Richard E. Wiley had suggested the TV executives reduce violence *and* sex in their programming, particularly during the early evening when families might be watching. All the new guidelines said was that the Family Viewing Hour shouldn't include programs "deemed inappropriate for viewing by a general family audience," leaving "appropriate" open to wide interpretation. Programming codes at CBS and NBC at the time, for instance, allowed *hell* and *dammit,* while ABC did not; CBS let *Good Times* character J.J. use the phrase "big mother" all the time, while ABC nixed that one as well.

Moore said at the time that the change had "set television back drastically." For the medium to thrive, she felt, the envelope had to be pushed.

But fearful of FCC sanctions, the networks reshuffled their fall 1975 schedules to avoid infractions of the new policy. Norman Lear's shows *All in the Family* and *Maude* were particularly stung. After five seasons, *All in the Family* moved from leading off CBS's powerhouse Saturday lineup to 9 p.m. on Mondays, while *Maude* plunged from a top-five program to well below the top thirty when it was moved out of the way of "family" time. Lear joined with *M*A*S*H* producer Larry Gelbart, *Barney Miller* producer Danny Arnold, and Burns to form the Writers Guild Committee on the Family Viewing Hour. Arnold learned that a story line on his show from the previous season, in which a detective fell in love with a prostitute, would no longer be allowed at ABC. A script he was planning, in which a man was to be arrested because he "shacked up with a minor," was nixed; the phrase "shacked up" was banned. The concern over family-viewing time did, in fact, affect the way Brooks and Burns made decisions about their shows, Brooks confessed in a *New York Times* piece at the time. "It scares me that we have been intimidated like that," he said. "I'm ashamed to admit it, but [we have]."

In October 1975, the Writers Guild group filed a lawsuit against the FCC's new policy. "If the networks were to make a sincere effort, it seems to me they would have called a series of meetings with the creative community to talk about excesses," Lear said. "No such meetings were even asked for. Part of the deceit is also the fact that we all know children of all ages are awake long after 9—so if they are all to be protected, cutting off family viewing time at 9 doesn't do it." Indeed, 11 million children still watched TV past 9 p.m. That was exactly why several religious groups complained that the change didn't go far enough, leaving twenty-three of twenty-four hours open to "anything-goes" content. Lear added, facetiously: "And 9 on the coasts is 8 in the Midwest. Why are the networks abandoning the little ones in the heart of the Bible Belt?" The networks countered, in all seriousness, that lots of families went to bed earlier in the farm states anyway. They had to tend to the crops, you know.

The power of the Christian right in American culture and politics would only grow from there. Iowa Democrat Harold Hughes resigned from the U.S. Senate to become an evangelist. Astronaut Jim Irwin joined forces with a different evangelist to start an organization called High Flight. Singers Pat Boone and Anita Bryant spoke about their own Christian beliefs—and spoke, and spoke.

The 1976 Democratic presidential primaries would pit Georgia governor Jimmy Carter, a down-home evangelical Baptist-turned-born-again-Christian, against California governor Jerry Brown, a former Jesuit seminarian who freely aired his religious beliefs, both Buddhist and Christian, during the primary campaign. Carter won the nomination. And in a moment that indirectly summarized TV's new views on risqué content, the presidential candidate talked openly of his Christian beliefs and also famously admitted to having "looked on a lot of women with lust" in an interview with *Playboy*. He beat Gerald Ford in the election a few weeks later.

Nielsen reported that the daily average home viewing of television slipped seven minutes in 1975—the second-largest decline in a generation—which sent TV leadership into a further panic. NBC promoted executive Herb Schlosser to lead the network in trying to attract younger viewers, but his efforts tanked—none of his new fall 1975 shows earned a second season, but they did manage to alienate older viewers. (His only bright spot: signing *Saturday Night Live*.) "Most critics agree this has been the most disastrous television season in the history of broadcasting," Johnny Carson said during a *Tonight Show* bit. He jokingly listed his suggested shows for the next season: *The Bionic Dog, Frontier Proctologist, Monday Night Cockfighting,* and *The Minority Next Door,* a Lear-esque proposal featuring a Jewish family, the Margolises, who move in next door to the Vatican. "The comedy high jinks begin," Carson deadpanned, "when Mr. Margolis runs into the pope and says, 'How's the missus?'"

No one, least of all writers and producers of longtime hits, knew what their network bosses wanted anymore. "I'd like to thank a lot of people at CBS," Burns quipped while he accepted an Emmy in May 1976, "but unfortunately, none of them are there anymore."

Just a few years earlier the industry media had hailed a sitcom "golden age." Now miniseries were the hot new thing, thanks in large part to the success of ABC's *Roots*—an adaptation of Alex Haley's novel about slave life, and another smashing success for Silverman. TV also struck a new ratings gold mine with more showings of films such as *Gone With the Wind* and *The Wizard of Oz,* a rare treat around which families would plan their evenings. At a time when movies essentially disappeared once they'd finished their theatrical runs, with no VCRs to replay them, big movies made for effortless event programming.

In this shifting TV market, Grant Tinker started to feel his company's flagship show would be better off ending than soldiering through. *Rhoda* and *Phyllis* were on the wane in terms of both ratings and quality, and MTM had lost four writer-producers to Silverman's new network. A fadeout in a terrible time slot seemed all wrong for the sophisticated, groundbreaking *Mary Tyler Moore Show.* And with five seasons in the can, the show would easily sell on the increasingly lucrative syndication market—studios were now making millions by selling reruns as a package to local television stations to fill slots outside of prime time, but they usually needed at least one hundred episodes to make the deal worthwhile. It was time, Tinker reluctantly concluded, to quit. But he wasn't sure how his producers or actors would feel about that.

He approached Brooks and Burns with his argument: To quit the show would be difficult, he said, but to go out on top would be better—in its fifth season, *The Mary Tyler Moore Show* still ranked in television's top twenty. But Mary Richards was now thirty-six, which made it a very different show from what it was when it began. There had been "a drying up of the creative thrust," as he said. Harper and Leachman had left, and Asner wanted his own show. MacLeod was getting tentative offers for other shows.

The producers agreed: Either major changes would have to come to the show soon, or they'd have to end it. Burns himself looked forward to the chance to give his long-neglected movie-writing career its due once he was away from the grind of weekly television. Tinker and Burns proposed ending the show the next season, at the end of its sixth year. Brooks pushed for a seventh, hoping to hold on to his success just a little longer. He was sure he and the other producers and writers could squeeze one more good year's worth of stories out of their beloved characters. Tinker and Burns agreed, and it was settled. They had become a workplace family like the one on their own show, but now they would have to leave it behind, for everyone's best interest.

Moore didn't quite feel the same drive to end things, but she understood that Brooks, Burns, and their staff craved new creative challenges. As the imminent end of the show was announced late in its sixth season—the seventh would be its last—she told the public that she, too, hungered for more substantial roles. She did, in fact, want to get back to dancing more, perhaps in a musical variety series, as she admitted to her friend Betty White. She was scared, but she fired up her trademark smile and told curious reporters, "Yes, this is a creatively healthy move we're making. Quit while you're still on top!"

She didn't discuss her future with any of her other coworkers. She didn't want to lose one moment of their remaining time together in the present.

A year after announcing the end of her show, and with a year left to go, Moore decided to try taking on a variety show. It would allow her to return to singing and dancing, which was what she'd always envisioned doing with her career. Even better, it was an idea she could test out before *The Mary Tyler Moore Show* ended. CBS happily handed an hour of airtime over to one of its biggest stars for a variety special in January 1976, a time of year normally stuffed with reruns anyway.

Moore hired Jack Good, who'd created the Monkees' *33⅓ Revolutions Per Monkee* special. He presented her with his concept: The show,

Mary's Incredible Dream, would tell the history of the world through song and dance numbers, from creation through World War II to the present—bookended by Moore slipping into and out of a dream state. Moore thought the idea was divine—edgy, mind-blowing, avant-garde kind of stuff. She gushed about it to all of her friends. She told every interviewer she spoke to about it. Hollywood columnist Marilyn Beck reported that Moore had shown screener tapes to so many friends that White teased her, "It's a shame you don't put it on TV, instead of showing it door to door."

However, when it finally did air, it turned out viewers and critics weren't quite ready for such a mishmash of songs, glitz, production numbers, religion, philosophy, angel-versus-devil battle, history, and psychedelic dream sequence. They did not appreciate spending an hour watching Moore as a pink angel, floating among religious symbols and singing "Morning Has Broken"; Broadway star Ben Vereen as a singing, dancing, glittery green devil; a version of the "Hallelujah Chorus" set in heaven; a review-of-history version of "Sh-Boom"; and Jerome Kern's "She Didn't Say Yes" rewritten to tell the story of Eve. It bombed in the ratings, and reviewers deemed it indulgent and weird. The *New York Times* called it "a landmark in TV vulgarity." It ran once, never to be repeated.

One of its few fans was Joe Rainone, who'd gotten too busy with working full-time at his family's printing business to write his detailed weekly letters to *Mary Tyler Moore* anymore. He'd thought a little more about Tinker's interest in him, the possibility of trying to work for the show, but he just didn't see himself going into television as a career. He was the accountant for the family business. That was what he did.

He still tuned into the show every week, however, and didn't miss *Mary's Incredible Dream.* When he read the vitriolic reviews of the special, he decided to write to Moore again to tell her he'd loved the production. Moore returned to the United States from Russia, where she'd hosted a network special about the Bolshoi Ballet, facing a barrage of criticism for her beloved project—and that nice letter from Rainone.

She sent a handwritten thank-you note in reply: "It seems like you were the only one who got what we were trying to do."

Rainone was inspired to take up his weekly letter-writing to *The Mary Tyler Moore Show* again, continuing it until the end of the series.

Luckily, at the time, Moore still had her sitcom to return to. And even in its final seasons, *The Mary Tyler Moore Show* wasn't finished making television history. In some ways, it seemed invigorated by approaching the finish line, especially compared with *All in the Family*. *The Mary Tyler Moore Show*'s longtime partner in history-making TV limped along, a shadow of its former self, no end in sight. Rob Reiner and Sally Struthers were preparing to leave the show, and Archie's purchase of Kelsey's Bar would do little to revive the flagging series. *All in the Family* was reinforcing Tinker's and the producers' decision to name an end date.

The sixth-season episode of *Mary Tyler Moore* that would become many viewers' favorite of all time started out as just another half hour of television. The show scheduled to air October 25, 1975, had a funny plot, sure, but so did many *Mary Tyler Moore* episodes. This particular script featured the funeral of Chuckles the Clown, a recurring character who hosted the children's show on WJM.

Producer David Lloyd had written the script at home, just as he wrote all of his scripts, stopping occasionally to laugh at something he'd written. He knew in this case that what he was writing was at least a little daring, and pretty funny. As Moore recalled, "It was the first time anybody had attempted a comedy episode about a tragic situation: the nervous giggles some people get in the midst of a funeral, out of an awareness that this is the one time you should never, ever laugh."

The idea came from a variety of sources. One was Brooks's memory of what his mother and aunt once did: "They got the giggles at a funeral when I was a kid, like nine years old," Brooks says. "I was humiliated." Another was something one of the writers had recently read about a guy who had died when, for unknown reasons, he'd put a large, empty stewed tomato can over his head. His fellow workers couldn't get over what a funny way that was to die. Lloyd turned in a script Brooks and Burns loved, full of his "mordant take on what is funny and what isn't," as Burns says. A line from Lou, as written by Lloyd, elegantly summed up the deeper meaning of the episode— finding humor in the inevitable end. "It's a release," he explains to Murray. "A kind of defense mechanism. It's like whistling in a grave- yard. You try to make light of something because it scares you. We laugh at death because we know death will have the last laugh on us."

The first sign that the episode would be something truly memora- ble came when Moore fretted over the subject matter, worrying it was "too sad." But Tinker, Brooks, and Burns outvoted her and proceeded with the script. She conceded to their expertise.

But then Sandrich declined to direct it. Joan Darling, who'd left behind an acting career on television and in the theater to join the growing number of women pursuing directing, took the reins for "Chuckles Bites the Dust" from Sandrich. She had gotten her start directing the pilot of Lear's *Mary Hartman, Mary Hartman,* and had gone on to direct other shows for Lear as well as MTM's *Doc.* Despite a legend to the contrary, Sandrich insists he didn't object to the mate- rial. "That's been so distorted," he says. Every season, he'd direct only sixteen of the twenty-two *Mary Tyler Moore* episodes so that he could have the freedom to do other shows occasionally. He was scheduled to work at about the same time on the American version of *Upstairs Downstairs,* called *Beacon Hill.* Weinberger asked Sandrich, "The week you're gone, would you like us to do 'Chuckles Bites the Dust'? Or do you want us to do the Eileen Heckart episode?" Heckart occasionally appeared on the show as Mary's brash aunt, and Sandrich particularly loved working with her. He chose her episode.

This immediately gave much of the cast and crew the impression that he was worried the topic was too sensitive. The network, too, had balked, though, as usual, Brooks and Burns forged ahead with Tinker's blessing.

Darling, however, was thrilled to get the assignment—not because she knew it would be a classic, but because the work would get her a much-needed paycheck. She was also happy for every chance she got to prove that women could direct. The first time she drove to the studio, she had to pull off to the side of the road to calm her nerves.

The episode itself posed its share of challenges. Moore pulled Brooks and Burns aside during rehearsal and told them, "I can't do this." They worried she was backtracking to her original concerns about the episode, but now she had a different problem: She could barely keep herself from cracking up every time she had to refer to one of Chuckles's characters, "Mr. Fee-Fi-Fo." And if she laughed too early in the episode, it would ruin the effect of her losing control at the funeral; she had to contain herself even while everyone in the scenes with her was laughing. Every time she'd make eye contact with Asner or MacLeod, she'd lose it.

Then the pretaping run-through had several problems that echoed the infamous pilot disaster five years earlier. Moore was still laughing, while the crew was . . . not. "We had a fairly elderly crew, and as we rehearsed it, they were not laughing their asses off," Asner recalls. The reaction of the crew was usually a reliable indicator of how a show would play, so now the producers and actors were getting worried. Perhaps laughing at mortality *was* pushing beyond the limit, but it was now Friday, too late to scrap the episode. "Just do the best you can," Brooks told the cast. "We'll try to write new stuff later and see if we can salvage it, but for now we're at a complete loss."

Not only that, but the run-through had timed out at about five minutes under the required airtime. Burns instructed the actors to "go out there and play the hell out of it" so the audience's laughter would fill the time. If there was still a deficit, they shouldn't worry too much—the writers would likely be adding new material in later weeks, anyway.

But somehow, the episode magically coalesced at showtime. The audience actually did laugh when Murray, Lou, and Mary found out about Chuckles's death, caused by an overzealous parade elephant that mistook the clown, costumed as Peter Peanut, for a real snack. They laughed even more when Murray started rattling off one-liners about the ridiculous incident. "Each time he'd do one, I'd force myself to create the biggest belly laugh I could, which evidently infected the audience pretty well because by the time we finished the scene, we'd extended it by a minute," Asner recalls. "By the end of the show, the audience had laughed so much, we had extended it five minutes."

Luckily, Moore didn't join the audience in those extra guffaws until her well-timed breakdown in the middle of Chuckles's funeral. Her costars did their best not to talk to her between scenes, or even look at her, for fear of setting her off on another of her giggling fits.

The episode won praise as soon as it aired—in fact, as soon as it was shot. *M*A*S*H* writer Ken Levine was in the studio audience that night, and he knew while he was sitting in the bleachers that he was watching what might be the single greatest half-hour comedy in television history. He and his writing partner, David Isaacs—who'd recently gotten a rejection letter from Lloyd—walked out of the studio in awe. "Do you think we could ever write anything that good?" Levine asked. Isaacs responded, "No one can."

Future *TV Guide* critic Bruce Fretts, nine years old at the time, watched the episode at home with his family—the CBS Saturday night lineup, with *Bob Newhart* and *Carol Burnett*, had become a weekly ritual for them, as for so many other families across the country. They called the stars "the Holy Trinity of Comedy." Not every episode of *Mary Tyler Moore* was allowed on when Bruce was in the room; his parents would decide each week based on the synopsis in *TV Guide*. (You know, the one you'd check to see if it was an (R)—for rerun—or not.) When Mary met a hooker in jail, for instance, that was a no-go.

But when Bruce saw the "Chuckles" episode, even at his young age, he knew something special had happened. He didn't know yet how to articulate why it was so funny, so memorable, but he would figure out why—and grow up to write for that Holy Bible of television.

(He would even think of that episode when attending his mother's funeral thirty-seven years later. "I chuckled a bit, albeit quietly, at the memory of my mom crying with laughter at her beloved Mary bursting out in guffaws," Fretts recalls. "It was an oddly comforting reminiscence that brought a smile to my face on an otherwise sad day.")

In his *Los Angeles Times* column, Cecil Smith raved about the "rare experience" the episode provided: "It was not only a very funny show, but . . . it actually disturbed you, which TV comedy almost never does. . . . It had a bizarre reality that grabbed you where you live—it bothered you. To bring a story like this off in the confines of TV's comic strips is really quite exceptional. It points up again the high degree of skillful ensemble acting that sets *The Mary Tyler Moore Show* apart." *Time* magazine said: "In another moving and improbably funny show, Chuckles the Clown, while dressed up as a peanut, was stomped to death by an elephant. Divorce, death and departure were part of the show's workings; MTM possessed at least that much realism." *Washington Post* critic Tom Shales later remembered the episode as a "bittersweet riot about laughing in the face of death. . . . Watching this and other perfectly crafted [*Mary Tyler Moore* episodes], one is reminded not only of the show's high standards and high quality, but of how caught up we were in the lives of the characters, and how caught up they seemed to be in ours." Just a year after the show had aired, *Newsday* writer Bruce Cook had already deemed it "a classic."

Darling earned her first Emmy nomination for the show, and Lloyd won for the script. Darling's reputation as a director got such a boost that she started receiving film scripts from major studios to consider. The episode would show up on virtually every future list of "greatest episodes of all time," usually at the top.

It also got the producers an invitation to the Cannes Television Festival's competition, another one of those bizarre real-life incidents that played out like an episode of their own show. Weinberger, Davis, and Brooks headed to France for the occasion. "We go in, and they're showing the show," Brooks recalls. "There are around sixty people in the room. They have things where you can put what language you want, because it was a dubbed French version. So we're listening to it in English and they're listening to it in whatever language they want to listen to it in, and we didn't get one laugh. Except at a certain point, because we were getting no laughs, we were falling on the floor laughing. It was as inappropriate as the show itself!"

When the cast returned to the set in late summer of 1976, they knew the clock was ticking. "This is the first day of the first week of the last year!" Mary announced.

MacLeod was standing next to her. "Mary, I just want to thank you for all this," he said.

"Gavs, don't start now," she joked. "We have a whole season to get through."

Moore still wasn't sure what she'd do after the finale. Those blank pages in her calendar after the show's end loomed. She felt whatever came next would be a true test of her talent: If she didn't make good, it would seem she'd just been lucky up until now. Asner was anxious, too—he'd rather stick around for a year at least, he thought. He had the best of both worlds, a steady comedy job and summers off to shoot dramatic movies and guest roles. He'd had his best hiatus the year before, in 1975: He played a Chicano bush pilot in the TV movie *Hey, I'm Alive* (with *All in the Family*'s Sally Struthers); the owner of a pro football team that hires a mule as a kicker in Disney's *Gus;* and a Nazi army escapee in the miniseries *Rich Man, Poor Man.* He didn't want to have to find a new day job—Tinker had shifted *Mary Tyler Moore*'s production schedule just to accommodate some of Asner's *Rich Man* shooting, a rare gesture he might not get from future employers.

But for now, they had a show to do, and *Mary Tyler Moore* wasn't about to take things easy, even in its last stretch: Two of the show's highest-profile guest stars were booked to appear in its final days.

The cast didn't think it could get more exciting than landing Walter Cronkite in the show's fourth season—until First Lady Betty

Ford signed on for an appearance in the show's final year. Ford was famously drunk when she turned up on the series as herself in its seventh season, taping her appearance not long before she checked into Long Beach Naval Hospital for rehab and then subsequently founded her own clinic. The scene called for a brief phone call between her and Mary, with Moore's half filmed on the set and Ford's shot at a hotel in Washington, D.C. Moore and a crew flew to the capital for the occasion, and were welcomed at the White House by a smiling, but slurring, First Lady. The fifteen-minute shoot was an hour and a half behind schedule, and rehearsals fizzled since Ford couldn't remember her lines.

Finally, Moore recalled an approach her costar Julie Andrews had used on the movie *Thoroughly Modern Millie* when she worked with Alzheimer's-stricken costar Bea Lillie. Moore stood next to the camera and said each of Ford's lines, one by one, and had her repeat them: "Hello, Mary?" she began. "This is Betty Ford." The scene came out just fine on film. Ford recalled the experience of television stardom as "so much fun."

For the show's third-to-last episode, the producers figured out an ingenious way to use guest star Johnny Carson to spruce up what could have been a standard "flashback" episode full of clips from previous shows. Mary gives one of her infamous parties and is sure this will finally be a good one; her friend, a congresswoman, is bringing none other than the famous talk show host as her guest. But before Carson arrives, the lights in Mary's building go out, and the cast sits in the dark reminiscing. When Carson finally makes an "appearance," it's still pitch black, and all we hear is his voice before he has to leave. Even though it was a "clip show," the episode served as the perfect denouement to one of the show's long-running gags, Mary's rotten parties.

The Carson appearance was a particular point of pride for Brooks: "a huge guest star, who never guest-starred on anything, and we never showed his face." Carson agreed to do the show because Weinberger used to write for him, and the writers thought it would be particularly funny if they reversed what would be the standard reaction to booking such a great cameo in their show's waning days. For the record, Carson really did come to the stage to shoot the appearance live—but only the studio audience that night, who saw him once the lights came up, knew for sure.

One giant question was imminent for the writing staff: How would they end the esteemed *Mary Tyler Moore Show*? The producers knew the ending would *not* have anything to do with her finding a husband. In the six years they'd been on the air, they'd yet to find a date who was right for Mary to go the distance with, so they weren't about to start trying now. Every time they'd thought, *Maybe this will be the guy*, they'd see the actor in question on the screen with Mary and think, *No.* They felt more frustrated by Mary's dating options than Mary Richards herself did. Talented, good-looking, comedic actors in their thirties were hard to come by in television. All the best ones preferred film. The producers finally acknowledged, *This is never going to happen.* Unlike their forced miscasting of Rhoda's husband Joe, a character intrinsic to that show's original premise, they never needed to give Mary a love interest if they didn't find the right one.

Only one gentleman ever had a shot with Mary, as far as the producers were concerned: Lou Grant. During the final seasons, Brooks and Burns purposely built in hints that Mary and Lou might get together in the end. Their relationship tension culminated—or, more accurately, fizzled—in an episode in which Mary asks Lou on a date. (Yes, she calls him "Lou" on their date, without incident.) But they find only friendly feelings between them. The deal is sealed with an attempted kiss that ends in hysterical laughter—and an immediate return to calling him "Mr. Grant." "That moment when they kissed was a cop-out for me," Brooks says. "I thought Ed was sexy, I thought people saw him as sexy, and they had great chemistry."

Moore, however, would have no talk of Mary and Lou as a couple, and the producers respected her wishes. "We thought it would be interesting to get a Tracy-Hepburn thing going on," Burns recalls. "It was not far-fetched to us. But it was one of the few times Mary ever told us she couldn't get behind one of our ideas. She said no, so we wrote the episode where they tried to kiss instead."

That episode was the show's second-to-last. Which meant the producers still had no idea what would happen in the finale.

Treva Silverman returned to the States in early 1977, first stopping in her hometown of New York. She called Allan Burns from across the country, just to say hi and tell him she was back on U.S. soil. She was preparing to move back to Los Angeles and return to writing pilots and movie scripts. "We're doing the last taping in two weeks," he told her. "Come." Two weeks later, she was on a plane back to Los Angeles.

Around the same time, Joe Rainone wrote to Carol Straughn, Brooks and Burns's assistant, asking if he could attend one of the last season's tapings. He understood that the finale would be a hot ticket and by invitation only, but he'd love to squeeze onto the bleachers for one of the other remaining episodes if possible. Straughn, a glamorous beauty with massive black curls, wrote back with great news: She'd gotten two tickets, so he could come as her date. It wasn't a *date* date, of course, but he didn't mind. He set off across the country in his Corvette, timing his arrival a few days before the finale.

Brooks, Burns, Weinberger, Daniels, Lloyd, and Ellison—those who had written the bulk of the episodes of the last few seasons—all gathered to write that last episode, their 168th. They were petrified by the pressure. They knew that whatever they did at work that week would be seen and discussed by all of America. As for plot, they were stumped, mortified at the level of scrutiny. They knew they'd bring Rhoda and Phyllis back one way or another for a final appearance. Beyond that, they weren't sure.

Meanwhile, as February 1977 began, the cast was gathering for their final week of work together, whether or not they had a script. "It's been a great seven years," Sandrich told the cast in a pep talk of sorts. "And we'll probably never have another job like this." They spent all of their time together—no lunches apart, no dance class, no alone time in dressing rooms. Finally, word came down from the office: The final half hour would revolve around massive layoffs at WJM after a new owner takes over. Everyone would be fired except Ted. The final joke would be on everyone *except* the man who'd played the buffoon for so long. A good joke, sure, but also a sly indictment of the local news business, which, in the time that *Mary Tyler Moore* had been on the air, had become as ratings-obsessed as the national network giants. Vincent Gardenia, known best for his role as Frank Lorenzo on *All in the Family*, guest-starred as the new station owner, a thankless role. The cast tried to include him in their lunches and be as friendly as possible, though Gardenia was in an awkward position, crashing the funeral of one of America's favorite shows.

The writers managed to churn out three-quarters of a final script in time for the scheduled rehearsal on Wednesday that week. The actors struggled not to cry through the whole first reading, they were so charged with emotion. But the script itself didn't quite work. Betty White wasn't in it, and neither was Georgia Engel. Jay Sandrich, after reading it through with the cast, called Brooks and Burns to tell them, "Here's what we on the stage think." That night, the writers rewrote.

The major problem, however, remained: The writers still didn't have a killer idea for the final scene. At last, one of them—no one is sure who—came up with having Ted recite the lyrics to the World War I–era marching song "It's a Long Way to Tipperary" on the air in a ridiculous effort to be profound. From there, the final scene built: The whole cast could sing it in the end as a poignant-but-funny good-bye. White and Engel could join the newsroom cast in the tearful send-off.

A complete and revised script appeared on Thursday, the day the cast was set to do blocking with the cameras. Sandrich sent the camera operators away anyway, to give the actors private time with the scenes. When Asner said his final line for the first time—"I treasure you people"—he did it so well that everyone on the stage broke up in tears.

Sandrich told Asner, "Don't do that line reading again until it's time," and told Moore, "Hold off on your tears as long as you can."

The final touch on the scene came from an improvised moment. During the rehearsal, the entire cast embraced in the newsroom, and one of them said they needed a Kleenex, at which point they all shuffled over to the tissue box on Mary's desk together. Sandrich wanted to put that group hug, complete with Kleenex-shuffle, on the show. Burns thought it was a little maudlin. But after the producers discussed it, they decided it would stay in. Sometimes maudlin worked.

Leachman squeezed in a final clash with Sandrich for her triumphant return. In the scene in which Lou brings Rhoda and Phyllis to Mary's apartment to cheer her up, Leachman jumped in front of Harper without warning, going off script. Phyllis, Leachman explained, was the one who did it. Cloris didn't. Sandrich screamed his final, *"Cloris!!!"* Leachman continued to explain: Phyllis could not let Rhoda in front of her, and she would play the scene no other way. It was hard to argue with her logic.

Getting through the taping of the final episode was another matter altogether, one that required periodic sobbing breaks for cast members, crew, producers, and writers alike. Moore felt like she was reliving every moment of the past seven years with every line. It didn't help that the plot so closely mirrored the real-life situation: Sandrich lost it when Moore's eyes teared up in the final newsroom scene. So did most of the writers who'd come back to watch the final taping, including Treva Silverman. Treva passed Brooks a note during the taping that said, simply: "Transcendent." It was the first time Brooks had seen that word; he would go look it up later, but he got the general idea.

Mary gave a tearjerker of a final speech: "I just wanted you to know that sometimes I get concerned about being a career woman. I get to thinking my job is too important to me, and I tell myself that the people I work with are just the people I work with, and not my family. And last night, I thought, 'What is a family, anyway?' They're just people who make you feel less alone and really loved. And that's what you've done for me. Thank you for being my family."

In a final scene that would become legendary, Moore is the last out the newsroom door, looking back one more time before turning out the lights. During the taping, the crewman who was in charge of dimming the lights was so enraptured that he forgot to do it, so those final few seconds had to be reshot.

The wrap party, held on the lot in the commissary—cleared of its trays and cafeteria lines for the occasion—was charged with excitement, relief, nostalgia, and grief. Their seven-year-long collaboration was now over. Those seven years had encompassed the most important events of most of the cast's, crew's, producers', and directors' lives. Their relationships had extended far past the show itself. Those who made *Mary Tyler Moore*, and their families and friends, mingled among dinner, drinks, and a huge, TV-shaped cake. Treva Silverman reminisced about her time on the show, which seemed several lifetimes away at that point. Pat Nardo visited with old friends and filled them in on how things were going on *Rhoda*. She made peace with Joe Rainone for, years earlier, blocking his letters from circulating to the staff.

As the evening wound down, Moore received a steady stream of well-wishers at the door. Rainone said what might be his last good-bye to her, then turned to head back to his hotel for the night. Allen Ludden was standing nearby, waiting for wife Betty White. "Are you the guy who came from Rhode Island?" Ludden asked a startled Rainone. The *Password* host knew who *he* was? "I've heard all about you!" It was the perfect end to Rainone's strange, seven-year trip through Hollywood.

As MacLeod loaded his dressing room odds and ends into the trunk of his car in the studio parking lot, MTM executive Arthur Price said, "I'm so sorry this is over. What are you going to do now?"

MacLeod, ever the optimist, said, "Don't worry, I'm not going to stop now. My career has always been blessed." He closed the trunk and added, "But nothing will ever be the same as this, either."

Brooks was so wired that he couldn't go home. He and his girl-friend, Holly, slept at the nearby Century Plaza hotel just to come down from the buzz before heading back into real life.

Moore spent the next three weeks with a lump in her throat, mourning the fall of her Camelot. White couldn't think about the last episode without crying.

The *Mary Tyler Moore* team left a permanent reminder of their presence on Soundstage 2, a plaque with an inscription written by Tin-ker: "On this stage a company of loving and talented friends produced a television classic."

The finale would become the benchmark for greatness in the par-ticularly fraught feat of wrapping up multiple years of a popular televi-sion series. And the show itself was instantly recognized as something special, the likes of which were rare. *Time* magazine summed up the show's legacy when its finale aired: "In many places around the U.S., *The Mary Tyler Moore Show* changed the nature of Saturday nights; it even became fashionable to spend them at home. The show turned the situation comedy into something like an art form—a slight art form perhaps, but a highly polished one. MTM was the sitcom that was intellectually respectable. The writing, acting and directing on MTM have been the best ever displayed in TV comedy. Owing much to Moore, who always set a tone of perfectionism, the show has been technically superb and beautifully paced. Former CBS Executive James Aubrey used to say, 'The American public is something I fly over.' But unlike 90% of TV's sitcoms, MTM has always transmitted intel-ligence, along with a rather unique respect for its characters and its audience."

The show had come a long way from the "disaster" *Time* had pre-dicted on the occasion of its premiere seven years earlier.

PART five
PART five
PART five
PART five
PART five
PART five
PART five
PART five

"I don't want anybody to make any fuss.
When I go, I just want to be stood outside
in the garbage with my hat on."
—Lou Grant

Leaving Camelot

(1977–present)

In the summer of 1977, Joe Rainone quit his job at the family business. Intrigued by his adventures with *Mary Tyler Moore*, he wanted to see more of the country. With the show over, he felt his "anchor was gone," he says. He told his family, "I'm just going to be gone one day, and then you'll know I left. No good-byes." (Howard Arnell would be proud.) In July, he got into his 1973 yellow Corvette and wandered west from Rhode Island, armed with a crate full of brochures he'd collected by writing away to tourist sites for information.

Throughout the Midwest, and on toward the coast, he sent postcards to a list of his favorite people. Mary Tyler Moore and Grant Tinker got one from the Grand Canyon.

When he reached Los Angeles, he stopped by the MTM studio. He walked over from his seedy motel on Ventura Boulevard, the kind of place that usually rents by the hour. But the *Mary Tyler Moore* set was gone, its staff and cast dispersed. He went to the office to say hi to Carol Straughn, who'd so generously brought him to the finale five months earlier. She was friendly, but busy helping her boss, Allan Burns, with a new project—Ed Asner's spin-off, *Lou Grant*.

Rainone wandered over to the MTM administration building and found Tinker's secretary. He introduced himself: "I'm an old friend of Grant's from *The Mary Tyler Moore Show*."

Tinker came right out and welcomed Rainone into his office. The two sat and chatted, Tinker propping his white-sneakered feet up on his executive desk. Tinker told Rainone tales from his own post-college drive around the country. After about twenty minutes of small talk, Tinker asked, "What are you going to do now?"

"I think I'll head back," Joe said. It was time to move on.

At the same time, James L. Brooks and Allan Burns faced perhaps the toughest decision of their careers: What does one do once one has created a television classic and guided it to a perfect end? What does one do after leaving the best job of one's life?

Brooks had no doubt: He wanted to keep working with their team, to stay with at least part of the family they'd built over the previous seven years—Stan Daniels, Dave Davis, and Ed. Weinberger—to keep making great television. But the group felt that MTM Enterprises, their onetime Camelot, had gotten too big for its own good. As *Mary Tyler Moore* came to an end, the company still had a slew of shows on the air: *The Bob Newhart Show, Rhoda, The Tony Randall Show,* and Ed Asner's and Betty White's own new series coming soon. Many more were in the works, and Brooks wanted his group to follow in the steps of their hero, Grant Tinker, instead of continuing to work for his growing company. He wanted them to run their own production company.

But when they asked Burns to join them, he decided to stick with MTM and *Lou Grant*. He and Brooks had talked their old boss at *Room 222*, Gene Reynolds, into executive-producing the new show. He'd been working on *M*A*S*H* since *Room 222*, and they knew he'd be a great asset to their spin-off, which would be an hour-long, issue-driven drama. Brooks and Burns had gone to Reynolds's office at *M*A*S*H,* which was now in its fifth season on the air, to ask for his help on *Lou Grant.* When they walked in, he was ending a tense phone call that seemed to be about his contract. They knew then that they had a shot.

Once they pitched the show concept to him, they could see his eyes sparkling with excitement. They asked him to join them. He demurred, saying he was mid-negotiation but would consider it. After a few tense weeks, he called them: He was in.

But in the meantime, Brooks decided he was out. Burns objected to the idea of leaving MTM behind, and to abandoning their character's spin-off. He decided to run *Lou Grant* with Reynolds while working on his long-abandoned movie scripts on the side.

Brooks left MTM with Daniels, Davis, and Weinberger, a formidable team. Each was now regarded as a giant in sitcom writing in his own right, and the group's first project was on the air the very next fall: the sitcom *Taxi,* based, in fact, on an article Grant Tinker had owned the rights to. When they read the *New York* magazine piece, "Night-Shifting for the Hip Fleet," they knew that was what they wanted for their show. Brooks in particular wanted to do a "real male show" after years of concentrating so much on women. But Tinker had already optioned the 1975 story. Brooks called his old boss and asked, "Hey, can I have it?"

MTM may have grown, but it hadn't gotten too large for Tinker to lose his familial spirit. He gave the article to them without a second thought, once again renewing Brooks's faith in him as a person and a businessman. Tinker was, Brooks thought, what it meant to be a righteous man, a standard to live up to. With that one gesture, Brooks knew he would always be able to count on his *Mary Tyler Moore* family to back him up, even when he was on his own.

The show, about a ragtag group of cabdrivers in New York City, built on the tradition of *The Mary Tyler Moore Show* with its intricate characters and the workplace family at its center. The character of Elaine Nardo, an art gallery receptionist/driver played by Marilu Henner, was named for Brooks and Burns's onetime secretary, Pat Nardo. Actor Tony Danza's character, a losing boxer named Tony Banta, paid tribute to Nardo's writing partner, Gloria Banta. The producers threw themselves into the project, scared of the inevitable comparisons with *Mary Tyler Moore*. They also found themselves on a completely different scene, with a predominantly young, predominantly male cast. "The *Taxi* group was a very different, gritty, lively, raucous group," Brooks said. "*Taxi* parties were always great parties. *Mary* parties you got home early."

Burns, meanwhile, was ready to be himself instead of part of the group, after years of writing with the powerful force known as Jim Brooks. He got his shot at running a show without Brooks when *Lou Grant* debuted in 1977. Brooks and Burns worked together to create the show before Brooks's departure, and decided the best way to make it stick was by moving their sitcom character into his own drama. The outlook was promising: The show, which followed Lou as he tackled issues at a new newspaper job, earned great reviews right away, unlike its predecessor. "Ed Asner finally brings something fresh to the beat—an original, multidimensional character," *Newsweek* said.

Even though TV was now officially the populist medium—it was in a staggering 71 million homes—Burns was still dreaming of writing for film. He loved doing *Lou Grant,* but, as ever, felt that it was stalling his longtime ambition. He handed over most of the daily show-running duties to Gene Reynolds while he carved out some extra writing time and got to work. Finally, the screenwriting career he'd been putting off for the past decade came to life when he wrote the script for the 1979 drama *A Little Romance,* based on the novel *E=Mc2 Mon Amour.* The story follows a teen, played by Diane Lane, who falls in love in France and runs away from her objecting mother with the help of a pickpocket, played by Laurence Olivier. The film made Lane a celebrated wunderkind, landing her on the cover of *Time* magazine as one of "Hollywood's Whiz Kids," and secured Burns an Oscar nomination for Best Adapted Screenplay. (He ultimately lost to *Kramer vs. Kramer.*)

It was also the work Burns was most proud of in his life thus far. Clearly, he had at least a little talent of his own.

His other concurrent script, for *Butch and Sundance: The Early Years,* came out a few months later and bombed. Still, it seemed Burns had achieved his ideal career, shuttling between *Lou Grant* and movie writing. The occasional fizzle was to be expected in *any* movie career. With *Rhoda* over by 1978, his ties to Brooks were severed, but both were now well on their way to their own separate, if parallel, trajectories.

The same year Burns's two films came out, Brooks's first screenplay made it to the big screen as well. The romantic comedy *Starting Over,* featuring Candice Bergen, Burt Reynolds, and Jill Clayburgh in a love triangle, jump-started Brooks's big-screen career, with *New York Times* critic Janet Maslin saying it was "fast and funny while break[ing] new ground." *All the Presidents' Men* director Alan J. Pakula brought it to the screen and allowed Brooks to be more involved in the filmmaking process than most screenwriters normally were, but Brooks did not enjoy being far more sidelined from his own creation than he ever was in television. From then on, he determined, he'd be a writer-director. But he watched Pakula closely in anticipation of his own directing career, and learned one piece of invaluable directing wisdom from him: "Take that nap. Every man's a master of his own energy."

Both Brooks and Burns were nominated for Writers Guild of America awards in 1980 for their scripts. They attended the awards together, but lost to Jerzy Kosinski, who wrote the adaptation of his own novel *Being There* for a comedy starring Peter Sellers and Shirley MacLaine.

While Brooks and Burns forged promising careers beyond television, most of the *Mary Tyler Moore* writers whom Brooks and Burns had so caringly mentored were discovering the hard truth—that the time they'd spent on such a successful show was a fluke, a freak occurrence in an industry that usually manufactured failure.

When Treva Silverman got back from Europe, she was dazzled by how the TV business had changed in the two and a half years that she had been away. Many more women were now TV executives, with the power to be decision makers. She was getting a lot of offers. She wrote and produced several sitcoms, wrote innumerable pilots, and got involved as a script doctor for movies, which she found she liked. To her surprise, diving into someone else's drafts appealed to her.

Michael Douglas phoned her. He had an unreleasable film. The name was *Romancing the Stone*. The script was good, the acting was good; the problem was that nobody liked the female lead, the character of Joan Wilder, played by his costar, Kathleen Turner. Focus groups found her icy and cold and couldn't relate to her, much less root for her. As producer, Douglas had only a limited amount of money he could spend on retakes—they had to make her likable in her first scene or else the picture was going to fail. The problem was Kathleen Turner was alone in her apartment in that first scene; there was nobody to talk to.

Aha. Silverman rewrote the first scene so that Turner had a sweet little cat. Turner talked baby talk to the cat. She gave the cat specially prepared cat food. She adored that cat, and the audiences adored *Romancing the Stone*. It was shades of the unlikable Rhoda, saved by Phyllis's daughter's affection, all over again.

Treva then wrote her own romantic comedy script; lyricist Ed Kleban read it and showed it to the creator-choreographer-director of *A Chorus Line,* Michael Bennett. Bennett read it and flew her to New York to meet him. They clicked, and Bennett told her he wanted her to write his next musical. Thrilled, she moved back to New York to work with him. After searching around for a topic, Bennett was intrigued by the idea of her taking off and living in Europe, and decided he wanted her to write a musical based on her European adventures.

Working with Bennett was one of the happiest and most creative times of her life. There was an eight-month workshop period where she wrote and rewrote and rewrote her play, and that was "as close," she says, "as she could come to heaven." Michael taught her to explore a character from an actor's point of view, to mine the truth of one's experience, and to be fearless. They worked together for four years, and at one point Michael asked her to come to Boston to work on *Dream Girls* with him. She realized she felt totally at home in theater. Her show was headed to Broadway and it was all coming true.

As she was getting dressed one morning to go to a meeting with Michael, she got a call—Michael had disappeared, nobody knew where he was, he had abandoned the show. Nobody knew why. As the weeks passed and Michael was unfindable, it turned out that he had become ill with AIDS. He never came back to theater work and spent the rest of his short life seeking a cure. Treva was devastated by his illness and by the sudden out-of-the-blue crashing of the world around her. She says that she divides her life into two sections: before Michael and after Michael.

Every now and then, she wonders what her life would have been if she hadn't taken those years off, if she had stayed on with *The Mary Tyler Moore Show*. Did it harm her career? Did she leave at the wrong time? The best answer she can come up with is that, yes, it most likely hurt her career. But then again, how do you weigh one turn in the road against another? If she hadn't left, she never would have worked with Michael, never would have had those four glorious years of learning from a master, never would have written what she considers the best thing she's ever done.

Recently she revisited her play and fell in love with it all over again. She decided that she was going back to the theater world, has rewritten and updated her play, and is having a first reading in New York. And she is looking forward to another turn in the road.

Susan Silver worked on the teen TV comedy *Square Pegs* in the '80s, growing increasingly annoyed with the disorganization in the industry, not to mention the drugs, before getting fed up with Hollywood for good. She moved back to New York to work in political campaigns and nonprofits instead. Gail Parent was one of the few *Mary Tyler Moore* alumnae to strike gold again: She wrote for *The Golden Girls,* where she was once again the only woman in the writers' room—even on a groundbreaking show that focused on four older women.

The women's personal lives were more fraught than those of their peers as well. Silver never married again; ironically, her ex-husband went on to produce *Married with Children.* Parent married four times, but she appreciated the precious years in between when she was single: "I would lie in a king-size bed and think, *How could somebody else fit in here?*" she says. "I had complete control over my life."

None of the women were sure whether they were running from marriage because of their feminist instincts, or if marriage wasn't built for driven women like them. For Marilyn Suzanne Miller, it seemed like the latter: She lived with one boyfriend who told her the home office was off-limits to her. "If you want to write," he told her, "you've got to leave." Another boyfriend, a press secretary, whispered lovingly to her, "There'll only be one career in my house." She had plenty of boyfriends and lived with several of them, but she always felt like she was "stuffing herself away." She often made more than they did. "I was dating guys in their thirties and surpassing them, and that made things rough."

When Pat Nardo got married a few years after *The Mary Tyler Moore Show* ended, she and writer Sybil Adelman (now Sybil Sage) took a photo of their left hands with their wedding rings on, just to document what they knew was a rare moment: The two of them were married at the same time.

Nardo, naturally, saw the professional opportunity in her new life circumstances. She hadn't forgotten what she'd learned on *Mary Tyler Moore*: Real life is always rife with sitcom possibilities. She spun her marriage into TV comedy—and *almost* made it big. When she and Banta left *Rhoda* in 1977, that marked the end of their partnership, and Banta's writing career. (She instead went into producing, which eventually led her into the executive ranks at the Comedy Central network in its early years.) But Nardo started her own production company and in 1983 sold her dream project to ABC. *It's Not Easy* was loosely based on Nardo's experiences marrying a Warren Beatty–gorgeous, wealthy man she met in London named Richard Black. She fell for him so hard that she didn't pay much heed to the massive complications his ex-wife and children would bring to her life.

The show was to star Gerald McRaney and Larry Breeding as the former and new husbands of a character played by Carlene Watkins (Ed. Weinberger's real-life wife). The pilot went beautifully, and the network immediately committed to thirteen episodes of the series. But then *Simon & Simon,* McRaney's series on CBS, got a last-minute reprieve from cancellation, which meant he had to pull out of Nardo's project. Soon afterward, Breeding was killed in a car accident. Nardo was in production with a thirteen-episode commitment and no cast.

Bert Convy and Ken Howard stepped into the leading roles, but the show was never quite the same. Even though the *New York Times* called it "one of the more promising" series of the season, the all-important cast chemistry Nardo had learned so much about on *Mary Tyler Moore* had vanished from the project. *It's Not Easy* lived out its on-air commitment, then ended, one more cautionary tale about the unpredictability of the TV business.

Nardo and Black eventually divorced.

Of course, the MTM cachet did lead plenty of its alumni into long and respectable television careers. Writer-producer Ed. Weinberger created *The Cosby Show* and *Amen.* Director Jay Sandrich went on to oversee most episodes of *The Cosby Show* as well as episodes of *Two and a Half Men* and *The Golden Girls.* Writer David Lloyd worked on *Frasier* and *Cheers.* Writer Monica Johnson wrote the Albert Brooks film *Lost in America.* Writer Karyl Geld (now Karyl Miller) went on to pen episodes of *My Sister Sam, Kate & Allie,* and *The Cosby Show.* And writer Sybil Sage went on to *Northern Exposure* and *Growing Pains.*

In all, being a former MTMer wasn't a bad life. "We got a lot because of the MTM name," Nardo says. "We were stars."

After their concurrent string of awards nominations for their post–*Mary Tyler Moore* screenplays, Brooks and Burns drifted apart. They stayed in touch but didn't see each other as often.

Brooks was consumed in a new project. After he collected his accolades for *Starting Over,* Paramount sent him Larry McMurtry's book *Terms of Endearment,* which follows thirty years of a contentious relationship between an overprotective mother and her stubborn daughter. The studio saw it as a potential vehicle for a specific actress—Brooks would never reveal who—but he didn't want to write it with any "preconditions." He did, however, want to write the script—he had wanted to do a mother-daughter story for some time, ever since writing scenes for Rhoda and her mother—and he convinced Paramount to option it without their actress attached. The studio's president, Michael Eisner, had faith in Brooks's abilities: "I think you'll do a good enough job so that if we don't want to make it I can sell it someplace else," the executive told the writer.

Once again, Brooks was back to writing distinctive leading lady roles, with men as their supporting players—though he did invent one standout male role, Garrett Breedlove, a swaggering astronaut and randy suitor to the mother character. When Brooks turned his finished script in, he found himself in slightly familiar territory: The executives didn't get that it was funny. "No, no, that's a funny line," he told them on more than one occasion.

"Yes, you mean witty," they would say.

"No," he would answer, "I mean ha-ha." It was the early days of *Mary Tyler Moore* all over again.

Finally, however, Eisner gave Brooks the go-ahead on his pet project via a note: "*Terms of Endearment.* Go picture at 7½ million. Delivery Xmas of '82." Brooks framed the scrawl and hung it on his office wall.

But the $7.5 million wasn't enough, and Brooks wouldn't do it as a low-budget shoot that wasn't on location. So the film got stuck in turnaround. He tried to sell it elsewhere, but no one bit. Eisner told him, "I still like it. I still like it for seven and a half."

Then Brooks's agent had an idea: Ask MTM Enterprises for the extra money he needed. Arthur Price agreed on the company's behalf, even though his colleagues told him it was a crazy investment. He didn't expect it to make the company money, but he thought it had a chance of breaking even. MTM put up $1 million, and in the end Paramount agreed to spend $9 million.

When it was finally made, the family drama became a showpiece for Shirley MacLaine, whom Brooks wanted for the role of the widowed mother, Aurora Greenway, because she shared his view that the film was a comedy (aside from the tragic ending). Debra Winger played her daughter. And Jack Nicholson took the part of Breedlove, deemed "uncastable" by Brooks himself. To Brooks's relief, Nicholson was happy to take a supporting role, because that willingness had served him well in *Easy Rider* and *Reds*. Even though Brooks had worked with some of the biggest names in TV comedy, bossing around movie stars of such caliber intimidated him. He told Nicholson as much when they started working together. "You can say anything you want to me," Nicholson drawled, setting Brooks at ease. MacLaine proved a gifted on-the-spot comedian, and Nicholson ad-libbed a few of his character's funniest lines.

Nicholson, in turn, was impressed with Brooks's TV-honed ability to figure out right away what was wrong with a scene. "Jim has got that brutal 'Does it work?' very firmly implanted in his mind," Nicholson said at the time. "Even if your mother's dying and this is your favorite line, you still ask, 'Does it work?' " Brooks knew from his long days at *Mary Tyler Moore* in front of a studio audience what would work, what would get a laugh, and what would get a cheap laugh. He excised cheap laughs on the spot.

When the movie finally hit theaters, MacLaine, Nicholson, and

Winger made audiences weep as well as laugh (like ha-ha, especially Nicholson). In the early months of 1984, Los Angeles Film Critics plaques—for best picture, best direction, and best screenplay—piled up on the extra bed in Brooks's office on the Paramount lot. Then the film garnered more Oscar nominations than any other that year, eleven. On the big night, it netted five Oscars, three of which went to Brooks himself: Best Screenplay, Best Director, and Best Picture, beating out *The Right Stuff* and *The Big Chill* among others. In the director category, Brooks beat out Ingmar Bergman, a fact that particularly impressed his old pal Allan Burns.

Even as his life reached this glamorous peak, however, Brooks missed television and didn't rule out returning to the medium where he'd begun his career. In fact, one fleeting moment with his cast from *Terms of Endearment,* during its onslaught of awards, made him miss his *Mary Tyler Moore* family even more. After the New York Film Critics dinner, where the movie had racked up a few more statues, he headed to a crewmember's nearby apartment with Nicholson and MacLaine. Winger hadn't been able to make it, so she called to check in with her costars. When Brooks looked around the room during the phone call, he got choked up: He felt the same camaraderie he'd experienced working late nights on television, but it shimmered and then disappeared before he could take it all in.

He missed the protective bubble he'd lived in back in the *Mary Tyler Moore* days, where he didn't have to obsess over budgets and ticket sales. He found himself constantly dividing the box office take of *Terms of Endearment* by the average $3.20 movie ticket to figure out how many people had seen his film. He didn't like that kind of pressure to perform.

And yet four years later, he found himself writing and directing another Oscar-caliber movie, *Broadcast News,* starring William Hurt, Albert Brooks, and Holly Hunter. Some critics loved its commentary on news-as-entertainment culture, while others thought it was nothing more than a long, slightly updated version of a *Mary Tyler Moore Show* script. It did touch on similar themes, with a twist, namely the timely question of whether working women could "have it all"—a great career and love life and children. It was a theme that would recur in both Brooks's and Burns's post–*Mary Tyler Moore* work.

Brooks invited Burns to an early screening of the film on the studio lot, and Burns thought it was terrific. It felt like watching *Room 222* for the first time all over again. Allan and his wife, Joan, headed to their car afterward and were talking about how much they'd liked it when a woman Allan knew, a fellow writer, caught up with them. "That must kill you," the writer said.

Burns was taken aback. "That's kind of insulting," he said. "Why would I be angry or upset at the fact that he's written a great film? I'm feeling good about it, and you're telling me I should feel bad?" It was an insinuation that would follow him through Hollywood for the rest of his life.

But Burns was still thrilled when *Broadcast News* was nominated for seven Oscars, including Best Screenplay and Best Picture. In all, Brooks would direct nine different actors in Oscar-nominated performances as his career stretched on. He went on to produce several films as well, including *Big* and *Say Anything . . .*, and TV's *The Tracey Ullman Show*, which led to the massive pop cultural force of *The Simpsons*.

Brooks's success didn't surprise his former producing and writing partner one bit. Burns had seen Brooks's talent close up. Occasionally, Burns wished he were still writing with Brooks, though he also knew they likely wouldn't have written screenplays together. It had been the time for them to part professional ways when they did. He felt wistful sometimes, but he wouldn't say he was envious of Brooks's success. He was, in fact, happy for his old friend.

Around the same time, however, Brooks ran into personal troubles: He split with his partner of twenty-seven years, Holly Holmberg Brooks—the flight attendant he'd met while filming *The Mary Tyler Moore Show*. The two endured a nasty-at-times breakup made public by Holmberg Brooks's $100 million lawsuit against the producer.

Holmberg, fifteen years his junior, accused him of not giving her half of their "cohabitation property" from that time, as he'd promised. "As an older man and professional writer," the suit said, "James was powerfully persuasive and exploited plaintiff's relative youth and lack of business and financial experience." They never legally married, but they'd lived as spouses, with Holly even going so far as to take his last name. The two had a son and a daughter, along with Brooks's daughter from his first marriage.

Holmberg Brooks went on to make a career for herself in Hollywood, founding a production company. She'd honed her skills writing for Brooks on *Taxi*. The couple eventually resolved their differences and were friendly again by 2010, when she attended the premiere of his romantic comedy *How Do You Know*.

As Allan Burns's once jet-black hair turned to gray and then to white, he found his initial luck in Hollywood fading away. He did a few projects, in both movies and television, but nothing as successful as Brooks's works of the same era. Many of Burns's TV endeavors lasted for a year or so, nothing more.

His 1989 sitcom on NBC, *FM,* followed an unlucky-in-love radio programming director played by Robert Hays. Though it was produced by MTM, the company didn't have the clout it used to. NBC decided not to pick the show up, and there was little MTM could do about it. Burns appealed to NBC president Brandon Tartikoff, who'd just taken over the job from onetime *Mary Tyler Moore* booster Fred Silverman. Burns recalls Tartikoff telling him, "I like it. I just don't need it right now. I've got *Cheers* and I've got *Cosby*."

After fifteen episodes on the air, *FM* found itself competing for a slot on the schedule with another struggling sitcom, *Seinfeld.* The ratings numbers were about equal, but NBC decided to gamble on a guy named Jerry Seinfeld instead of Bob Hays.

It was hard, afterward, for Burns to hold it against NBC, when *Seinfeld* eventually built to number one in the Nielsen ratings and became one of the '90s' most influential shows, redefining the sitcom as much as *Mary Tyler Moore* had.

Things had not gone like Burns had thought they would after his Oscar nomination for *A Little Romance* back in 1979. Weren't Oscar nominations supposed to get you somewhere? Instead, pursuing a film-writing career grew harder and harder. By the time he was in his sixties and seventies, he still had plenty of ideas, but movie and television studios are notorious for wanting only young talent, even behind the camera. In 2010, many of the *Mary Tyler Moore* writers and producers, now in their sixties and seventies, got a cut of a $70 million settlement the Writers Guild of America struck with major TV networks, movie studios, and talent agencies after filing an age discrimination lawsuit.

They all had their own stories about being iced out of jobs because of their advancing years, and Burns had his. Just a few years before the suit, he had gotten a meeting with some junior studio executives on a script he'd written. But when he walked into the room, he could see the faces of the two twenty-something women drop at the sight of his gray hair and wrinkles. Nonetheless, they told him they loved his movie—it was so castable!

"Your name sounds familiar," one of them said. "What else have you done?"

"The Mary Tyler Moore Show," he told them.

"Oh my God," one of them said. *"That* Allan Burns."

His answer had clearly garnered him great respect, but he felt he could also see them do the math before their eyes: That made him *how old*? Despite the graying and the wrinkles, he was well preserved, with thick hair and twinkling eyes. The script was never made. He has since taken comfort in the fact that he was once part of such a remarkable show—and the fact that he still lives in that beautiful house that he bought at the height of *Mary Tyler Moore,* with his wife of almost five decades, Joan. Nearly every flat surface of their home is crammed with photos of their two sons and five grandchildren.

No matter what came afterward for its creators and writers, *The*

Mary Tyler Moore Show remains one of the most acclaimed TV shows ever, with twenty-nine total Emmys. It also remains the best job any of its writers and producers have ever had, no matter their subsequent successes or failures. "Every year we'd be nominated, and we'd either win or we wouldn't," Brooks recalls. "But we'd have a party that was good whether we did or didn't."

SIXTEEN
SIXTEEN
SIXTEEN
SIXTEEN
SIXTEEN
SIXTEEN
SIXTEEN
SIXTEEN

MAKING IT ON THEIR OWN

(1977–PRESENT)

In the summer of 1986, Ted Knight was sick enough that word spread to his old friends from *The Mary Tyler Moore Show*: He had cancer, and his treatments were not going well.

When Gavin MacLeod heard how badly things were going for his old costar, he and his wife, Patti, went to Knight's house to visit him. The show MacLeod had been starring in, *The Love Boat*, had just ended its nine-year run, and he had recently reconciled with his wife, whom Ted knew and loved from the *Mary Tyler Moore* years. Patti was about to go on the road with a play, and Gavin would be accompanying her for the summer. They worried it would be their last chance to see Knight, who lived just a few blocks away from them in the exclusive Los Angeles neighborhood of Pacific Palisades. The men had stayed in touch over the years, both serving as honorary "mayors" of the neighborhood. Knight had become well loved in the role, going to a local restaurant and setting up a sign that said, "The Mayor Is In" while receiving concerned citizens, neighbors, and, of course, the fans who always bolstered his confidence.

Knight was now living in the sprawling house he'd always wanted, with the wife he'd long loved. When Gavin and Patti MacLeod arrived, Knight's wife, Dottie, answered the door and admitted things weren't looking good for her husband. Knight called from his bed on the second floor for them to come on up.

They found him in his bedroom, his cane propped next to him, self-help books surrounding him. They hugged him. "Look at you two," Gavin remembers Knight saying. "You're back together!" Seeing Knight in such a state, Gavin couldn't help thinking about his own father, who died of cancer when he was thirty-eight, but he tried to keep his emotions in check and focus on his friend. "What's going on?" Knight continued. "What caused you to get back together? You seem so happy."

Gavin was nervous about revealing the truth of their reconciliation: They'd recently found religion together. "Don't get scared," Gavin joked, "but we became born-again Christians."

The three discussed spirituality, and its particular pull as death approached. Knight told them he'd been reading all of the books surrounding him in hopes of finding some guidance, which emboldened Gavin to tell him, "You can have the peace of knowing where to go."

Dottie came in, and the four of them held hands and prayed. Gavin let his tears come.

Afterward, Knight quipped, "I don't feel any different!" But it was enough for Gavin. "You will," he promised as he helped his old friend to the bathroom.

Later, Patti and Gavin supported Ted down the stairs so he could show them his prized possession: his pool. "I've always wanted to have a black-bottom pool," Knight said, as proud as he'd ever been.

Weeks later, Ed Asner came by Knight's house for a visit as well. The two hadn't spoken in five years, since Asner's spin-off, *Lou Grant,* had been canceled. The show had ended in part because Asner had publicly supported medical aid for communist-leaning rebel troops in El Salvador, and Knight, when asked about it in interviews promoting his own new show, *Too Close for Comfort,* had failed to defend his friend. (Asner can't remember what specifically Knight said or didn't say that upset him, but he remembers that whatever it was, it was an "outrageous" breach of their friendship.) Asner refused to have anything more to do with Knight, until he heard Knight was dying.

His visit to his ailing friend that day "had nothing to do with making up," Asner says. "I went to pay my respects." By this time, Knight had slipped much closer to death; he couldn't communicate, and showed no signs of recognizing Asner.

"You're still my brother," Asner told him. Asner did not apologize. He didn't feel he needed forgiveness. He didn't visit Knight to make himself feel better; he went in hopes of making Knight feel a little better. He had no idea if it worked. "The sin was his," Asner says. "I hope he left this veil of tears a little more lighthearted."

It would, as the MacLeods had feared and Asner had known, be the last time any of them saw their friend. Two months later, Gavin got an urgent phone call while on the road with Patti in Cape Cod, Massachusetts. The play's producer came to him, crying, and said, "The Associated Press wants to talk to you right away." Gavin knew immediately that the news service was writing his friend's obituary.

Ted Knight died on August 26, 1986, at just sixty-two years old, after being stricken with an aggressive form of cancer. The Connecticut native and son of a Polish immigrant barman had served in the U.S. Army in World War II, worked as a disc jockey, become a ventriloquist, and, finally, found his calling as an actor. In all, he'd played three hundred parts in various television shows, including *Gunsmoke, The FBI,* and *Get Smart,* but he would never quite separate himself from the role of buffoonish anchorman Ted Baxter on *The Mary Tyler Moore Show.*

He'd remained married to his wife, Dorothy, throughout his career, and left behind two sons, Ted and Eric, as well as a daughter, Elyse. His real-life family reached out to his professional family when it came time to plan the funeral. They asked his *Mary Tyler Moore* co-star, Gavin MacLeod, to be among the speakers at the service.

MacLeod was anxious. He knew his strong religious beliefs could make some people feel uncomfortable. But he couldn't turn down the chance to memorialize the friend he'd known since they met in that agent's office back in 1957, when neither of them had a career or a proper business manager.

On August 28, 1986, the cast of *The Mary Tyler Moore Show* reunited for the first time since they'd gone off the air nine years earlier, to attend the funeral of one of their own. The private service in Glendale, California, prompted more laughter than tears as the mourners remembered Knight's comic gifts. It also allowed the cast members to reflect on their own lives since the show. Some of them had continued success, some of them didn't—but either way, everything had seemed a little harder, a little more painful, than it had when they'd spent seven years cocooned together in the protective shell of Soundstage 2.

The summer after *The Mary Tyler Moore Show* had ended, Mary Tyler Moore didn't know what to do with herself. The show had been her whole life. She had no real hobbies besides dancing, and all of her closest friends had been on the set. Ballet classes filled some of the void, as did therapy, but she mostly wandered through her days until Tinker returned home from work at night.

Tinker was off running the company that bore her name, MTM Enterprises. MTM was now hitting its zenith, producing hits such as *Newhart,* starring the company's old favorite, Bob Newhart, this time as an author-turned-inn operator in New England. MTM's medical drama, *St. Elsewhere,* earned lukewarm ratings but great critical acclaim, and its police drama *Hill Street Blues* was an across-the-board success that redefined the cop genre. The hit crime-solving dramedy

Remington Steele, starring Stephanie Zimbalist and Pierce Brosnan as sexy detectives, added to the company's long list of accomplishments.

Moore was now the official queen of a quality-TV kingdom, but she preferred to let her talented husband and producers do what they did best without her interference. "Mary's not a Lucille Ball," one MTM executive said at the time. "She doesn't get involved with the lights and the props and every aspect of production." Soon, Tinker left the company's everyday operations as well, figuring it could hum along just fine under the supervision of others. After eleven years of running MTM, he took a new job heading NBC. He'd had his first job at the network, and he'd returned for that brief period in the '60s in New York. He thought it would be great to go back in the '80s and end up on top. He liked ending up on top. As he would say, "It's better than the other way, right?"

But he hadn't forgotten the show that had made his company. In 1982, when ABC canceled *Taxi,* he lent a major assist to Jim Brooks when his old producer called him to commiserate. By the end of the conversation, Tinker had saved Brooks's post–*Mary Tyler Moore* baby. He offered to put it on his new network, where it ran for another year. Tinker's "extraordinary manners," as Brooks says, had come to the rescue once again.

At the same time, however, Moore was dealing with a quick succession of tragedies. Her sister Elizabeth, nineteen years her junior, died of a drug overdose in 1978. Her son, Richie, died two years later when he accidentally shot himself with a faulty gun.

She and Tinker split up for good shortly thereafter.

Moore also experienced wild fluctuations in her post–*Mary Tyler Moore* career. More than anyone else on the show, she'd become entwined with her America's-sweetheart character. She *was* her character in viewers' minds, and there was little she could do to stop that. Having her name in the title of her now-classic show didn't help matters.

Nonetheless, she tried to live down that legacy with another show bearing her name. Once again, she returned to her original dream: to sing and dance. A variety series seemed like a good idea at the time, despite the critical drubbing of her variety special a few years back, *Mary's Incredible Dream*. She maintained that *Incredible Dream* had been brilliant, if too avant-garde for TV audiences, and was willing to try again with a more traditional variety format. It would allow her to perform musical numbers and comedy skits, and it would, Moore thought, allow a natural transition from Mary Richards into other roles. This way, audiences wouldn't be forced to accept Moore immediately as some *other* person, just as herself.

Alas, her show, *Mary,* lasted only three episodes, despite having ratings powerhouse *60 Minutes* as its lead-in, and despite a cast that included Michael Keaton, Swoosie Kurtz, and David Letterman. Letterman, a struggling young comedian, was thrilled to work with Moore, whom he'd admired since *The Dick Van Dyke Show*. Hell, he was thrilled just to get a name badge that got him into CBS Television City and its commissary full of stars, where he could see the likes of Bob Newhart or Ted Knight eating tuna, corned beef sandwiches, and salad bar fixings. But the show didn't make the best use of its future all-stars, particularly Letterman, whose sardonic humor was reduced to smirking through perky song-and-dance numbers. "That was tough," Letterman later said. "I knew my limitations, but this really brought them home. You know, it was, 'You're not a singer. You're not a dancer. You're not an actor. Get out of here. What are you doing? Get away from Mary. That's her fruit. Don't try and eat her fruit.'"

The show faltered from the start, trying to combine sincere musical numbers with the "edgy" humor that made *Saturday Night Live* popular. To wit, one memorable number had Keaton and Letterman dressed up like characters from a scene in *Deliverance,* singing the Village People song "Macho Man." "It's enough to make you cry," critic Bob Moore wrote in *The Palm Beach Post*. "After five fabulous years with Dick Van Dyke and seven equally enjoyable ones with her own show, Mary Tyler Moore is in trouble. Deep trouble . . . As for Michael Keaton, Swoosie Kurtz and David Letterman, they should be thankful they have jobs at all, because it seems inconceivable people with the comedy acumen of MTM could so miscast their No. 1 star with such inferior talent."

Variety shows were also falling out of favor, though the youthful *Donny & Marie* was still going strong. Even Carol Burnett ended her show that year.

Moore regrouped with another idea: She would turn her variety show into what she called a "sit-var." Later that season, she returned to TV in *The Mary Tyler Moore Hour*, a sitcom *about* a singing, dancing variety show star. "Surprisingly enough, that failed, too," she later joked. Despite attempts to shore up ratings with crowd-pleasing cameos by the likes of Bea Arthur, Lucille Ball, and Dick Van Dyke, TV viewers wouldn't accept her as a new Mary. The show premiered on March 4—hardly an auspicious start, as it came near the end of the "midseason replacement" season, when networks were already preparing their schedules for the following fall—and was canceled by June after eleven episodes.

Just one year later, however, Moore achieved one of her greatest career heights: She starred in Robert Redford's screen adaptation of *Ordinary People,* playing against type. She got her first Oscar nomination with her portrayal of distant mother Beth Jarrett, who grows even colder after the death of one of her two sons. Redford said he got the idea to cast her when he saw her walking on the beach in Malibu and wondered about "the dark side of Mary Tyler Moore." Moore said at the time, "I guess he was right to wonder about that, because there is, in fact, a dark side." She related to the role, she later said, of a woman who was so brittle inside that she could alienate her own son, because of her "self-expectation for perfectionistic, unachievable dreams" and her "inability to be a whole person and give it freely."

Moore and Redford met to discuss the role early in the casting process, before Redford went on to audition other actresses for three months. Finally, he came back to his original choice and offered her the part. After the film was released to great acclaim and award nominations, Moore ran into Jim Brooks on the street. *"Mary,"* was all he had to say for her to know what he meant. She accepted the compliment gratefully.

Though Moore had planned to attempt yet another sitcom in 1980, she decided instead to take a unique part in the Broadway play *Whose Life Is It Anyway?* The experimental piece features a quadriplegic main character who spends the play arguing for euthanasia, never moving during the performance. Tom Conti had originally played the role and won a Tony for it, but Moore agreed to take over for him instead of pressing her luck at another sitcom. She, too, won a Tony for her effort, a special award from the academy acknowledging the risk she'd taken with the role. The victory took on extra significance for Moore because of her awful earlier experience with the stage adaptation of *Breakfast at Tiffany's.* She'd finally conquered the unforgiving Broadway stage—for herself, and for television actors who weren't taken seriously by the New York theater snobs. Joe Rainone visited her backstage at one performance to congratulate her, and she never failed to make him feel she was glad to see him.

Now single for the first significant period of time since she was nineteen, Moore remained in New York City to live alone and find herself. She spent a few years finally playing Mary Richards in real life, feeling what it was like to make it on her own, renting a house on East Sixty-fourth Street. That didn't last too long, however: Three years later, in 1983, as Brooks's *Terms of Endearment* opened in theaters, she married her third husband, Dr. Robert Levine, whom she met when he treated her mother for heart trouble.

Over time, Moore developed a habit of unwinding with a drink or two before dinner and a brandy after, a pattern that started to catch up with her because of her diabetes. Her blood sugar would fluctuate with each drink, exhausting her. In 1984, she read about Elizabeth Taylor and Liza Minnelli seeking help for their addictions at the center run by Betty Ford. Inspired, she decided to check in to break what Levine called a "social drinking" habit.

The next year, she was back on television, ready for a fresh start with the medium that had built her career. Again, the show was called *Mary*. She was still under her long-term contract with CBS, signed after the end of *The Mary Tyler Moore Show,* and hoped to redeem her name in television after her failures of the last eight years. She decided to return to her beloved sitcom format, even though she still didn't think she was a comedian. "I'm not an innately funny person," she told the *New York Times* then. "I find it an almost overbearing responsibility when I think about having to be funny. . . . I like simply standing next to the funny person. Just being part of what caused the laughter is great fun for me." The concept for *Mary* felt strangely familiar: Following the adventures of a fortyish divorcée who worked at a struggling tabloid newspaper, it sounded a lot like Brooks and Burns's first proposal for *The Mary Tyler Moore Show.*

But the MTM luster was fading now, sixteen years after the company began and without Tinker to lend his vision. *Mary* lasted just half a season. Moore tried yet again two seasons later with *Annie McGuire,* which followed a couple married later in life. Her first show not bearing some form of her name, however, didn't do any better, and lasted just ten episodes. A few years later, MTM Enterprises went on the stock market and flopped. MTM never returned to its heights of television production, and the company was at last absorbed into Twentieth Century Fox by the '90s.

She had some minor success during the same period by revisiting her *Mary Tyler Moore* roots: She reunited with Burns on a movie script he'd written for her, *Just Between Friends.* In it, Moore plays an uptight housewife-turned-aerobics-instructor who finds out, after her husband's death, that he'd been cheating with her best friend. The film, directed by Burns and costarring Christine Lahti and Ted Danson, explored a theme that had become mainstream since *Mary Tyler Moore*: the divide between working, single women and stay-at-home moms.

Moore was now playing the stay-at-home mom. But the movie didn't make enough impact to help anyone forget she was Mary Richards first.

Back in the early '70s, with *Phyllis* and *Rhoda* on the wane and plagued with troubles of their own, what once seemed like a sure thing for Betty White—a spin-off show for her belovedly bitchy Sue Ann—now looked like a huge gamble. So much so, in fact, that MTM Enterprises issued an edict: Yes, there would be a show starring Betty White. No, it would not be about Sue Ann Nivens. To soften her up enough to be a leading lady would destroy her character, à la *Phyllis*; to marry her off was a chance they weren't about to take after *Rhoda*. They would, instead, build a whole new show around White.

In *The Betty White Show,* she would play a character named Joyce Whitman, a TV actress who has to work with her ex-husband as the director of her new show. Georgia Engel would play Joyce's best friend. White had watched *Star Trek* from its beginning in 1966, often to her husband's chagrin, so she pitched the idea of Joyce's series being a space show. It would not only provide two contrasting worlds for Joyce, but it would also be hilarious, she thought. David Lloyd wrote the pilot script, with Ed. Weinberger and Stan Daniels producing; but the guys decided to put Joyce in a second-rate crime show called *Undercover Woman* instead, to play off the recent success of Angie Dickinson's *Police Woman.*

Despite all of those efforts, the show would last only half a season. Just two months later, in April 1978, *Maude* ended its six-year run, and *All in the Family* said good-bye to the cast that had made it famous (attempts at reboots and spin-offs of the show would never reach the same heights as the original). By that December, *Rhoda* was over as well.

The Golden Age of Comedy that *Time* had declared in 1974 had officially ended.

Gavin MacLeod cracked the code of the changing TV landscape in the late '70s better than anyone else who came out of *The Mary Tyler Moore Show.* He turned down a pilot in which he would have played a character who, he says, was "like Murray in a cowboy suit," to instead take his dream job, costarring in a production of *Annie Get Your Gun* with Debbie Reynolds in San Francisco. Then his agent told him about a script for a pilot called *The Love Boat.* "I think it stinks," his agent said. "But do you want to read it?"

MacLeod agreed to take a look despite that unenthusiastic endorsement. As he read it at his house in Palm Springs, and saw the simple but compelling premise— a show following different romantic stories each week, set on the same cruise ship with the same amiable staff—he thought, *No one has ever done anything like this before.* He handed it over to his wife, and within the first ten pages, she told him, "I think if you get the right people, it could be interesting."

MacLeod agreed to a meeting with producer Aaron Spelling about the role of Captain Merrill Stubing since he was driving to Los Angeles to meet with NBC about another pilot anyway. When he got to Spelling's mansion, he found a producer who'd done his homework. "I know you like to do other things," MacLeod recalls Spelling saying. "So I can structure this so you're not doing the lead."

MacLeod's agent had warned him about saying yes right away to Spelling. "Aaron," he said, "gives great interview." His agent had been right: "Just say yes," Spelling now implored MacLeod.

"I promised my agent I wouldn't say yes," MacLeod said. But he *wanted* to say yes, and he told his agent so as soon as he could get to a phone after meeting with Spelling. "I like Aaron," MacLeod told him. "And I read the other pilot script you gave me, and they're in like a Salvation Army place, and they're knocking Jimmy Carter, they're knocking this and that. I don't want to do that."

He went back to *Annie Get Your Gun* after filming the *Love Boat* pilot and loved the stage work even more than he'd expected to. He thought, *Wow, this is great. I get to do a musical! I'm used to seven pieces in the orchestra, and they have twenty-eight pieces!* Then he got the call that he was, in all honesty, dreading: Spelling telling him *The Love Boat* had gotten picked up for the fall. Spelling had promised to work around the actor's schedule, but daily performances nearly four hundred miles from Los Angeles seemed a bit much.

"Isn't it great?" Spelling said to MacLeod of *Love Boat*'s prospects. "The focus groups saw you in the pilot, and they pressed those buttons [to indicate their love for a character], and it went through the roof!"

"Aaron," MacLeod remembers saying, "I'm going to open in San Francisco in a week and a half."

"Didn't I say I'd work around you?"

Indeed, every afternoon for the duration of the play, one of Spelling's drivers would take MacLeod from the *Love Boat* set to Los Angeles International Airport, and MacLeod would fly to San Francisco, where he'd be taken from the airport to the theater. He would eat dinner, do the show, and fly home. Spelling may have been accused of watering down television with his soapy, guilty pleasures, but he was a man of his word.

And MacLeod was thrilled when *The Love Boat* became a huge hit, an icon of '80s television and a mainstay of family viewing on Saturday nights. He didn't mind that people called it "mindless television." It was what viewers wanted to see. He had been part of a show that got more Emmys in seven years than any other show, and now he got to be part of a show that made people happy and provided them some escape from their everyday lives. Was that so bad?

Many of his former *Mary Tyler Moore* costars took a voyage or two on the vessel of romance as well: Georgia Engel, Harold Gould, Valerie Harper, Ted Knight, Cloris Leachman, Nancy Walker, and Betty White all showed up in guest spots. Harper appeared on a show in which the ship was traveling the Nile, and she brought her new husband, personal trainer Tony Cacciotti, with her for the shoot. Mac-Leod tried to give the couple his expansive suite so they wouldn't have to sleep on bunk beds in a cramped cabin, but Harper would have none of that. "No, no, you worked hard for this," she told him. "It's yours."

White appeared twice, both times having the damnedest time keeping her hands off MacLeod's bald head—she missed Sue Ann's signature caress, but she knew that time was over. You just don't do that to Captain Stubing. Somehow it felt as if nothing, and yet everything, had changed.

Ed Asner had changed as well. He had become a feminist.

Yes, the man behind the gruff Lou Grant had been converted to a full-fledged women's rights advocate after witnessing Mary Richards's ascent for seven seasons. He was a vocal ERA supporter. And, on a more personal level, his agent added a clause to his *Lou Grant* contract that required progressive hiring practices on the show. Asner may have acted macho—some midwestern football player habits don't die easily—but he did his best to support and speak out for women's equality. In 1986, he would even deliver the National Organization for Women's 20th Anniversary radio broadcast, a tribute to male feminists like Alan Alda.

Asner was growing ever more outspoken about his political beliefs by 1982. While he'd become a fervent women's libber during his time on *The Mary Tyler Moore Show,* it was his more extreme-left views that got the most attention, culminating in controversial fund-raising efforts to send medical aid to rebels in El Salvador fighting against the U.S.-supported regime. Asner even went so far as to send out a letter asking for donations that began, "My name is Ed Asner. I play Lou Grant on television." That raised the hackles of conservative Screen Actors Guild members such as Charlton Heston, who objected to Asner's use of a character to push a political agenda.

Right-wing sentiment turned even more against Asner when he

answered a question in a press conference: Would he support free elections in El Salvador even if the result was a communist government there? At first, he demurred. Then, given a few more seconds to think, he changed his mind, just as he had years earlier when he gave a poor reading for his Lou Grant audition. He said to himself, *You came all this way to give that kind of bullshit answer?* So he stepped back to the microphone and told the reporters what he really thought: If that's what the people chose, he answered, he would have to support it. He felt like the dog in the *Tom and Jerry* cartoons: *Boom!* Incinerated by his own words. He realized he could be ending his own career, and he made peace with that in the moment.

He was labeled "communist swine" and "the Jane Fonda of Latin America." ("I didn't know I was that cute," he quipped in response.) Burns and the other *Lou Grant* producers tried to talk Asner into toning down his rhetoric. Asner remembers producer Seth Freeman telling him, "We think there are two ways to present ideas: One is the way you're doing it and one is the way we do it. We think our way is better." (Burns remembers the incident differently and says neither he nor his fellow producers tried to talk Asner out of speaking out, but simply expressed concern for his safety.)

Asner appreciated the sentiment but felt trapped by his situation. "What do you want me to do?" he said. "They're attacking me. Do you want me to shut up?"

They had no answer, but soon they didn't need one. *Lou Grant*—despite its continuing place in the top ten—was canceled by the fall of 1982. CBS executives maintained that the decision had nothing to do with politics, though Asner pointed out that actor Howard Hesseman, who'd also participated in the rally for the rebels, found his equally popular *WKRP in Cincinnati* axed as well. The network never acknowledged a tie between the political uproar and the cancellations, but Asner will always believe there was one.

Asner felt he was "blacklisted" by some after the event, and his agent advised him to stop responding to accusations because it "kept the game alive." But Asner wasn't as concerned about his own career prospects as he was sorry to put the cast, crew, producers, and writers out of work. He thought the ensemble on *Lou Grant* was as good as that on *Mary Tyler Moore,* and he felt badly that they didn't get to continue. But he would never admit he regretted saying what he did. He simply regretted the consequences.

He would also never admit he regretted his fallout with Knight when Knight failed to defend him in interviews about the controversy. But it was a shame nonetheless.

At the Church of the Recessional, in Forest Lawn Cemetery, just outside Los Angeles, on a perfect August day, Knight's body lay in a flag-draped casket. The *Mary Tyler Moore* writers had taken out a full-page ad in that morning's *Variety,* showing a photo of Knight as Baxter and saying, "Bye, Guy." Mourners filled the pews to capacity. Asner was among them, along with Moore, Leachman, Harper, and MacLeod. Producer David Lloyd, who'd written the "Chuckles Bites the Dust" episode, spoke. Nancy Dussault, Knight's *Too Close for Comfort* co-star, read a telegram from President Reagan: "All America joins us in mourning the loss of this fine man, who gave us the best of his talents and captured our affection and admiration."

MacLeod then stood before the congregation and told them about his thirty-year journey with the man who was Ted Baxter. He told them about working with Knight, and about their final prayer together. Then he cited none other than Chuckles the Clown's oft-quoted motto: "A little song, a little dance, a little seltzer down your pants," he said. "That's how I'll remember you, Ted. Oh, the fun we had together."

epilogue
epilogue
epilogue
epilogue
epilogue
epilogue
epilogue
epilogue

mary, rhoda, and the modern girl

On May 19, 2008, all of the surviving cast members from *The Mary Tyler Moore Show*—Mary Tyler Moore, Ed Asner, Gavin MacLeod, Valerie Harper, Betty White, Cloris Leachman, and Georgia Engel—gathered on the Chicago set of *The Oprah Winfrey Show*. Winfrey had watched every episode throughout her teens "like my life depended on it," she said. Now that Winfrey had become the most powerful person in media—an unthinkable feat for a woman when *The Mary Tyler Moore Show* had begun—she used her clout to make one of her own dreams come true. She was reuniting the cast of the show that had inspired her to become the woman she was. In 1997, a surprise appearance by Moore on *Oprah* had rendered Winfrey sobbing and speechless. Now she wanted the whole cast there for a real interview. "The show was a light in my life, and Mary was a trailblazer for my generation," she said. "She's the reason I wanted my own production company."

Her staff re-created the newsroom set of WJM and Mary's first studio apartment. The seventy-five-member crew assigned to the task pored over DVDs of the show to get every detail correct. They found out how tall Moore was, then scaled their sketches as close as possible to the originals. They scoured thrift stores, antique shops, and eBay for the right furnishings. The wood-burning stove in the corner of Mary's apartment came from a museum. Lou Grant's office coffeepot came from the art director's grandma. With every new score, the staff did a jig to celebrate—'70s phones, a hand-painted spice rack, the exact mirror and pumpkin cookie jar from the original set. The *M* on the wall was the easy part.

After thousands of man-hours, they had versions of both sets that were up to Winfrey standards. "I wanted to walk through those doors and sit at Mary's desk," she said. "And today, I get to do it."

With the clone of Mary's apartment as their backdrop, the cast reminisced with Winfrey about their part in making a TV classic. "From this small and neighborhood-like studio [came] these little gems of shows that were well-written and people who respected each other and who did their very best not to get the bucks, but to make a good show," Moore said of MTM. Winfrey told Moore she'd spent years wondering what might have happened to Mary Richards once she'd left WJM in the finale. Moore had a simple answer: "She continued working, and then she met and fell in love with a wonderful man and they got married and had wonderful children."

Winfrey broke into tears when Moore presented her with a gold *O*, just like Mary's *M*, signed by the cast. After a tribute to Ted Knight's memory, the cast and Winfrey shared a group hug like the one that had ended the series.

After the show wrapped, Winfrey walked with MacLeod back to where the cast had their guest dressing rooms, recalling an appearance Winfrey had made on *The Love Boat* before she was famous. She wanted to write her phone number down for MacLeod. While Winfrey stepped away into her own office for paper and pen, MacLeod slipped into the wrong dressing room, thinking it was his, but finding Leachman there naked. She screamed at him, but after the initial shock, they made up, yet again. It helped to soothe her nerves when MacLeod later cracked, "I've known you for fifty years. Why did I wait so long?"

Through the years, Moore tried—but failed—to play down talk of her being a "symbol" to women. She tried to shed her Mary Richards image, her efforts to do so culminating with an autobiography, *After All,* in 1996. In it, she revealed every imperfection in her life: her struggle with alcoholism, the death of her son, her regrets about spending so much time at work in his formative years, her divorces, her diabetes. She proved that no matter what the world thought, Mary Tyler Moore was not the sweet, perfect, inspiring Mary Richards. She was simply a flawed actress doing the best she could.

She knew, however, that Mary Richards would always follow her. She would have to learn to live with it, and she would have to acknowledge her own influence: Female comedians and producers cited her as the reason they'd known they could succeed in the business; single, working women everywhere hummed her theme song to themselves whenever they were feeling overwhelmed by life's challenges. (If you think this is an overstatement, you are not a woman who grew up in the '70s idolizing Mary Richards.) Because of her show, women had infiltrated the television industry until, by the end of the 1970s, professional women's groups proliferated throughout Hollywood and were filled with high-powered producers, directors, writers, and executives.

Moore put all of this out of her mind the same way she let herself forget that when she was on camera, millions of people were watching her, planning their entire evenings around her show. She liked to joke that the only time she thought about being a symbol was when she tried to get a good table at a restaurant. Then she found herself suddenly hoping the maitre d' had seen *Dick Van Dyke* or *Mary Tyler Moore* or *Ordinary People.*

She just wanted to be remembered as someone who always looked for the truth. Even, as she once said, if it wasn't funny.

The television of the 1980s had made it feel as if the previous decade's progressive television revolution had been nothing more than Mary's Impossible Dream. A return to vapid female roles and token people of color marked the superficial programming of an empty-calorie decade. *Three's Company, Dallas, The Dukes of Hazzard, Charlie's Angels,* and *Dynasty* outweighed the gains in that same decade of *Kate & Allie* or *The Cosby Show.*

Women's comedies had a brief moment again in the late '80s and early '90s: Murphy Brown upset a vice president with her plans for single motherhood, Ally McBeal single-handedly killed feminism (according to a *Time* magazine cover story with echoes of the '70s feminist backlash against *Mary Tyler Moore*), and no one missed the parallels to Mary Richards. In 1998, another major milestone in Mary Richards's afterlife came in the form of a bawdy HBO sitcom about, not one, but four single women over thirty: *Sex and the City.* Though that show's graphic sex and naughty girl talk went far beyond what we saw of Mary's dating life, the influence of *Mary Tyler Moore* was clear. Where once Mary had broken ground by casually mentioning her Pill use and staying out all night with a man, these women went through a man a week. A sly reference to birth control would've been the tamest part of any episode.

That's why it made all too much sense when Moore brought the idea of a Mary-and-Rhoda revival to CBS. And yet the network that had supported her for so long declined. But she wouldn't give up. She was visibly excited when she talked about this project, despite her previous efforts to disentangle herself from her character. Now she was ready to make the best of her legacy. She wanted to bring the characters back to television, twenty years after *The Mary Tyler Moore Show* had gone off the air, to follow their adventures as once-again-single women.

ABC, as it turned out, did share her enthusiasm—at least at first—and plans came together in 1997 for a new series set to start the next year featuring Moore and Harper as middle-aged versions of their memorable characters. They would reunite after living separate lives, and both would have college-age daughters. Moore talked it up to the press: It could be an innovative series, she proclaimed. It would take long-known and -loved characters and catch up with them twenty-five years later. It would be *The Golden Girls* meets *Mary Tyler Moore*. What could be better?

But the problems soon mounted. The actresses and the network couldn't agree on a version of a pilot script they all liked, and the development dragged on for two more years. Eventually ABC president Jamie Tarses had to admit in 1999, "This was one of those cases where the stars didn't line up correctly."

To make up for the time and resources spent on the idea, the network decided to expand the pilot script into a TV movie, then gauge audience reaction to determine whether to pursue a series. Harper and Moore had a blast filming it, with a sixty-two-year-old Moore even doing her own stunt when she had to sprint down a New York sidewalk, jump over a rolled-up carpet being carried by two workmen, and skid to a stop—all in high heels, chasing a stray dog. She broke her right wrist in the process, perhaps a sign of the project's fate.

When it eventually aired in 2000, *Time* pronounced it "ultimately disappointing," though it called Moore "still one of the most brilliant and sadly underutilized comedic actresses around." *Variety* had mixed feelings as well. "Rhoda, you haven't changed a bit," a review said. "The sarcasm, the wishy-washiness, the inner-turmoil surrounding a mother-daughter relationship—it's still boiling over and inviting as ever. Mary, you're a whole lot harder to write for, and attempting to put a few scars on the smile that turned everyone on is a tricky proposition." The *San Francisco Chronicle* had harsher words still: "*Mary and Rhoda* is to be savored, ever so briefly, for its reunion of Mary Richards and Rhoda Morgenstern. And then it should be spat out like sour milk, in hopes of preserving the happier memory of Mary and Rhoda in their 1970s sitcom heaven."

How could anything—even if it starred Mary and Rhoda themselves—live up to the memory of *The Mary Tyler Moore Show*? Perhaps, as that review suggested, the series was better left to hall-of-fame reminiscences. Then again, maybe *Mary Tyler Moore* itself had helped to advance television so much that a safe, by-the-numbers revival failed to live up to its legacy. Not long after *Mary and Rhoda* aired, the spirit of *The Mary Tyler Moore Show* experienced a renaissance of sorts. When those who grew up watching *Mary Tyler Moore* started making television themselves, a new golden age—in television, and particularly television comedy made by women—dawned.

The fact that tributes to *The Mary Tyler Moore Show* materialized with ever more frequency in the years to follow was no coincidence. In the mid-1990s, just as '70s nostalgia was reaching a peak among the Baby Boomers who lived through the decade, a new generation discovered the show when kids' network Nickelodeon added it to its popular Nick at Nite lineup of classic sitcoms. In 1998, *Entertainment Weekly* named it the best TV show of all time. In 2002, cable network TV Land sponsored a Mary Richards statue to be built in the spot where she famously tossed her beret on Nicollet Mall in Minneapolis. That same year, CBS ran yet another reunion special, with a lengthy tribute to Knight. In 2006, Moore made a guest appearance on *That '70s Show,* which happened to be filmed in the old *Mary Tyler Moore* studio. The sitcom proudly gave her back her old dressing room for the weeks she was there.

Still more hints of a *Mary Tyler Moore* resurgence came in 2009, with the massive comeback of Betty White. At the age of eighty-seven, the television veteran made a sudden succession of scene-stealing appearances: first, in the romantic comedy *The Proposal,* then in a Snickers commercial that premiered during the 2010 Super Bowl, and finally in an online petition drive to get her to host *Saturday Night Live.* She

topped it off with a new show, *Hot in Cleveland,* and a special tribute from the Academy of Television Arts & Sciences. Her *Mary Tyler
Moore* costars all showed up to salute her, with MacLeod declaring her
a "national treasure." When the two hugged later, she told him, "You'll
have to forgive me for being so overexposed." He quipped, "Honey,
you've always been overexposed."

Cloris Leachman experienced a parallel rebirth in Hollywood,
first gaining attention as a 2008 contestant on *Dancing with the Stars,*
then playing a grandma whose dementia garners laughs on Fox's edgy
comedy *Raising Hope.* She even appeared on the 2011 MTV Video
Music Awards, joking about how everyone kept confusing her with
Betty White.

Ed Asner continued to score a ludicrous amount of work for
an actor in his eighties, guest-starring on White's *Hot in Cleveland,*
ABC's sitcom *The Middle,* and USA Network's *Royal Pains.* He played
financier Warren Buffett in HBO's film *Too Big to Fail;* he toured the
country doing a one-man show about FDR; and he voiced the lead
character in the Oscar-nominated animated film *Up* in 2009.

What's amazing is that so many of the best minds in the business still
cite *The Mary Tyler Moore Show* as their inspiration, and their benchmark for greatness. The *Onion*'s AV Club website declared in 2010
that "*All in the Family* and *The Mary Tyler Moore Show* are among the
handful of TV series that altered the medium so profoundly that it can
be divided roughly into periods before and after their arrival. . . . both
would change the face of television radically and influence virtually
every television comedy up through the present." True enough, its
influence goes beyond simply bringing single women into the sitcom
sphere. Its dedication to realism—death and divorce were real and
possible in its world, unlike the comedies that came before it—made
way for real stakes on television, even in comedy. Whether it was
Mr. Hooper dying on *Sesame Street,* Coach dying on *Cheers,* or everyone dying on *The Sopranos, The Mary Tyler Moore Show* did it first. The

fact that bad things could happen in its world didn't turn viewers off; it only made them even more invested in its characters, large and small.

Similarly, the revelation that a show could combine the melancholy with the comedic reverberates throughout more recent shows, including *The Office, Louie,* even *The Simpsons.* Power ensembles such as those on *Friends* and *Seinfeld* show how wise it was for Moore to surround herself with talent, rather than keeping the spotlight on herself.

At the same time, Mary Richards's cultural daughters were multiplying on the airwaves like never before in a new wave of single, professional female comedy heroines. In 2006, *Saturday Night Live*'s Tina Fey—its first female head writer—got her own sitcom, *30 Rock,* and deliberately structured it like a funhouse-mirror version of *The Mary Tyler Moore Show.* Her character, Liz Lemon, works in television and struggles to balance her work and personal lives, but work always wins. (That part is very Mary Richards. The fact that Liz is also a slob who loves junk food and struggles to find appropriate dates is less so.) Her primary relationship is with the gruff network boss played by Alec Baldwin. She's surrounded by characters even crazier than she is. And she represents single women of the era perfectly—there is something painfully relatable about a woman who's great at her job but can't control her sub sandwich and white wine habits or maintain a romantic connection.

Throughout the first season, Fey taught herself to write sitcoms— rather than the freer form of sketch comedy in which she was well trained—by watching DVDs of *The Mary Tyler Moore Show.* She and her fellow writers talked about the show all the time, particularly the way it focused on the relationships among colleagues who happened to make a TV show for a living. Like Brooks and Burns before her, the married Fey deferred to her single writers on story lines exploring Liz Lemon's dating life.

The show, in one way, surpassed even *The Mary Tyler Moore Show*'s first season: It won an Emmy for Best Comedy Series. In the next few years, Fey's popularity soared, even though her show got only 5.4 million viewers per week in its first season—less than a fifth of what *The Mary Tyler Moore Show* once got, a testament to the changes in the media and entertainment landscape since then. Nonetheless, Fey's success spawned a new era in which funny women starred in and created more shows than they ever had before—the next few years' media coverage felt a lot like the heights of lady-writer-mania that *The Mary Tyler Moore Show* inspired (minus the hot pants).

Grey's Anatomy, created by Shonda Rhimes, focused on a core cast of prickly female doctors; *Ugly Betty* celebrated the life of a gawky girl from Queens working at a fashion magazine. By 2011, the TV schedule boasted so many Mary Richards acolytes that it had reached what one male sitcom producer griped was "peak vagina": Among the biggest breakouts of the season were Zooey Deschanel in *New Girl*, a show about a lovable single girl living with three guys, created by writer Liz Meriwether; and *2 Broke Girls*, created by comic Whitney Cummings and following the adventures of a modern-day (and much raunchier) Mary and Rhoda. Even TV's edgier and quirkier heroines showed shades of Mary Richards. *Parks and Recreation*'s Hillary Clinton–worshipping, small-town government wonk Leslie Knope (Amy Poehler) is just your basic single girl trying to make it. *Nurse Jackie* (played by Edie Falco) has a workplace full of goofballs, an acerbic best friend, and a less-than-perfect love life; she just also happens to have a pill-popping problem and a disintegrating marriage.

Then, in 2012, as *30 Rock* prepared its predetermined final season—its seventh, like *The Mary Tyler Moore Show*—we got a glimpse of the next generation of Mary Richardses. At just twenty-six, Lena Dunham created HBO's *Girls*, which follows an aspiring writer in Brooklyn and her cringingly realistic exploits with boys, booze, drugs, and sometimes, even, jobs. The premiere had critics panting about "the next *Sex and the City*" and stoked deafening media buzz. The first episode pointedly referenced *The Mary Tyler Moore Show*, as if to point out both its similarities—single girl takes on city!—as well as its stark differences—Mary Richards would likely blanch over the flagrant nudity, raw sex scenes, and coarse language.

These days, those female-centric shows have one thing *The Mary Tyler Moore Show* never did, nor could have: a woman running the show *and* starring in it. Thanks to the work of Treva Silverman, Susan Silver, Pat Nardo, Gloria Banta, and others, Fey, Dunham, and their ilk have the chance to write their own words. Fey watches *Mary Tyler Moore* to stoke her creativity when she writes. Dunham looks to Rhoda as a role model; *Seinfeld*'s Julia Louis-Dreyfus says the same of Mary. "I love Mary Tyler Moore and, of course, Lucille Ball, too," Louis-Dreyfus said while playing the neurotic Elaine Benes on the '90s hit. "But Mary was more accessible. I liked her because she was funny, and she was feminine. She didn't compromise her femininity to be humorous, which is an easy trap for women to fall into." Rhimes says *Mary Tyler Moore* is among her top TV influences of all time. "There was something about the humor," she says, "but it was also really moving."

Mary Richards was so real to so many, it's easy to imagine her still living her life today. But what we imagine her doing says more about us—and what she meant to us—than it does about her. *Mary Tyler Moore* writer Pat Nardo imagines Mary Richards as an executive, unmarried and childless. Her writing partner, Gloria Banta, agrees. "I think she'd be head of a nonprofit because she was such a good person." Susan Silver has no doubt: "Plastic surgery. That's what Mary would be doing right now." Silver also figures Mary is divorced, and grappling with the same questions she finds herself facing every day. "Are we still visible, women after a certain age? And where are all the men? And how do we age gracefully?" She adds, "The answer to all of that is plastic surgery." Silver wishes Mary were still around—and on television, where she belongs, continuing to make life better for her cohorts. "There is life between fifty and eighty," she says. "But it's not on television. I think Mary would be trying to fix that."

Or perhaps she'd just be happy to relax into her later years, knowing she'd changed the lives of millions of people in a million different ways. She gave Treva Silverman a female character worth writing for. She launched the careers of dozens of female comedy writers. She brought the words and humor of Jim Brooks and Allan Burns to as many people as possible. She gave Joe Rainone five double-spaced pages of inspiration every week for seven years. And she gave everyone who watched the unexpected laughs and tears they had come to expect. Not bad for a single girl from Roseburg, Minnesota.

AUTHOR'S NOTE
AUTHOR'S NOTE
AUTHOR'S NOTE
AUTHOR'S NOTE
AUTHOR'S NOTE
AUTHOR'S NOTE
AUTHOR'S NOTE

AUTHOR'S NOTE

When I was five years old, I loved to play Mary and Rhoda. Sometimes I was Mary, sometimes I was Rhoda, depending on my mood. If I wanted to indulge my love of office supplies, I was Mary, sharpening pencils like she did on her very first day on the job; if I wanted to tie a scarf around my head, that was Rhoda.

As I sat in my red paisley scarf with my legal pad and watched the women of *The Mary Tyler Moore Show*, I didn't know that these icons of female independence would influence the rest of my life. I just liked the way they looked, the way they loved and supported each other, and the glamorous adult lives they led. To mention now that my "Mary and Rhoda" games supplanted the use of baby dolls and tiny lightbulb-powered ovens, that playing Mom and House gave direct way to pretending to be a single working woman or a bohemian creative spirit, feels a little too perfectly feminist, too women's libby, too ERA era. But it is what happened to me in the late 1970s and early 1980s, during my formative years, as I watched endless reruns of the most respected sitcom of the previous decade. To mention that my mother bought a giant wooden *J,* her own first initial, spray-painted it gold, and hung it on her bedroom wall just like Mary did with her *M,* well, that feels even more pat. But that happened just the same. My mother and I, two decades apart, embraced the props of the only enviable, unapologetic single women we knew in our insular suburban existence. We hoped to catch a little of that spirit in our own lives, even though we were both too young to realize what it meant.

acknowledgments
acknowledgments
acknowledgments
acknowledgments
acknowledgments
acknowledgments
acknowledgments

I'm honored that those who helped to create Mary, Rhoda, and the rest of the indelible *Mary Tyler Moore* characters shared their stories with me. This book is based on published accounts and other research materials (specified in the endnotes to follow) as well as hours of interviews, email conversations, phone calls, and more email conversations with creators James L. Brooks and Allan Burns, MTM executive Grant Tinker, former CBS executives Fred Silverman and Michael Dann, and many of the writers and cast members (not to mention superfan Joe Rainone, an invaluable resource). I cannot thank them enough for helping me with this dream project. I must in particular mention my deepest gratitude to those who went above and beyond, helping me to secure interviews with others, sending me photos, calling in favors, giving me detailed feedback on memories, and sharing very personal stories with me: Valerie Harper, Allan Burns, Treva Silverman, Pat Nardo, Gloria Banta—your generosity knows no bounds. If there's a reason *Mary Tyler Moore* succeeded, it is because of wonderful spirits like you. If this book is any good, it's for the same reason.

While I'm at it, I must thank my own wacky cast of characters. Thank you to: Jesse Davis, for two years of editing on demand and endless conversations about this one damn TV show from the '70s; the most inspiring editor/publisher ever, Jonathan Karp; the agent who changed my life, Laurie Abkemeier; Simon & Schuster MVP Nicholas Greene; my readers, Heather Wood Rudúlph, A. K. Whitney, Allison Hantschel, and Gavin Edwards; my transcriber, Katie Lucas; those who gave me shelter, food, and wine during research trips, John and Diane Katz, Carter Covington, and Patrick Sean Smith; those who gave me shelter on my self-imposed writing retreat, the nuns at the Grail; and the ever-helpful librarians who got me everything I needed from Smith College's Gloria Steinem Papers.

NOTES
NOTES
NOTES
NOTES
NOTES
NOTES
NOTES
NOTES

All quotations and recollections in this book come from the author's interviews with the major, surviving participants in the scenes and incidents recollected, unless otherwise noted here. Quotes at the beginning of each section and attributed to characters from *The Mary Tyler Moore Show* come from episodes of the series. Sources follow for other quotes and information from publications not attributed in the text.

INTRODUCTION: COMEDY AND THE SINGLE GIRL

2   "platinum blonde": Graham Greene, quoted by Rhoda Koenig, "The Queen of Comedy," *Independent,* June 24, 2005.

5   "Theoretically a 'nice' single woman": Helen Gurley Brown, *Sex and the Single Girl* (Open Road Integrated Media ebook, 2012), p. 23.

5   "glamour girl": Ibid., p. 21.

5   "not to stay back home": Katherine J. Lehman, *Those Girls: Single Women in Sixties and Seventies Popular Culture* (Lawrence: University Press of Kansas, 2011), p. 73.

CHAPTER 1. THE COMEBACK (1961–70)

12   first national live television broadcast: "This Day in History," http://www .history.com/this-day-in-history/president-truman-makes-first-transconti nental-television-broadcast.

12 commercial television had its first live television broadcast: "CBS at 75," http://www.cbs.com/specials/cbs_75/timeline/1950.shtml.

13 The former dancer had grown up watching Milton Berle: Mary Tyler Moore interview, Archive of American Television.

13 "This child will either end up on stage": Ibid.

13 moved with her family to Los Angeles: Mary Tyler Moore, *After All* (New York: Dell, 1995), p. 29.

13 "straight woman": Mary Tyler Moore, Museum of Broadcast Communications, http://www.museum.tv/eotvsection.php?entrycode=mooremaryt.

14 first tested it out: Vince Waldron, *The Official Dick Van Dyke Show Book* (New York: Applause Theatre Books, 2001), p. 125.

14 "very egalitarian": Mary Tyler Moore interview, Archive of American Television.

15 word *pregnant* was not allowed: Ibid.

15 "You're very good": Ibid.

15 "rather than subject the drama critics": Steven Suskin, *Second Act Trouble* (New York: Applause Theatre & Cinema Books, 2006), p. 54.

15 when Reiner and Van Dyke started craving more variety: Carl Reiner interview, Archive of American Television.

16 Moore felt insecure: Moore interview, Archive of American Television.

16 "a nervous chorus girl": Mary Tyler Moore, *Growing Up Again* (New York: St. Martin's Press, 2009), p. 3.

16 "the fantasy girl of the American dream": "Moore: Healthy, Zany, Sexy," *Newsweek,* Aug. 1, 1966.

17 closed in sixteen days: *Playbill* Vault, http://www.playbillvault.com/Show/Detail/4498/The-Loves-of-Cass-McGuire.

17 lasted only a week: *Playbill* Vault, http://www.playbillvault.com/Show/Detail/4360/We-Have-Always-Lived-in-the-Castle.

17 airplane-ride argument: Howard Kissel, *David Merrick: The Abominable Showman* (New York: Applause Books, 1993), p. 338.

18 "Get me Abe Burrows!": *Webster's Online Dictionary,* http://www.websters-online-dictionary.org/definitions/Abe+Burrows?cx=partner-pub-0939450753529744%3Av0qd01-tdlq&cof=FORID%3A9&ie=UTF-8&q=Abe+Burrows&sa=Search#906.

18 Moore grew terrified: Sheilah Graham, "Boston and Philadelphia Critics Broke Mary Tyler Moore's Heart," *Milwaukee Journal,* Dec. 4, 1966.

18 lack of TV's retakes: Moore, *After All,* p. 154.

18 admired her intense work ethic: Kissel, *David Merrick: The Abominable Showman,* p. 340.

18 trashed the original script: Ibid., p. 341.

18 looking for Moore's old boss: Moore, *After All*, p. 156.

18 "Why drown in two feet of water?": Kissel, *David Merrick: The Abominable Showman*, p. 341.

18 "All those awful jokes": Ibid.

19 "masterful": Moore interview, Archive of American Television.

19 ran four hours: Koenig, "The Queen of Comedy."

19 "a vocal range": Moore, *After All*, p. 154.

19 Audiences in Philadelphia: Kissel, *David Merrick: The Abominable Showman*, p. 340.

19 *Who's Afraid of Holly Golightly?*: Ibid., p. 343.

19 "She was a dream": Ibid., p. 340.

19 throw her arms around the stage manager: Josh Wolk, "The King of Comedies," *Entertainment Weekly*, March 26, 2004.

19 "What have I done wrong?": Kissel, *David Merrick: The Abominable Showman*, p. 343.

19 thought she was always about to be fired: Moore, *After All*, p. 155.

19 $1 million in advance ticket sales: Frank Rich, "David Merrick, 88, Showman Who Ruled Broadway, Dies," *New York Times*, April 27, 2000.

19 "my Bay of Pigs": "Quotable Quotes," *Ocala Star-Banner*, Feb. 19, 1967.

19 "I told everybody": "Rhoda and Mary—Love and Laughs," *Time*, Oct. 28, 1974.

20 "Step aside": Ibid.

20 smoking and drinking: Moore, *Growing Up Again*, p. 9.

20 doctors discovered she was diabetic: Ibid., p. 7.

20 "caved in": Moore, *After All*, p. 170.

21 forget about the *Breakfast at Tiffany's* debacle: Ibid., p. 177.

21 As soon as CBS executives saw: Ibid., p. 178.

23 2,063 feet: "N.D. TV Tower No Longer World's Tallest," NPR, *All Things Considered*, Jan. 5, 2010.

CHAPTER 2. THE PRODUCERS (1969–70)

32 only skyscraper ever designed: Jayson Blair, "CBS's 'Black Rock' Building Is Said to Be for Sale," *New York Times*, Aug. 30, 232.

32 83 million TV sets: Les Brown, *Televi$ion* (New York: Harcourt Brace Jovanovich, 1971), p. 3.

33 particularly his competition: Seth Scheisel, "Paul L. Klein, 69, a Developer of Pay-Per-View TV Channels," *New York Times*, July 13, 1998.

33 Ratings were born: Martin Mayer, *About Television* (New York: Harper & Row, 1972), p. 33.

34 $8,389 annual average: http://www.infoplease.com/year/1969.html.

34 NBC's 1970 "Product Usage Highlights": Mayer, *About Television*, p. 47.

34   "You are scum!": "Television: Dann v. Klein: The Best Game in Town,"
       Time, May 25, 1970.

34   To pull off a last-minute victory: Brown, *Televi$ion,* p. 92.

34   "My [contract] option is coming due shortly": "Television: Dann v. Klein."

34   20.3 percent to 20 percent: Ibid.

34   "HAPPINESS IS BEING": Ibid.

34   "I've never known": Ibid.

39   "a bit of wire": Cecil Smith, "Tough Sledding for New Concepts," *Los An-
       geles Times,* Jan. 28, 1970.

39   "A stirring up of the schedule": Ibid.

40   "broads, bosoms, and fun": Andrew Grossman, "The Smiling Cobra," *Vari-
       ety Life,* June–July 2004.

40   "The American public": Lance Morrow, "Goodbye to 'Our Mary,' " *Time,*
       March 14, 1977.

40   moon landing was viewed: "1969: Man Takes First Steps on the Moon,"
       http://news.bbc.co.uk/onthisday/hi/dates/stories/july/21/newsid_263541
       /2635845.stm.

41   two failed pilot episodes: Museum of Broadcast Communications, http://
       www.museum.tv/eotvsection.php?entrycode=allinthefa.

chapter 3. not quite making it yet (1970)

47   met Holly in the '50s: Ellis Amburn, *Buddy Holly* (New York: St. Martin's
       Griffin, 1995), p. 25.

49   from Iran to the United States in 1955: "Reza Badiyi, Set Record for Di-
       recting Most Hours of Episodic Television," Academy of Television Arts
       and Sciences, Aug. 22, 2011.

50   wear a wig: Moore interview, Archive of American Television.

50   would symbolize Mary's graduation: Reza Badiyi interview, Archive of
       American Television.

51   "Run out into the middle": Moore interview, Archive of American Televi-
       sion.

53   pronounced *Mary Tyler Moore*'s fate: Cecil Smith, "A Gloom Sayer Could
       Be Wrong," *Los Angeles Times,* April 29, 1970.

chapter 4. casting call (1970)

55   CBS casting executive Ethel Winant: Ethel Winant's pieces of the *Mary
       Tyler Moore* story are constructed from others' recollections of her, most
       notably her son, Bruce Winant.

56   Anne Nelson: Josef Adalian, "CBS Loses Its Longest Serving Staffer," *TV
       Week,* June 24, 2009.

56 dropped out of high school: Burt A. Folkart, "Hollywood Star Walk: Ted Knight," *Los Angeles Times,* Aug. 27, 1986.

56 host of a kids' show: Kenneth W. Parker, "WJAR-TV's Ted Knight," *Providence Journal,* Feb. 23, 1955.

59 Jack Cassidy: David Cassidy, *C'mon Get Happy: Fear and Loathing on the Partridge Family Bus* (New York: Grand Central, 1994), p. 50.

72 channeled her own aunt: "Love Is All Around," Oprah.com, http://www.oprah.com/oprahshow/The-Cast-of-The-Mary-Tyler-Moore-Show-Reunites_1/2.

chapter 5. technical difficulties (1970)

73 careful not to leave stray syringes: "The Needle That Keeps Mary Tyler Moore Alive," *Photoplay,* March 1971.

74 "Having worked with Mary": John Rich interview, Archive of American Television.

76 Marilyn Monroe and Marlene Dietrich: Ann O'Neill, "Marilyn Monroe Slept Here," CNN.com, Nov. 30, 2011.

79 could feel the audience's patience dwindling: Moore, *After All,* p. 197.

80 pulled herself together: Ibid., p. 199.

83 made Tinker and Moore an offer: Ibid., p. 203.

85 "I firmly believe": Mayer, *About Television,* p. 67.

85 "cancelled everything with a tree": Anthony Harkins, *Hillbilly: A Cultural History of an American Icon* (New York: Oxford University Press, 2004), p. 203.

86 a group of about one hundred feminists: Megan Gibson, "A Brief History of Women's Protests," *Time,* Aug. 12, 2011.

87 "wholesale upheaval": Percy Shain, "CBS Shifts Six Shows to Different Time Slots," *Boston Globe,* July 22, 1970.

chapter 7. pulling through (1970–71)

100 Nixon's approval rating: "Nixon: The Pursuit of Peace and Politics," *Time,* Sept. 28, 1970.

100 "*The Mary Tyler Moore Show,* on opening night at least": Richard Burgheim, "The New Season: Perspiring with Relevance," *Time,* Sept. 28, 1970.

101 "unmarried and getting a little desperate": "Fall Preview," *TV Guide,* September 12, 1970.

101 "preposterous": Tom Shales, "The Mary Memory Tour," *Washington Post,* Feb. 18, 1991.

101 "the return of a delightful and talented actress": "Comedies Appear Back to Back," *St. Petersburg Times,* Sept. 19, 1970.

101 "may take getting used to": "Tube Filled with Series Openers," *Eugene Register-Guard,* Sept. 19, 1970.

107 "she seemed to act": Alan Rafkin, *Cue the Bunny on the Rainbow: Tales from TV's Most Prolific Sitcom Director* (Syracuse, NY: Syracuse University Press, 1998), p. 69.

108 "Mary should be presented with a problem": Dwight Whitney, "Mary, It Needs Just One Beat of Wistfulness," *TV Guide,* Feb. 26, 1972.

110 hated it: Fred Silverman interview, Archive of American Television.

110 had reduced earnings: Mayer, *About Television,* p. 251.

111 "patient capital": Norman Lear speech at the Securities Industry Association, Wharton School, March 13, 1986.

112 Wood killed more programs: "CBS, in Big Sweep, to Drop Sullivan Show, Oldest in TV History," *Wall Street Journal,* March 17, 1971.

112 "You know there'll be other times": Rafkin, *Cue the Bunny on the Rainbow,* p. 69.

ChAptER 8. SUCCESS (1971-72)

115 "thirty-three, unmarried, and unworried": Mary Tyler Moore, http://www .encyclopedia.com/topic/Mary_Tyler_Moore.aspx.

115 20 million viewers: Verne Gay, "Cronkite Was Lucky, but So Were We," *Newsday,* July 18, 2009.

119 "of singular value": Cecil Smith, "Ed Asner Comedy Find of the Year," *Los Angeles Times,* March 15, 1971.

125 During the week, Moore: Details of Moore's habits on set are from Whitney, "Mary, It Needs Just One Beat of Wistfulness," as well as Robert Kerwin, "Can You Find the Boss in This Picture?," *Chicago Tribune,* Nov. 24, 1974.

125 "when people don't do their work right": Kerwin, "Can You Find the Boss in This Picture?"

126 "A television job": James L. Brooks, "What I've Learned," *Esquire,* January 2011.

127 "the best show on television": Benjamin Stein, "A Slice of Life Every Saturday," *Wall Street Journal,* Jan. 4, 1974.

ChAptER 9. Girls' Club (1970-73)

129 Leslie Hall: Leslie Hall's story is told from the recollections of her son, Gary Hall, and those who knew her on the set.

132 promised its readers: *Ladies' Home Journal,* September 1976.

132 "I do interviews": Kerwin, "Can You Find the Boss in This Picture?"

138 asked Holly Holmberg out: Ann W. O'Neill, "The Court Files," *Los Angeles Times,* Oct. 1, 2000.

138 five foot seven and 118 pounds: "Editor TV Times," *Los Angeles Times,* Aug. 30, 1970.

139 "It's a discipline in itself": "Mary Tyler Moore: Enjoying Her Three Ds," *Edmonton Journal,* Nov. 30, 1973.

139 encasing her thighs: Susan Cheever Cowley, "The Scavullo Look," *Newsweek,* Nov. 22, 1976.

139 comparing herself to the models: Moore, *After All,* p. 368.

139 crab salad with diet cola: Kerwin, "Can You Find the Boss in This Picture?"

139 "It's all well and good": "Rhoda and Mary—Love and Laughs," *Time.*

139 "I love her": Mark Goodman, "TV's Reigning Queen," *People,* Sept. 30, 1974.

139 "it's like Dorian Gray": "Rhoda and Mary—Love and Laughs," *Time.*

139 "On the big screen": Kerwin, "Can You Find the Boss in This Picture?"

CHAPTER 10. THE WRITERS WORE HOT PANTS (1972–74)

155 "breakthrough": Mary Murphy, "Lou, Wife Split," *Los Angeles Times,* Oct. 5, 1973.

156 "On MTM": "Victorious Loser," *Time,* Sept. 3, 1973.

159 "We're going to do a story about women": Mollie Gregory, *Women Who Run the Show: How a Brilliant and Creative New Generation of Women Stormed Hollywood* (New York: St. Martin's Press, 2002), p. 91.

163 could still find talk show host Jack Paar: Don Shirley, "Sexism on Television Crumbling in Laughter," *Los Angeles Times,* June 10, 1973.

163 Of the Writers Guild's nearly three thousand members: Gregory, *Women Who Run the Show,* p. 7.

164 "you never hear people say": Marcia Seligson, "Being Rhoda Is No Joke," *McCall's,* January 1975.

164 cover of *Ms.* magazine: Gloria Steinem, "An Interview with Valerie Harper," *Ms.,* May 1978.

164 had just opened in 1972: Comedy Store, Club History, http://hollywood .thecomedystore.com/page.cfm?id=872.

164 Leno would soon meet David Letterman: David Letterman, Museum of Broadcast Communications, http://www.museum.tv/eotvsection.php?entry code=lettermanda.

165 Led Zeppelin, the Who, and the Rolling Stones: Andaz West Hollywood, Hotel Overview, http://www.westhollywood.andaz.hyatt.com/hyatt/hotels -westhollywood-andaz/index.jsp?hyattprop=yes.

chapter 11. pot and the pill (1972-73)

170 "As a writer and producer": Norman Lear on Business, Politics, and Culture, http://normanlear.com/backstory_speeches.html.

172 first won approval: "The Birth Control Pill," *Embryo Project Encyclopedia*, Arizona State University, http://embryo.asu.edu/view/embryo:123917.

172 *Time* magazine cover story: *Time*, April 7, 1967.

173 "Now she's aggressively feminine": Bill Davidson, "*The Mary Tyler Moore Show*—After Three Seasons," *TV Guide*, May 19, 1973.

173 "In the romantic glow of sunrise": Lehman, *Those Girls*, p. 149.

173 producers decided to nix a dialogue: Ibid., p. 150.

174 "It was awfully old-fashioned": Ibid., p. 155.

175 Two CBS affiliates: Bruce Weber, "Bea Arthur, Star of Two TV Comedies, Dies at 86," *New York Times*, April 25, 2009.

175 "Maude is commercial TV's first striking manifestation": Shirley, "Sexism on Television Crumbling in Laughter."

175 "We're not *Maude*": Davidson, "*The Mary Tyler Moore Show*—After Three Seasons."

176 "The show is opening up": Kerwin, "Can You Find the Boss in This Picture?"

178 "Be careful": Davidson, "*The Mary Tyler Moore Show*—After Three Seasons."

180 "I think women are okay": Kerwin, "Can You Find the Boss in This Picture?"

180 Conference on Women in Public Life: Gloria Steinem Papers, 1940–2000, Sophia Smith Collection, Smith College, Northampton, MA.

181 "I'd like to ask each of us": Original recording courtesy of Sophia Smith Collection, Smith College, Northampton, MA.

183 "compromised and contradictory feminism": Bonnie J. Dow, *Prime-Time Feminism: Television, Media Culture, and the Women's Movement Since 1970* (Philadelphia: University of Pennsylvania Press, 1996), p. 51.

183 "girl-next-door sweetness": Ibid., p. 25.

183 "she hardly ever gets to write the news or report it": Judy Klemesrud, "TV's Women Are Dingbats," *New York Times*, May 27, 1973.

183 "challenging the family system": Caroline Bird, "What's Television Doing for Fifty Percent of Americans?," *TV Guide*, Feb. 27, 1971, quoted in Serafina Bathrick, "*The Mary Tyler Moore Show*: Women at Home and at Work," in Joanne Morreale, ed., *Critiquing the Sitcom: A Reader* (Syracuse, NY: Syracuse University Press, 2003), p. 158.

chapter 12. the georgia and betty story (1972-74)

187 like she was starting her career all over again: Cecil Smith, "After 25 Years, the 'Real' Betty White," *Los Angeles Times*, Dec. 21, 1973.

195 "I don't think I should": Moore interview, Archive of American Television.

195 cook to handle dinner: Kerwin, "Can You Find the Boss in This Picture?"

196 the emptier it became: Moore, *After All,* p. 121.

197 she'd wave to Tinker: Grant Tinker, *Tinker in Television: From General Sarnoff to General Electric* (New York: Simon & Schuster, 1994), p. 123.

197 one of the few people Moore had felt comfortable opening up to: Kerwin, "Can You Find the Boss in This Picture?"

197 moved into a new Bel Air home: Tinker, *Tinker in Television.*

CHAPTER 13. GIRL, THIS TIME YOU'RE ALL ALONE (1974)

204 had existed since at least 1941: John Dunning, *On the Air: The Encyclopedia of Old-Time Radio* (New York: Oxford University Press, 1998), p. 293.

206 used the hiatus: William Glover, "Change of Pace Role for Valerie," *Hartford Courant,* March 17, 1974.

206 "a friend": Steinem, "An Interview with Valerie Harper."

207 making twenty-five thousand dollars a week: Seligson, "Being Rhoda Is No Joke."

207 hated talking or thinking about money: Steinem, "An Interview with Valerie Harper."

207 sent her a gift: Kerwin, "Can You Find the Boss in This Picture?"

208 sneaked back over: "Rhoda and Mary—Love and Laughs," *Time.*

209 size fluctuated enough: Valerie Harper, *Today I Am a Ma'am* (New York: HarperCollins, 2001), p. 38.

209 Tinker was so uncharacteristically anxious: "Rhoda and Mary—Love and Laughs," *Time.*

209 "It would have been": Clifford Terry, "Psyching Out Bob Newhart," *Chicago Tribune,* Sept. 23, 1973.

210 "a neatly balanced show business cartel": "Rhoda and Mary—Love and Laughs," *Time.*

211 "I'm thirty-three": Ibid.

215 raked in three hundred thousand dollars per year: "Hollywood's Hot Hyphens," *Time,* Oct. 28, 1974.

216 more than 50 million: Rick Mitz, *The Great TV Sitcom Book* (New York: R. Marek, 1980), p. 350.

218 shot by two men: Michael Newton, *The Encyclopedia of Unsolved Crimes* (New York: Facts on File, 2009), pp. 87–88.

218 "Barbara stories": Harry F. Waters, "TV's Fall Season," *Newsweek,* Sept. 8, 1975.

218 could spend hours debating: Ibid.

222 grossing more than $20 million: Goodman, "TV's Reigning Queen."

chapter 14. the best job of their lives (1975–77)

223 got ready to hit the stage: Elizabeth Peer, "The Rating Game," *Newsweek*, Oct. 13, 1975.

224 "I don't like having to write down": Susan Harris biography, Paley Center for Media, http://www.shemadeit.org/meet/biography.aspx?m=32.

228 "look like the Gestapo": Benjamin Stein, "The Old Taboos Fall, One by One," *Washington Post*, Sept. 19, 1975.

229 "I think of commercial television like Times Square": Harry F. Waters, "Why Is TV So Bad?," *Newsweek*, Feb. 16, 1976.

230 received two thousand complaints: *FCC Report on the Broadcast of Violent, Indecent, and Obscene Material*, Feb. 19, 1975.

230 In a December 1974 letter: David Black, "Inside TV's 'Family Hour' Feud," *New York Times*, Dec. 7, 1975.

230 "set television back drastically": Waters, "TV's Fall Season."

231 Lear joined with *M*A*S*H* producer Larry Gelbart: Black, "Inside TV's 'Family Hour' Feud."

231 In October 1975: Andrea Jane Grefe, "The Family Viewing Hour: An Assault on the First Amendment?," *Hastings Constitutional Law Quarterly*, Fall 1977.

231 "If the networks were to make a sincere effort": Black, "Inside TV's 'Family Hour' Feud."

232 Nielsen reported: Waters, "Why Is TV So Bad?"

232 "I'd like to thank a lot of people": "CBS Under Pressure," *Forbes*, June 15, 1976.

234 "Yes, this is a creatively healthy move": Moore, *After All*, p. 5.

235 Moore thought the idea was divine: Ibid., p. 235.

236 stopping occasionally to laugh: Christopher Lloyd, "Veteran Sitcom Writer David Lloyd," *Entertainment Weekly*, Dec. 4, 2009.

236 "It was the first time": Mary Tyler Moore, "David Lloyd," *Time*, Nov. 30, 2009.

239 Ken Levine was in the studio audience that night: Ken Levine, "In Memory of David Lloyd," http://kenlevine.blogspot.com/2009/11/in-memory-of-david-lloyd.html.

240 "It was not only a very funny show": Cecil Smith, "Altering the Asner Image," *Los Angeles Times*, Nov. 7, 1975.

240 "In another moving and improbably funny show": "Victorious Loser," *Time*.

240 "bittersweet riot": Tom Shales, "The Mary Memory Tour," *The Washington Post*, Feb. 18, 1991.

240 "a classic": Bruce Cook, "Now Women Are Calling the Shots," *Newsday*, Nov. 19, 1978.

241 Moore still wasn't sure: Moore, *After All*, p. 238.

242 Moore's half filmed on the set: Ibid., p. 351.

248 "In many places": "Victorious Loser," *Time*.

chapter 15. Leaving Camelot (1977–present)

254 "The *Taxi* group": Kenneth Turan, "On His Own 'Terms,' " *Film Comment*, March/April 1984.

254 "Ed Asner finally brings something fresh to the beat": Harry F. Waters, "Eyeballing the New Season," *Newsweek*, Sept. 26, 1977.

254 cover of *Time* magazine: *Time*, Aug. 13, 1979.

255 "fast and funny": Janet Maslin, "Burt Reynolds as Unmarried Husband," *New York Times*, Oct. 5, 1979.

255 "Take that nap": Turan, "On His Own 'Terms.' "

259 "one of the more promising": John J. O'Connor, "TV: Comedy of Divorce," *New York Times*, Sept. 29, 1983.

260 Paramount sent him: Turan, "On His Own 'Terms.' "

261 "uncastable": Stephen Farber, "Comedy Buoys 'Terms of Endearment,' " *New York Times*, Nov. 20, 1983.

262 After the New York Film Critics dinner: Turan, "On His Own 'Terms.' "

263 split with his partner of twenty-seven years: O'Neill, "The Court Files."

chapter 16. Making It on Their Own (1977–present)

269 Polish immigrant barman: Burt A. Folkart, " 'Mary Tyler Moore Show' Newscaster," *Los Angeles Times*, Aug. 27, 1986.

270 didn't know what to do with herself: Moore, *After All*, p. 238.

271 "Mary's not a Lucille Ball": Thomas O'Connor, "Mary Tyler Moore: 'I'm Not an Innately Funny Person,' " *New York Times*, Dec. 8, 1985.

272 "That was tough": Kliph Nesteroff, "The Early David Letterman," WFMU, http://blog.wfmu.org/freeform/2010/03/the-late-night-hosts-before-they -were-big.html.

273 "sit-var": Moore interview, Archive of American Television.

273 "the dark side": *Ordinary People* entry on Turner Classic Movies archive, http://www.tcm.com/this-month/article/18955/0/Ordinary-People.html.

273 "I guess he was right to wonder": Cole Kazdin and Imaeyen Ibanga, "Mary Tyler Moore: A Career Retrospective," ABC News, March 31, 2009.

273 "self-expectation": Moore interview, Archive of American Television.

274 took on extra significance: Moore, *After All*, p. 265.

274 remained in New York City: Ibid., p. 275.

274 when he treated her mother: Ibid., p. 313.

274 a drink or two before dinner: Louise Lague, "Addicted No Moore," *People*, Oct. 1, 1984.

275 read about Elizabeth Taylor and Liza Minnelli: Moore, *After All*, p. 351.

275 "social drinking": Lague, "Addicted No Moore."

275 "I'm not an innately funny person": O'Connor, "Mary Tyler Moore: 'I'm Not an Innately Funny Person.' "

276 White had watched *Star Trek*: Betty White, *Here We Go Again* (New York: Scribner, 1995), p. 206.

279 "My name is Ed Asner": Ed Asner, Museum of Broadcast Communications, http://www.museum.tv/eotvsection.php?entrycode=asnered.

280 "the Jane Fonda of Latin America": Pete Hamill, "What Does Lou Grant Know About El Salvador?," *New York*, March 15, 1982.

281 At the Church of the Recessional: "Laughter Wins over Tears at Funeral of Ted Knight," *Eugene Register-Guard*, Aug. 29, 1986.

epilogue: MARY, RhodA, ANd ThE ModERN GiRl

284 seventy-five-member crew: "Recreating History," http://www.oprah.com/oprahshow/Recreating-History_1/11.

285 when she tried to get a good table at a restaurant: O'Connor, "Mary Tyler Moore: 'I'm Not an Innately Funny Person.' "

286 if it wasn't funny: Moore interview, Archive of American Television.

286 *Time* magazine cover story: *Time*, June 29, 1998.

286 visibly excited: Moore interview, Archive of American Television.

287 plans came together in 1997: Frank DeCaro, "Mary and Rhoda," *New York Times*, Dec. 29, 1997.

287 "This was one of those cases": "Mary, Rhoda Are Dead," *People*, May 17, 1999.

287 doing her own stunt: James Poniewozik, "Doing Less With Moore," *Time*, Feb. 7, 2000.

287 "Rhoda, you haven't changed a bit": Phil Gallo, "Mary and Rhoda," *Variety*, Feb. 6, 2000.

287 "*Mary and Rhoda* is to be savored": John Carman, "Mary, Rhoda Should've Just Sent E-Mails," *San Francisco Chronicle*, Feb. 7, 2000.

288 best TV show of all time: Alison Gwynn, *Entertainment Weekly's The 100 Greatest TV Shows of All Time* (New York: Entertainment Weekly Books, 1998).

289 "*All in the Family* and *The Mary Tyler Moore Show*": Todd VanDerWerff, " '70s Sitcoms," *AV Club*, http://www.avclub.com/articles/70s-sitcoms,45254/.

290 deliberately structured it: Jacques Steinberg, " '30 Rock' Lives, and Tina Fey Laughs," *New York Times*, Sept. 23, 2007.

292 "I love Mary Tyler Moore": Nancy Randle, "Actress Will Be Real-Life Mother," *Chicago Tribune*, July 7, 1992.

index
index
index
index
index
index
index

Note: Asterisks (*) denote fictional/TV characters.

ABOUT THE AUTHOR
ABOUT THE AUTHOR
ABOUT THE AUTHOR
ABOUT THE AUTHOR
ABOUT THE AUTHOR
ABOUT THE AUTHOR
ABOUT THE AUTHOR

ABOUT THE AUTHOR

JENNIFER KEISHIN ARMSTRONG grew up deep in the southwest suburbs of Chicago, then escaped to New York to live in a succession of very small apartments and write about pop culture. In the process, she became a feminist, a Buddhist, and the singer/guitarist in an amateur rock band. She also spent a decade on staff at *Entertainment Weekly,* cofounded SexyFeminist.com, and now writes for several publications, including *Women's Health, Runner's World, Writer's Digest, Fast Company,* and *New York*'s Vulture. She's the co-author (with Heather Wood Rudúlph) of *Sexy Feminism* and the author of a history of the original *Mickey Mouse Club.* She has provided pop culture commentary for CNN, VH1, A&E, and ABC, and teaches article writing and creative writing. Visit her online at JenniferKArmstrong.com, or follow her on Twitter: @jmkarmstrong.